EARL WARREN

A Life of Truth and Justice

D. J. HERDA

Prometheus Books

Guilford, Connecticut

Published 2019 by Prometheus Books

Cover image © Library of Congress
Cover design by Liz Mills
Cover design © Prometheus Books

Trademarked names appear throughout this book. Prometheus Books recognizes all registered trademarks, trademarks, and service marks mentioned in the text.

The internet addresses listed in the text were accurate at the time of publication. The inclusion of a website does not indicate an endorsement by the author or by Prometheus Books, and Prometheus Books does not guarantee the accuracy of the information presented at these sites.

Distributed by NATIONAL BOOK NETWORK

Library of Congress Cataloging-in-Publication Data
Names: Herda, D. J., 1948-, author.
Title: Earl Warren: a life of truth and justice / D. J. Herda.
Description: Amherst, New York: Prometheus Books, 2019. | Includes index.
Identifiers: LCCN 2019019046 (print) | LCCN 2019020364 (ebook) | ISBN 9781633885813 (ebook) | ISBN 9781633885806 (hardback)
Subjects: LCSH: Warren, Earl, 1891-1974 | Judges—United States—Biography. | Governors—California—Biography. | United States. Supreme Court—Officials and employees—Biography. | BISAC: BIOGRAPHY & AUTOBIOGRAPHY / Lawyers & Judges. | POLITICAL SCIENCE / Government / Judicial Branch. | BIOGRAPHY & AUTOBIOGRAPHY / Political.
Classification: LCC KF8745.W3 (ebook) | LCC KF8745.W3 H475 2019 (print) | DDC 347.73/2634 [B]—dc23
LC record available at https://lccn.loc.gov/2019019046

To Judge James Warren (Jimmy Lee) for his invaluable input of personal family history and for sharing his intimate knowledge of his grandparents, Papa and Mama Warren. Also, to Faye Swetky of the Swetky Literary Agency for believing in this book and in me and for supporting my writing for the past twenty years.

CONTENTS

Author's Note

SOURCES AND ACKNOWLEDGMENTS

For the resources used in creating this book, I relied upon both written and oral documentation provided by researchers, archivists, editors, fellow authors, interviewers, and the keepers of a wide range of historical materials repositories. In addition, I reviewed numerous historic radio and television tapes and transcripts, as well as various magazine and newspaper articles and personal correspondence written and published over the past several decades. I found the correspondence between Warren Court justices, their friends and associates, and their coworkers and staff to be particularly enlightening, and I utilized the notes, diaries, memoranda, and draft opinions of members of the court to provide details that otherwise may have been unavailable to me. I am grateful for the papers and other documentation furnished by the Harry S. Truman, Dwight D. Eisenhower, John F. Kennedy, and Lyndon B. Johnson Presidential Libraries, as well as the Library of Congress with its accommodating and endlessly patient staff.

Particularly helpful in researching and writing this book were the oral history projects undertaken and maintained by the Bancroft Library, Regional Oral History Office, at the University of California, Berkeley, to whose interviewers, miscellaneous staff, transcriptionists, and editors everyone is grateful. The library is a rich larder of unedited, raw, historically valuable source material for which researchers and writers around the world are thankful.

I would also like to acknowledge the tremendously generous act by Judge Earl Warren Jr., who, in 1995, broke with a lifelong policy of never commenting on anything written about his father, the chief justice. In praising my young adult book *Earl Warren: Chief Justice for Social Change*, he awakened in me a fervor to discover more about this extraordinary man, the cases over which his court presided, and the Supreme Court in general.

Finally, I am most grateful for the selfless sharing of family history by the grandson of Earl and Nina Warren, Judge James Warren (Jimmy Lee), without whose cooperation much of the original material in this book—from photographs to little-known and less-reported family facts, traditions, and insights—may have been lost to the world. For his gracious sharing and his expansion of the knowledge of Earl Warren and his court, I am forever indebted.

Introduction

LIFE, DEATH, LOVE, ETC.

In the late twelfth century BCE, the Old Testament prophet Samuel appointed the tribe of Benjamin to elect a new monarch. They chose from within the clan of Matrites a man named Saul, whose reign marked Israel's transformation from tribal society to statehood. After Saul led his army to victory over the Ammonites, the people congregated at Gilgal to crown him king. The newly elected monarch proclaimed as his first act that he would not rain retribution against those who had contested his authority.[1]

Just as the prescient biblical king, Earl Warren, too, was a prophet—but of a different sort. Climbing the ladder of political ascendancy culminated with his crowning as chief justice of the Supreme Court of the United States, he ascended the highest judicial position in the land. And he promptly found himself mired in controversy, disunity, and fractious dissension. As with Saul, Warren, too, forbade retribution against his opposing armies—not by decree but rather by the stealth of his intellect and his time-tempered statesmanship.

It worked. For the first time in decades, harmony sprang from chaos, and the US Supreme Court came together as one.

Born of Scandinavian immigrants, Warren led a sober, studied life of temperance, tolerance, and justice. His parents taught him these attributes, directing him and his sister toward the stewardship of truth. Only through truth, they believed, could justice be achieved. It was a lesson in which the boy placed his faith, and he carried it to his grave eighty-three years later.

On his long and winding journey through life, Warren—ostensibly a conservative Republican—created the most liberal Supreme Court in modern history, best known for outlawing segregation in public schools and transforming several areas of American law. In particular, he established the rights of the accused, ended sponsored prayers in public schools, and required "one man, one vote" rules for apportionment of election districts. He

1

made the court more equal in power to Congress and the Executive Branch through four landmark decisions: *Brown v. Board of Education* (1954), *Gideon v. Wainwright* (1963), *Reynolds v. Sims* (1964), and *Miranda v. Arizona* (1966).

To millions of people around the world, Earl Warren was the poster child for the American ideal that "all men are created equal." To millions more, who feared the potential overreach of a government embodiment of Big Brother, he was perceived as the very personification of evil.

Neither the first nor the last chief justice to project one particular ideological bent while embracing another, Warren was an enigma of contradictions. While history prophesied one thing of him, his ingrained sense of humanity often delivered something else. In the process, the Warren Court, as the press soon dubbed it, added essential phrases to the lexicon of American jurisprudence: "Separate is not equal." "One man, one vote." "Mirandize him!"

A former prosecutor, Warren was no great legal mind, judicial pontificator, or boisterous advocate for the poor and the downtrodden. Instead, he approached the shortcomings of society with a well-seasoned, well-reasoned approach to resolution. His personal experiences had taught him right from wrong, truth from lie, justice from iniquity. As a three-time California governor and a former candidate for vice president, he was among the first modern-day elected officials to temper his decision-making process with a strong moral compass honed by reality. He was one of the first to amass secret files on suspected subversives for potential legal action, making him a poster child for Big Government. Yet he later led the court to curtail Joseph McCarthy's Red Scare of the mid-1950s, shooting down the notion that the chief was but a shadowy shill for Washington politicos.

In one case after another, Earl Warren helped to reshape the very meaning of the Bill of Rights, insisting that the states, too—and not only the federal government—were bound to honor the integrity assured to every citizen, a revolutionary legal concept. Outside of his immediate family, even those who knew him best never fully understood the man or his thought processes. But everyone instinctively realized that Warren the man had been forged from the same steel as Warren the boy. Even Robert Kenny, a good friend, attorney, and politician who once lost the California governorship to Warren, commented upon his rival's slow but steadfast development into a political force of reckoning: "There was no sudden conversion like [that of] Saul of Tarsus"[2]; instead, he drew out his decision-making process tempered by the wisdom of experience. Newspaper columnist Drew Pearson, a close friend and an occasional summer traveling companion of Warren, saw things differently, comparing Warren to Saul on the road to Damascus, slicing his way decisively to victory.

These two different takes on the same man are both valid. Depending upon one's political view, Warren's career was a tangle of apparent contradictions. He proved so deliberate in weighing the elements involved in the making of a decision that some people thought him crudely ignorant. One politician who knew him well had a more realistic assessment: "Warren is and always was about two jumps ahead of where you thought he was. He'd anticipate what you were thinking."[3]

Earl Warren's rise to a larger-than-life figure is a uniquely American tale with a universal backstory, but the man cannot be studied, understood, or analyzed without an analysis of the roots of his personal development.

A person of unwavering family values, Warren remained in love with the same woman for forty-nine years. Throughout that time, he built a career unstained by public, political, or personal scandal, although he had been dropped into a seething cauldron of political intrigue and shame. Intensely antagonistic toward crime and corruption, he was personally targeted on numerous occasions by those who wanted him to "disappear." Yet, so concerned was he about the frightening effect such information might have on his family, he worked diligently to keep the truth of his personal endangerment from his wife and, particularly, his children.

As his son James once said, "I can remember when I first heard [about] it that I had seen a car parked up the street a couple of blocks but I didn't pay any attention to it. Sometime later I found out it was somebody keeping an eye on the house. But none of the kids were ever aware at any time that there were any problems going on like that."[4]

With his appointment to the Supreme Court in 1953, Warren caused liberals to groan out loud at the reactionary decisions destined to come down from the bench. When Warren retired sixteen years later, those same liberals bemoaned the nation's loss of Warren's brand of progressivism, while it was the conservatives who breathed a long-suffering sigh of relief.

Throughout Warren's sixteen years of service as chief justice, the Warren Court continued to confound its followers. In his postwar book, *Inside U.S.A.*, author John Gunther described Warren as "honest, likable and clean," someone "with the limitations of all Americans of his type with little intellectual background . . . or coherent political philosophy" who would "never set the world on fire."[5] Gunther later called his characterization of the chief justice "the most serious misjudgment of a personality I have ever made."[6]

Dwight D. Eisenhower, the president who had appointed Warren to the bench, later lamented that his decision had been "the biggest damned-fool mistake I ever made,"[7] while Harry S Truman, against whom Warren had fought bitterly and lost the office of president in 1948, never missed a chance to praise him.

James Warren once pointed out to an interviewer the dichotomy behind his father, the difference between the persona and the real man: "The first time Maggie [James's wife] and I went back to Washington, my mother put up a bed in my dad's library for us. On the wall there is framed his Appointment duly signed by President Eisenhower—his appointment as chief justice—and right underneath it is the original of the Interlandi cartoon that appeared in the *New Yorker* [showing] Whistler's mother embroidering, "Impeach Earl Warren." Mother said, 'Dad thinks it's funny.'"[8]

Warren, of course, loved his children unfailingly and missed being close to them throughout his Washington years, one of the most difficult things about being chief justice and moving away from their home in California. James commented on another trip he and his wife made to visit their mother and father in DC: "We went back there for a week. My mother and dad had given us a couple of suitcases as a Christmas present and Dad said, 'Now Jim, these aren't going to do you any good sitting in a closet collecting dust. We want you to pack them up and come on back there and see us. . . . As a matter of fact, in January there's . . . going to be a dinner . . . the Alfalfa dinner. We can bring guests to it, so if there's any way you and Maggie can get back there, you're invited.'"[9]

By the time his career as chief justice had come to an end, his cohorts who knew him best were unanimous in their accolades: Earl Warren had left his mark on history, and the world was a better place for it. Conservative justice Felix Frankfurter, with whom Warren often disagreed, reportedly said the Californian "will be remembered as a great chief justice."[10] The irascible William O. Douglas pronounced that Warren would rank "with Marshall and Hughes in the broad sweep of United States history."[11] Justice William Brennan nicknamed him "Super Chief" after the flagship Atchison, Topeka and Santa Fe rail liner "The Train of the Stars," which whisked its passengers between Chicago and Los Angeles.

CBS News commentator Eric Sevareid, a frequent visitor to the Warrens' Washington apartment, praised the chief justice for possessing "that certain quality that helps to hold a diverse people together and move a nation on." That characteristic was not necessarily eloquence or intellectual superiority, Sevareid explained, but what the Romans called *gravitas*—

"patience, stability, weight of judgment, breadth of shoulders. It means that strength of the few that makes life possible for many. It means manhood."[12]

And Warren went out of his way to help make life a little easier, a little more pleasant, for everyone with whom he came in contact—and millions more he would never meet. Among those he bent over backward to accommodate were the attorneys appearing before the bench in the Supreme Court building. As James recalled, "He was very friendly. He made these attorneys coming up there [before the court] just feel at home. They've got to be under an enormous strain, especially the young ones coming up who haven't appeared there before. He always made it a point to call them by name, and I suppose if he could have found anything about them ahead of time he did, to throw in an anecdote here and there. It's overwhelming in the sense that the things they talk about are so heavy."[13]

Overwhelming, too, was the notion that James and the other Warren children grew up with such an uncommon father "who was also such a regular guy. . . . He always encouraged everybody to go his own way, to go after his own [dreams] without any sort of arm-twisting, and this whole concept of don't ever settle for being average. I don't care what it is that you do, but when you do it, do it better than anybody else. These were never pep talks; they were just good solid guiding principles."[14]

Of course, not everyone shared that opinion of the chief justice. Richard Nixon, less than three years before his fall from grace and resignation from the White House, was both "surprised and bewildered" when a magazine poll of sixty-five academics ranked his longtime nemesis among the twelve greatest of the ninety-eight justices who had ever sat on the Supreme Court.

Alabama governor George Wallace fumed, "Earl Warren does not have enough brains to try a chicken thief in my home county!"[15] Although Warren had been a vocal anti-Communist all his life, he was viciously denounced by the right-wing John Birch Society for being a member of the Communist conspiracy. "Impeach Earl Warren" bumper stickers popped up across the nation. When far-right commentator Patrick J. Buchanan was invited onto a television show in St. Louis in the early sixties, the hostess asked if the political Right agreed that Warren should be impeached. "No," Buchanan snapped, "he should be hanged!"

For all of his critics, Warren seemed to thrive on the atmosphere, neither offended by nor delighted with the controversy swirling around him. Or perhaps a better description would be that he coexisted with it. For sixteen years, he marched through the halls and corridors of the Supreme

Court building where he triggered a revolution, guided not by astutely argued legal principles or even pressure from the populace or the press but, instead, by the simple question he had learned to ask as a child: Is it fair?

An unprepossessing man with a solid core based upon a genuine interest in his fellow human beings, he was once described by *Life* magazine journalist Robert Coughlan as a man of the people:

> He likes people individually and in large crowds, and people instinctively like him. When he meets some casual acquaintance on the street and says heartily, "Hello, there, glad to see yuh, how are yuh?" the person is left with the distinct impression that Warren actually is glad to see him and genuinely concerned about his health. Moreover, sometimes despite themselves, people trust him. Left-wingers may deplore his views; intellectuals may look down at what one of them calls his "middle-class mind"; but few people have ever come from a talk with Warren without feeling that he will always do the best he can, according to the lights of his conscience.
>
> If Warren's political philosophy is neither very profound nor very novel, it is because his conscience has led him in the same directions, and at the same pace, that the consciences of millions of average Republican voters have led them. He is probably as good a one-man Gallup poll as could be found.[16]

In his autobiography, *The Memoirs of Earl Warren*, Warren summed up the reasons behind his success as a Supreme Court justice: "My first job in public service was as a clerk of the Judiciary Committee of the California State Legislature. Thereafter, I served in the City Attorney's Office of Oakland. This was followed by fourteen years as district attorney of Alameda County; then four years as state's attorney general, and later eleven years as governor of California before coming to the United States Supreme Court. . . . From every such experience, I believe I learned something that could be fitted into some phase of my work as chief justice."[17]

While a world of experience may have primed him for the most critical role in his life, Warren never took himself too seriously. Once, when his son Earl Jr., then a sitting judge on the bench in California, asked his father just what he thought he had accomplished in life, the white-haired man who had spent his entire adulthood in public service paused for several moments before he replied in his usual self-effacing manner, "History is going to have to tell us that."[18]

He was right. And in time, history did.

1

UPON THIS ROCK

The year 1891 was a remarkable one by anybody's standards. Arthur Conan Doyle had just published *The Adventures of Sherlock Holmes*. Herman Melville, the author of *Moby Dick*, died at the age of seventy-two. Artist Paul Gauguin had recently moved to Tahiti, where he would paint some of his most significant works, contract a venereal disease, and die a pauper. Composer Sergei Rachmaninoff just finished his first piano concerto, while Gustav Mahler premiered his breathtaking orchestral, Symphony No. 1. The first wireless radio transmission took place that year, widespread famine ripped across Russia, and a massive earthquake killed ten thousand people in Japan. And in Los Angeles—perhaps most noteworthy of all—Chrystal and Methias Warren celebrated the birth of their first son.

Earl Warren entered the world in one of the most vibrant and exciting states in the Union. His birth came only four decades after Mexico had surrendered the sleepy, somniferous California Territory to the United States in the 1848 Treaty of Guadalupe-Hidalgo.

Los Angeles, where Warren was born at home on March 19, 1891, had been a drowsy little hamlet of a few hundred people. When a strike was made north of the city near Sacramento, the Gold Rush of 1849 began, and people from all across the land flooded the territory. Within two years, California was admitted to the Union with more than ninety thousand residents.

At the time of Warren's birth, Los Angeles County numbered some one hundred thousand people, nearly one-tenth of the population of the state. The infant made his debut courtesy of parents of Scandinavian design who had come to California the way so many of its early residents had: poor, attracted by the promise of good jobs, and hungry to settle in the land of opportunity.

Earl's father, Methias, eventually grew into a wiry, strong man built to the ax and the ox, a man of thin features and few words. But when Methias's mother and father, originally from the maritime city of Haugesund, Norway, emigrated to the United States in 1864, their son was still an infant. Matt was the youngest of two boys who included two-year-old Ole. Halvor and Inger Varran (or Varren), as they had been known in Norway, settled with their two children in Illinois before picking up and moving cross-state to neighboring Iowa, eschewing city life for the wide-open prairies of the Heartland. In that respect, they were like most other Scandinavian immigrants who lived either off the sea or the land and ended up in the midwestern states of Minnesota, Wisconsin, North or South Dakota, Nebraska, Iowa, and Illinois. Strangers in a strange land, the Warren family had settled, as Earl would proudly relate, in "the open spaces of the Middle West."

After Inger passed away when her eldest boy was barely four, Halvor remarried and moved his new wife and ten children to a farm in Eagle Grove, Iowa. Before long, the strain of caring for that large a family took its toll. When Halvor's health began to fade, he decided there were too many mouths to feed and too few dollars with which to feed them, so he sent the three eldest boys away. Burton, the youngest of the trio, went to live with relatives. Ole and Methias moved in with a neighboring family, where they worked in exchange for bed, board, and schooling.

Although the two boys toiled from morning to night, Matt somehow always found time for his studies. He stayed in school through the seventh grade, far longer than most children in the late nineteenth century. But when older brother Ole turned seventeen, he took fifteen-year-old Matt and left town, heading east.

On their own, the boys crisscrossed the Midwest, hiring themselves out as farmhands and unskilled laborers wherever they went. Eventually they worked their way to Chicago, where they had barely settled in when Ole contracted a "virulent form of tuberculosis," according to Warren biographer Ed Cray.[1] Unable to afford medical treatment for his brother, young Matt watched helplessly as Ole died in his arms on Christmas Eve 1844. Methias never got over the guilt he felt for his brother's death. A generation later, Earl Warren recalled of Methias, "Having lost the one most near and dear to him and being broke in a strange city, my father later told me he then swore that as long as he lived he would never be broke again. He said that, no matter how little he earned, he would save some of it. That became the guiding principle of his life. He would say, 'Earl, saving is a habit like drinking, smoking, or spending. Always save some part of what you earn.'"[2]

After Ole's death, Methias moved to the thriving metropole of Minneapolis to look for work. There he met and began dating another Scandinavian immigrant, Chrystal Hernlund. An attractive blonde of Swedish origin, she had changed her first name from Christine, which she'd always hated. Like Matt, she had come to America with her parents as a child. She settled with her family in Chicago, but they were forced out of the Windy City when their home burned to the ground in the Great Chicago Fire of 1871. In time, they moved north, resettling at the headwaters of the Mississippi River.

It was kismet. The young couple were drawn together by their shared backgrounds and values (both believed in hard work and eschewed alcohol and tobacco). Less than a year after they'd met, Matt Warren, twenty, asked Chrystal Hernlund, eighteen, to be his wife, and she accepted. They were married on Valentine's Day 1886. The couple's first child, Ethel, was born in Minneapolis one year later.

Shortly after that, the Warrens moved to California, the land of golden opportunity, where they lived briefly in San Diego before settling into a five-room rented cottage at 457 Turner Street near the bustling Los Angeles train depot. Methias found work with the Southern Pacific Railroad. And on March 19, 1891, Chrystal gave birth once more, this time to a son, Los Angeles's newest resident.

By 1891, the city, initially founded by the Spanish as El Pueblo de Nuestra Señora la Reina de los Ángeles de Porciúncula ("The Town of Our Lady the Queen of the Angels of Porciuncula"), had been an American possession for less than fifty years. During that time, it had grown in stature under the auspices of an oligarchy, in stark contrast to San Francisco to the north. While San Francisco, or "The City" as the locals called it, was liberal, Catholic, and organized around the sea and its workforce, Los Angeles was Protestant, conservative, geared to its dry desert valleys, and unionized. Methias would learn all too soon what being unionized meant to a working man in nineteenth-century Los Angeles.

When into this teeming cauldron the Warrens' bouncing baby boy made his debut, the family christened him simply "Earl Warren." Years later, young Earl asked his father why his parents had never given him a middle name. Methias thought for several moments before replying, "My boy, when you were born, we couldn't afford to give you a middle name."[3]

No strangers to hard work and physical labor, Matt and Chrystal Warren ran a fiscally conservative household whose typical Scandinavian values centered on the importance of a strong work ethic, an unshakable belief in God and the Ten Commandments, and a near-fanatical devotion to quality education.

Deprived of formal education due to his life's circumstances, Methias as a parent made providing education for Ethel and Earl his life's passion. Unfortunately, Ethel fell ill as a teenager and was unable to advance beyond high school, but Earl recalled his father's constant support of striving for more: "Not only did my father do everything possible to keep me interested in learning, but until he was well into middle age, he took correspondence courses himself in accounting and various phases of mechanics."[4]

For Methias, the courses paid off. He had worked on the night shift as a car inspector for several years before being promoted to foreman of the Bakersfield car repair shops and eventually named master car repairer for the San Joaquin Division, which extended from Fresno, a hundred miles to the north, to Los Angeles, a hundred miles to the south. He retained that position until his retirement.

At first, things went well for the young Warren family. But as the months crept toward a new century, their lives began to change. When a financial slump struck much of the country in the form of the Panic of 1893–1897, many Californians thought themselves immune. A large number of the state's working population were members of the vibrant, growing American Railway Union (ARU), whose members spread across railyards stretching from the Great Lakes to the Pacific Ocean. The ARU was the buffer that protected Californians from any threat of an economic depression. Or so they thought.

The union was headed by Eugene V. Debs, who steadily grew the membership of his all-white workers. (Blacks and other minorities were restricted from joining.) Debs was an American democratic socialist and a political activist, a trade unionist, and one of the founding members of the political party called the Industrial Workers of the World (IWW or the Wobblies). He'd run for the presidency of the United States five times under the banner of the Socialist Party of America. Through his presidential bids, as well as his work with labor movements, Debs eventually became one of the best-known and most influential socialists in America.[5]

One of the newest members of Debs's union, Methias Warren had joined in early 1894. Before long, he became aware of a large number of inequities within the railroad industry. The Pullman Palace Car Company had carved out a chilling reputation for abusing its workers. When the company cut wages to increase profits amid the tightening depression, its employees were already stretched to their financial limits. They turned to Debs, their union leader, for relief. He didn't want to strike, but after visiting the Pullman yards and seeing firsthand the deplorable conditions his workers faced, he had no choice but to support it.

So, shortly after Methias Warren joined the union, he found himself walking the picket line. As the work stoppage moved into its second week, Debs called for an emergency meeting with Pullman company executives to try to negotiate a settlement, but the executives flatly refused.

With no recourse, Debs ordered the ARU to send out a telegram calling for a boycott of all Pullman sleeping cars. At dawn the following morning, June 28, 1894, a switchman at the La Grande Station in Los Angeles refused to attach two Pullman sleepers to a train departing for San Francisco. Similar incidents unfolded across the country as other workers stood in solidarity with striking Pullman employees. Soon, the United States found itself embroiled in a nationwide labor dispute that impacted both its railway system and its postal service, which relied upon the rails to move its cargo.

After several more weeks of stagnation, the ARU at its national convention called for a nationwide boycott of all Pullman cars. Within four days, more than twenty-nine railroads west of Detroit and a quarter million workers in twenty-seven states had walked off their jobs rather than handle Pullman cars. Union Local 80 of Los Angeles joined in support of the boycott, refusing to process Pullman sleepers. Within days, more than three thousand union members in Los Angeles had joined the strike. Railroad service between Chicago and the West Coast was crippled. Thousands gathered at the prophetically named Hazard's Pavilion to hear speeches and demonstrate their solidarity. Other unions, including printers, pressmen, carpenters, and retail clerks, provided financial support.

On the other side of the stalemate, Harrison Gray Otis, publisher of the *Los Angeles Times*, used his influential newspaper to attack the ARU and its members. Fearing that his own employees might one day be emboldened to unionize with similarly catastrophic results, he pulled out all the stops, criticizing the ARU's work stoppage daily.

"In the great railroad strike of '94," a typical article read, "the *Times* was the only daily on the Pacific Coast which stood fast, stood firm, stood true . . . for law and order." The union responded by moving its picket lines over to the *Los Angeles Times* building.

Meanwhile, US Attorney General Richard Olney, who sat on the board of directors of several influential companies, intervened on behalf of the railroads. With the *Times*'s encouragement, the federal government moved against the unions. Olney relied on the Sherman Antitrust Act to place an injunction against the ARU, claiming that its members were interfering with interstate commerce and the delivery of mail. Authorities arrested ARU president Debs, the union's board, and local leaders who chose to disobey the injunction. Debs was sentenced to six months in federal prison, while the remaining board members served three. In Los Angeles, a grand jury indicted six local ARU leaders, all of whom were sentenced to eighteen months behind bars.

The strike was crushed.

While the union insurrection lasted only a few weeks, it ignited a war in the City of Angels that left behind a long trail of victims. Methias Warren was one of them. Although he was no activist, his loyalty to his coworkers cost him dearly: He was fired and blacklisted by the Southern Pacific as a socialist agitator.

Methias eventually found temporary employment working for the Santa Fe railroad in the desert to the east of Los Angeles, but in time, he saw the writing on the wall. He moved his family nearly one hundred hard, hot, dusty miles north and inland to the town of Bakersfield.

In 1895 the Warrens settled into a row house on Niles Street in Sumner, a tiny railroad town two miles outside of Bakersfield. At the time, the town was still a frontier settlement of railroaders, miners, oil workers, construction laborers, Basque sheepherders, gamblers, saloon keepers, promoters, pimps, and prostitutes, all of whom made up nearly 10 percent of Bakersfield's total population of seven thousand. Although the Warrens' place of residence had changed, Methias's family values hadn't. He still clung to the same intrinsic beliefs in God and family that he had known growing up. Each night before the children were tucked into bed, he took his Bible from the nightstand and read from it, a custom that had been passed down from father to son for generations.

While Earl Warren the boy grew into his new surroundings, Earl Warren the man later recalled those early years in the memoir he crafted. Two images in particular stood out, even three-quarters of a century later. One was Warren's hauntingly real memory of the sobs of a young neighbor stricken by polio or meningitis—he couldn't recall which. The young girl cried out in pain as she passed from one life into another, sobbing even as her family was unable to comfort her. The second was the railroad strike and a raucous evening when a group of protesters started a bonfire and burned an effigy above it. That night, Warren recalled, "gave me a horror of mob action which has remained with me to this day."[6]

The memories—so distant in nature and yet so ingrained in one man's mind—remained alive all those years because of the horror of his inability to stop them. Disorder. Disharmony. Abandonment of reason. They were terrifying concepts to the young boy growing up in Bakersfield, and their memory was destined to remain with him for the rest of his life.

For Methias Warren and his family in the 1890s, Bakersfield was a frontier town, the old West, the Wild West. It was Dodge City and Deadwood, it was Tombstone and every other ripped-and-randy place rolled into one. Its citizens were uniquely California chic offset by blue-collar grubby—romantic and foreboding at the same time. The town had no real scions of industry to whom to look for guidance. Just the opposite: It was chaotic and freewheeling. Its streets, one visitor recorded in 1882, were "generally full of horses, caparisoned in the Spanish style, tied to the hitching posts and awaiting their owners in the stores and taverns. The sheep-herders [were] a lonely class, who become morose and melancholy through long wanderings with their flocks far from the habitations of men and human speech." The city's shops, the writer noted, were "kept by Jews," while Chinatown stood apart, separated by an irrigation ditch "like a moat." Gypsies lived on the edge of town, while the "great ranches of the era were located just outside."[7]

Arriving in Bakersfield in 1895, Methias settled his family into a small rented house near the railroad tracks and took a job inspecting cars for the Southern Pacific. So eager was the company to attract workers to its new facilities that it chose to ignore its own blacklist.

While the Warrens embarked upon their new lives, the area was awakening all around them. Bakersfield was closing out the century with $4,347.24 in its treasury—a staggering amount at the time—with Big Oil bringing in more each day. The town council had voted to pave the sidewalks, and new roads were being laid. Respectable establishments were taking root, too—three major landholding companies ensured an endless supply of cattle, grain, and hay, while growers harvested peaches and apricots. One visiting editorial writer noted, "Substantial business buildings, an atmosphere of business thrift and engagement, a satisfied and unconcealed air of content, activity, briskness, good order on the streets and general observance of the dignity of the peace left upon the minds of the visitors . . . the impression that Bakersfield is a steady, growing, pushing and successful city."[8]

Despite all outward appearances, disorder and vice were still the underlying hallmarks of the town that boasted a hundred saloons "as thick as the leaves of autumn forest glades," according to one observer. The city's seven thousand residents—up from twenty-six hundred only five years earlier—included five hundred prostitutes. Crime was commonplace and widely reported in the *Daily Californian*, where coverage was splashy and at times revealing. A Wednesday evening knife battle made the headlines: "Mexican Stabbed in Leg Muscles." When three Native American men were arrested for public drunkenness, the paper cited the law against providing "Indians" with liquor and asked its readers the rhetorical question, "Who Gave Them Whiskey?"[9]

An even more shocking incident that captured the attention of the locals was a fatal Chinatown shooting. Jee Sheok, a Chinese resident of the quarter, shot and killed Jee Duck in the fall of 1899 over what witnesses reported as a business deal turned sour. The following January, Sheok came to trial, drawing huge crowds, including many local Chinese, an assemblage the Californian described as an "outpouring of heathendom."[10] The newspaper reported:

> Chinatowns, new and old, transferred themselves to the court house today, and the court room, the stairs, the corridors and the yard, were alive with Mongols representing all the tongs on the coast and every tribe from Manchuria to the sea. The occasion for this outpouring of heathendom is the trial in the superior court of Jee Sheok, who shot Jee Duck to death in new Chinatown in October last. Duck was a Chinese merchant and Sheok killed him over a business transaction.[11]

The paper went on to state that the defendant, a "villainous-faced Chinaman," sat without comment through the early days of the proceedings, which moved slowly in part because of the difficulty in swearing in twelve honest citizens willing to give equal credence to the testimony of both Asian and Caucasian.

Once a jury was finally seated, Sheok was convicted mostly on the testimony of a nine-year-old white boy, Percy Baker, who saw the shots fired and told the court that the dead man carried no gun, rebutting the defendant's argument that he had shot in self-defense. "This was the little fellow's story, and no amount of questioning by the defendant's attorney Mr. Emmons could shake it," the *Californian* reported. "The boy knew what he knew, he showed that he understood the oath, and his manner carried conviction to the listener." Sheok was sentenced to life in prison.[12] Warren, like young Percy Baker, was only nine years old when Jee Sheok was sent off to San Quentin, California's maximum-security prison. The image of the man as his sentence was read stayed with Warren for his remaining days.

As a boy, Earl was unusually quiet and mannerly—family traits he would carry with him through life. His father, although loving, caring, and devoted to providing the best for his family, was less than demonstrative.

Equipped with a biting sense of humor, he unleashed it only rarely, a Norwegian trait passed along from father to son. Expected to bear the rigors of life in stoic silence, men such as he felt obligated to work hard and achieve their goals, regardless of personal sacrifice. Laughter and overt expressions of happiness were not part of their agenda. Sudden bursts of emotion or giddiness were neither encouraged nor often shown.

Earl's mother, on the other hand, came from hearty Swedish stock. She loved everything she held dear with a passion, including her two children, and never shrank away from expressing her feelings. Equipped with stinging wit and elfish good humor, she was the perfect foil to her Norwegian husband and a constant reminder of why he toiled so hard to make a good living.

As a family, the Warrens' lives revolved around the kitchen. That was where the wood-burning stove stood against the wall, adjacent to the sink, pump, icebox, and table. That was where the family meals took place, and that was where the focal point of familial life exposed itself daily. Between meals, that table percolated with coffee klatches popping up like morels on a chilly, sunless morning. Whenever Methias was not off working, he joined his wife over a steaming cup of java to reminisce, dream, and plan for their future and that of their children or to share their largesse with friends and neighbors. If any one element of family life held the Warrens together, it was their early morning and late evening ritual of gathering around the table for a hot, steaming cup.

By the time young Earl turned five, his father had already made plans to enroll him in Washington Grade School. It was 1896, a full year before the customary age of enrollment. But education was the father's dream for his son—an unwavering hallmark of the Warren family—and Methias viewed Earl's formal schooling as the best gift he could bestow upon him. So he went down to the school and talked the principal into accepting into his tutelage an underage young Master Warren, most probably because Matt had already taught his son to read and write.

Chrystal, too, was anxious to see their boy enter school. She dressed him in the most stylish—if somewhat effeminate—clothes of the day. But young Warren's sartorial splendor only served to alienate him from his classmates, who were already a year older than Earl, further setting him apart as an oddity.

Something else that set him apart was the fact that he was left-handed in a right-handed world. But early in his academic career, an astute teacher noticed how awkwardly the boy handled himself and began tying his left hand behind his back, forcing Earl to learn to write right-handed. From that time on, he did everything left-handed except eat and write.[13]

Was what the boy experienced unnecessarily harsh treatment? Warren, writing years later, believed it was good training: "If a boy isn't made to obey . . . when he is young, he won't obey the laws of his country when he is older."[14]

His parents, who were better fixed financially than most of their neighbors, splurged in buying books to help fuel young Warren's appetite for knowledge. Later in life, he recalled receiving *Peck's Bad Boy* for Christmas in 1901 and a sequel the following year. His voracious appetite for literature helped him progress in proficiency tests well enough that his teachers recommended he skip the second grade, a practical decision that nonetheless failed to take into account Earl's lack of acculturation, thrusting him forward before his social skills had a chance to catch up with his intellect. As a result, he spent even *less* time with his classmates and more with his nose buried in his books. When a library was built only two blocks from the Warrens' home, Earl became one of its first and best customers, spending hours on end entombed there rather than going out to play with his classmates.

When young Earl wasn't reading, his father enlisted his help in building or repairing some of the dozens of small cottages Matt had purchased, renovated, and rented out to the railroaders. But the encouragement he gave his son failed to take root; Earl soon learned he wasn't cut out for working with his hands, although he appreciated those who were. So, from the age of nine, he dabbled in a variety of odd jobs to earn money to increase his college savings account—anything besides performing manual labor for his father! He delivered newspapers for the *Daily Californian*. He kept the accounts for the Ardizzi-Olcese Company, a local general merchandiser. He proved successful at selling ice (in the hundred-degree temperatures of Bakersfield's pre–air conditioning days, he would have been hard-pressed to fail). He even spent two summers driving a mule team for a grocery store.

That proved to be child's play for young Warren, who had spent most of his free time growing up surrounded by animals. His "pets" ranged from house dogs and hunting hounds to a sheep, an eagle, several chickens, numerous rabbits, and, most importantly, a burro named Jack. Earl thought of all of them as human, carefully digesting their actions and equating them with the corresponding human emotions and responses, but of all the animals, Jack was Earl's constant companion and favorite.

At that time, having a burro in Bakersfield wasn't unusual. Several of Warren's neighbors had them. They purchased them for a song from the sheepmen after the herders brought their flocks down from the mountains to overwinter on the scant patches of grass. Eager to rid themselves of the burden of having to feed the beasts costly hay, the herders sold them off for bargain-basement prices. Earl rode his mule around the countryside; he hopped on him to go swimming and fishing or to chase jackrabbits with his greyhounds. He rode him to go out trapping squirrels and occasionally merely to see what was happening around town.

While he may have been an excellent rider and a good judge of burro flesh, not every job Warren tackled as a boy panned out. One of his least successful ventures came after he received an advertisement in the mail. A company was looking for "enterprising young men" to sell books—one on the life of President William McKinley and another on "the Boer War in South Africa."[15] Both of those subjects had made a profound impression on Warren, who had been devastated with the news of the assassination of the president, almost as indelibly as by the courageous fight put up by the Boers against British attempts to subjugate them. With their poorly equipped soldiers and primitive techniques, the Boers had managed to stand off the better-armed, well-trained British forces until Great Britain was forced to give up the ghost.

Feeling as strongly as he did about two such dramatic world events, Earl was confident he could sell the books. The advertising materials to support his efforts were profoundly stirring! But instead of cleaning up, his efforts succeeded only in wearing down a couple pairs of shoes. He was too small of stature and too shy for his neighbors to take seriously, so they politely declined. He realized he'd never make a successful door-to-door salesman when he approached his father to buy a book and Matt turned him down. Earl gave up his fantasies of becoming a successful salesman that same day.

Although the Warrens were far from wealthy, Methias was a frugal man with a steady income, so the family managed to put away a tidy nest egg with which they were able to improve their standard of living. Matt bought a house and moved his family into it. Eventually, they had acquired enough money from working and renting out their income properties to enable Matt to retire from the railroad.

But not Earl. The Southern Pacific provided yet another opportunity for the boy to earn money. He later recalled that the railroad had been instrumental in his development. Working there taught him a lesson about monopolistic power, corruption, and political dominance that would eventually help to shape his judiciary career. At the time, though, the railroad appeared to be little more than another opportunity to make a buck.

As Earl grew into his teenage years, he discovered a newfound love: music—especially clarinet music. He learned a few basic notes and found he enjoyed the sounds coming out of the instrument. He also liked the fact that playing music enabled him to live inside himself instead of having to relate with others. Before long, his dedication to practicing paid off as he perfected his skills, developing uncanny virtuosity—that, despite Earl's insistence later that the neighbors for years thought the Warren family had an ailing cat.

As Earl's expertise as a clarinetist grew, his friend Albert Cuneo talked him into joining the local band with him. They were a welcome addition and soon were marching in ceremonial parades, performing Saturday night concerts in the park, and providing the backdrop for various political rallies and torchlight parades. Being a prominent figure in the band lent Earl a rare sense of security and self-confidence. As the group traveled around the city playing different venues, people came up to him, slapped him on the back, and congratulated him, telling him how much they appreciated the talent he had brought to the community. Suddenly, music became a means to an end, allowing him to escape from his shyness and step out of the shadows and into the limelight.

By the time Earl turned fifteen, he and Albert had been invited to join Local 263 of the American Federation of Musicians. "It wasn't that my playing was so good," he joked later, "it was just that the union needed members."[16] Earl was one of its youngest members and served as secretary at the group's organizational meetings. He carried his musician's union card proudly for the rest of his life.

With their teenage son showing so much ambition, the Warrens assured themselves that no matter what direction Earl's future might take, he was bound to be a success.

But Earl's musical prowess should have come as no surprise. Music had been an integral part of the Warren family for years. In a wide-open, reckless town, Methias proved to be a stable if somewhat grim source of constancy. He valued work and frugality. But when it came to music, that was something entirely different. The Warrens owned a Victrola and played it nearly every evening after dinner. Before long, Earl found himself emulating the rousing marches and organized rhythmic parlances of John Philip Sousa, "The March King."

Although the Warren family may have lacked some of the laughing and hugging and prancing around the living room in which other old Bakersfield families indulged, they were never short of one familial commodity: atonement. Whenever someone committed an infraction, Methias was there to dole out a suitable punishment—with a birch rod, if necessary. Honesty was the cornerstone of the family's heritage, nearly as much so as education. But, as Methias had learned the hard way years earlier, it didn't often come spontaneously. Honesty had to be taught; honesty had to be learned; honesty had to be practiced. Years later, when dealing with his own children and grandchildren,

Earl insisted upon the same, reminding his progeny that the measure of a man lay not in the number of dollars he had in the bank but rather in his refusal to tell a lie. It was an echo from Earl's past that had spanned three generations.

Surprisingly, for all the family's emphasis on virtue, the Warrens were not overtly religious. Earl and Ethel were raised Methodists, and the family kept and read a Bible, but they didn't attend weekly services. Methias chose instead to indoctrinate his children in a more corporal way: through moral upbringing and a demand for integrity that he taught by example. To Earl's father, organized religion did not rank high on the family's list of priorities. You could learn to be moral without going to church, Matt reasoned, but you couldn't learn to be smart without going to school!

As Earl moved through his academic years, Methias supported his son's every step, broadening the boy's exposure to life's experiences whenever and wherever. Beyond the classroom, the father often took his son to hear motivational speakers as they passed through the area—all in the hopes that young Earl would learn something more of life than existed within the four walls of a classroom.

And then it happened. On the evening of February 3, 1904, father and son left the house to hear an address that had received advance notice in the local *Daily Californian*. For young Earl, lightning struck.

It was billed as a lecture by Dr. Russell H. Conwell, a well-known minister and founder of Philadelphia's Temple University. Conwell crisscrossed America, delivering versions of his talk hundreds of times a year. In fact, he gave his speech more than five thousand times in twenty-five years. Whenever he arrived in a new town, he made time to chat with the local residents, hear the story of their town's founding, and learn about its people. By the time he actually rose to speak, Conwell was able to weave the locals' personal tales into his speech, identifying for the crowd the true gems in their own town and reminding them to treasure those unique aspects of their lives and communities.

When Conwell arrived in Bakersfield to deliver his "Acres of Diamonds" speech, he followed his usual protocol. The theme of his talk that evening was engaging and simple: There's no need to search the world for riches when they exist in your own backyard. He recounted the tale of a wealthy Persian who had heard from a stranger about vast riches in diamonds to be found in a faraway land. The fortune-seeker sold his property, deserted his family, and spent the rest of his life traveling the globe in search of the elusive treasure, only to wind up destitute. Meanwhile, the man who had bought the fortune-seeker's property was digging a garden in the backyard when he struck the wealthiest diamond field ever found.

Religious in fervor, moral in tenor, pragmatic in tone, Conwell's speech foreshadowed what Earl Warren wanted from life. "Greatness consists not in the holding of some future office," the speaker said, "but . . . in doing great deeds with little means and the accomplishment of vast purposes from the private ranks of life." He stopped to take a sip of water before continuing. "He who can give to this city better streets and better sidewalks, better schools and more colleges, more happiness and more civilization, more of *God*, he will be great anywhere."[17]

Sitting in front of the stage and looking up, Earl was spellbound. Half a century later, Warren recalled, "I can still see his towering form and hear his powerful voice as he told his never-to-be-forgotten story. Of all the lectures I heard in my youth, this one made the greatest impression on my young mind. The little town where we lived did not appear to offer too many advantages. It was located in an area covered largely by sagebrush and populated mainly by jackrabbits." But his father assured him that Conwell's story about diamonds applied to their own small town as well as to the largest sprawling city. He reinforced the message that people who were always planning to seek fortune in faraway places were overlooking the golden opportunities in their own backyards.

"He kept this picture before me through all the years I was growing into manhood," Warren said. "That little town is now the center of a population of a hundred and fifty thousand. Many who left there in search of oil and gold in Alaska, Mexico, and other distant places returned at a later date empty-handed, only to find that those who had remained had not only struck oil at home but, by harnessing mountain water and irrigating the parched land, had profitably made a veritable Garden of Eden out of the desert."[18]

Of course, it was one thing to fantasize about discovering riches in your own backyard and quite another to actually do so. Despite his father's mantra to work hard and achieve good results, Earl delivered on only the first of those two commandments. He had developed only mediocre study skills and barely managed to squeak by in school. When the final class bell rang for the day, Warren was first out the door, according to his classmates. Reflecting in 1969 upon Warren's less-than-stellar high school days, one fellow classmate called him "the bunk" in physics and described him, simply, as "never outstanding."[19]

Fortunately, there were other things to occupy Earl's time besides his schooling. One morning, on April 19, 1903, he learned of a shooting in Bakersfield; the city marshal and a deputy sheriff had been killed. That was enough to fire the boy's curiosity.

Hopping on Jack, Earl rode out to the scene of the crime. Crowds were still milling about as he arrived. "[S]ure enough," Warren recalled years later, "the city marshal, the deputy, and a notorious bandit had been slain. There was much speculation about the affair, and there was even talk about lynching another deputy who had been named by the dying marshal as the killer."[20]

At the time, a notorious outlaw named Jim McKinney had operated for years as a desperado throughout the Southwest. He had recently been jailed in Hanford, just north of Bakersfield, but escaped to resume his murderous spree. On the night of April 18, a deputy marshal named Al Hultse suggested to some townsfolk that McKinney was holed up in Bakersfield not more than a few hundred yards from the bar where they were drinking. The following morning, City Marshal Jeff Packard and his deputy, Will Tibbet—along with Tibbet's brother, Burt—tailed Hultse when he left his hotel after breakfast. As the two lawmen followed Hultse into a Chinese joss house, they were met by blasts from a twelve-gauge shotgun. Burt Tibbet returned fire from behind a woodpile and killed McKinney as he peeked out of the window. Marshal Packard, shot in the exchange, had just enough life in him to announce that it was Hultse and not McKinney who had done the shooting. Hultse was arrested later that morning and charged with the murder of officers Packard and Tibbet.

Several months later, after starting high school, Earl was passing the courthouse square on his way to school. He heard that Al Hultse was on trial for murdering his two fellow lawmen. Earl's curiosity got the better of him, and he sneaked into the courtroom to observe the murderer firsthand. Imagine his surprise when he realized that the killer was the same man who had once won several awards in a turkey shoot and given one of the prize birds to young Earl!

In the end, according to Warren, "the first trial resulted in a disagreement, [but] the second in a conviction for second-degree murder." Earl later learned that, while Hultse was in jail awaiting appeal, he slit his throat from ear to ear with a razor he had been given so he could shave. The image of that brutal act of desperation never left his mind.[21]

Fortunately, not all of young Warren's life was filled with such melodrama. One of seventy students enrolled in the Kern County High School class of 1908, he had gotten there by somehow squeaking through his grammar school courses and graduating among the lowest in his class. Although his father was less than pleased with his son's grades, he at least approved of his enrolling in a college preparatory program at Kern. Earl was thirteen at the time.

But Earl's high school transcripts turned out to be little better than his grammar school grades: a study in mediocrity. His motto might have been "Latin is my downfall; conjugation is my death." After two years of studying, Warren received no grade higher than a 77 on a test. Nor did he do much better in French or physics, which for Earl were a disaster. As one classmate's recollection confirmed, he was abysmal, receiving a 75, the second-lowest grade of his entire high school career, exceeded only by a 70 in junior year algebra.

One promising mark, though, was Warren's highest grade of all throughout his four years at Kern: a 94 in American history. That year, too, introduced him to poetry, to which he flocked like a goose to a ripening cornfield. In 1904 he received a collection of English poetry masterpieces in which he promptly inscribed his name. He retained the book to his grave.

But if his time in high school didn't do much to form Earl Warren's future, it did solidify within him one realization: He did best with those subjects that appealed to him. *Latin? French? Physics? Algebra?* No, thanks. *The history of America and the people who lived it?* Absolutely.

One more thing he discovered that appealed to him during those hectic years was hard work—or, rather, earning money by working hard. Throughout his high school years, he spent the summers toiling for the Southern Pacific, promising his father he would return to school at the end of each summer's break. Earl's job as a call boy consisted of running through town and gathering up crews for departing trains. It was an eye-opening education for the teenager. He tramped through the city's bowels to locate the men, sober them up whenever remotely possible, and deliver them to their posts. Along the way, he witnessed men gambling away their life's earnings and saw the Southern Pacific strip its poorest workers of most of their paychecks by luring them to the company store. He witnessed others blacklisted because of their union membership, as his father had been before the family relocated to Bakersfield.

But the most appalling things Warren witnessed were the injuries. He watched in horror as men were crushed between cars and carried, scream-ing, to the shop lathe, where they were held down by fellow workers as the operator cut off their arms or legs with the blade.

To a young man filled with dreams and hopes for a brighter tomorrow, it didn't seem fair. "My nature," he remembered years later, "always recoiled against these inequities. All my life, I wanted to see them wiped out."[22] Many years later, some of Warren's most liberal colleagues on the Supreme Court expressed surprise at Warren's insistence on the court's taking up even the most obscure cases involving workers seeking compensation for injuries. When they finally realized that Warren's concerns stemmed back to his childhood memories, they began to understand.

Of course, not all of Warren's memories were so gruesome. Earl's recollections of delivering newspapers for the *Daily Californian* were far more pleasant. It was easy money for a few hours' work after school. But even at that, his time away from home created problems. Earl's burro, Jack, became discontented because of his master's late arrivals and took to braying impatiently for hours on end. Earl's parents finally persuaded their son to find a new home for Jack with someone who could keep him both busy and happy. Warren recalled the outcome: "I was contacted by the owner of a shoe store that carried Packard shoes. He told me he would like to have Jack for use on a conveyance to advertise those shoes. He said Jack would be kept busy and would be well taken care of in a livery stable not far from the high school. Much as I hated to sell my burro, I did, and Jack went into the advertising business."

The "conveyance" to which he was harnessed was a replica of a giant shoe on a makeshift buggy chassis. A boy sat inside the shoe and handled the reins. But, as Warren recalled,

> It was only a partial success because they soon found that the contraption could not go to suburban Kern City, [because] Jack, if he came within a half mile of our home, would put his head in the air and run there as fast as he could. The bridle and bit could not hold him. His mouth was like iron, and his determination equally so. On arriving at our house, he would bray until my mother came out and fed him a little snack of some kind. Even then he would not leave, so [the company] abandoned trips to that part of the community.
>
> On my way home from school, I would always stop at the livery stable and give him scraps from my lunch basket. If he was not there, I would leave them in his feed box. One day when I arrived at the livery stable, I was informed that he was dead. Poisoned, they said. They did not know by whom, but I reasoned that his constant braying for me had irritated the neighbors so much that someone had decided to put a stop to it. My sorrow at his passing remains to this day.[23]

As the dog days of summer approached, the lingering weeks of Earl Warren's academic nightmare were likewise grinding to an end. If anything, he had learned during those four long, hard years of high school that his love of practical learning and his reliance on his personal experiences over academic integrity would serve as a mainstay for making his way through life: They were destined to ground his ideologies in real life and infuse his politics and jurisprudence with common sense.

By the time of his graduation, Earl had managed to develop a remarkably analytical mind, according to his sister, Ethel, something that would serve him well in his future. "At home," Ethel recalled, "Dad and Earl used to take opposite views of things. I think Dad was drawing Earl out to see what he was thinking."[24]

One of the things about which he was thinking most seriously was leaving home—for good.

Despite his aversion to schooling, Warren went to work for two months that summer following his high school graduation. He had resigned himself to enrolling in college. It was less a newfound love for education than his father's incessant drilling into him the requisites for obtaining as much knowledge as possible. So, as the summer ground to a close far more quickly than he might have preferred, Warren packed some belongings and boarded a train headed north in the brutal sweltering heat of August, riding on the free pass the railroad issued its employees.

The journey from Bakersfield to Oakland was long, hot, and dusty. For thirteen hours, the gawky young kid from the conservative blue-collar town sat sweating in the grimy Southern Pacific coach, watching the San Joaquin Valley pass by his open window. He'd never before realized just how large a state California was, and he began to wonder if he'd ever arrive in Oakland.

After his father had bid him a gruff good-bye, reminding him that he was a man now and would be expected to act like one, Earl felt a momentary swell of excitement and fulfillment before the specter of loneliness fell across him like a shroud. Feeling apprehensive and yet somehow empowered, he was uncertain of what the University of California held in store for him. Had he only had a crystal ball to foresee his future, he would have worried less and enjoyed the scenery more.

The university system in California in those days was in its unbridled infancy. The school in which young Warren had chosen to enroll was destined to test his mettle. He would see few familiar faces on campus at Berkeley. He was the first person ever from East Bakersfield to attend there. Four of his fellow Kern County High School graduates eventually joined him, including Reginald Stoner and Wilfred Forker—both from a privileged social class, both successful athletes, and neither the sort of young man likely to choose to chum around with the younger, unprepossessing Earl.

Shortly after arriving, he confronted another dilemma when he was forced to decide what electives to take. Warren wanted one thing; his father wanted another. Matt had looked at the situation objectively, concluding that his son should study mining. There was a good mining school at Berkeley and plenty of jobs for its graduates in a state overflowing with rich mineral deposits and oil fields. Stoner, Forker, and another acquaintance, Omar Cavins, were all planning on studying mining, each destined for a career as a geologist with Standard Oil.

But Earl clung to a different dream. He knew he wanted to be a lawyer—a trial lawyer like those he had seen arguing cases in the courthouse back home. He could never recall precisely when or how he had reached that decision, which initially surprised even his sister, who recalled that Earl initially wanted a career in medicine because a doctor could help people, but once he made up his mind to be a lawyer, he never changed it. That, according to Warren, was quite early in his life. "My determination to become a lawyer goes back so far that I can hardly remember ever having been without it," he often remarked to friends.[25]

It seemed a strange career choice for a youngster who found it difficult even to appear before strangers, let alone mount a persuasive argument. Perhaps it was the very gregariousness of the attorneys he had witnessed in the courtroom in his youth or the practiced ease with which they presented their cases that attracted him. Maybe he envisioned himself one day mastering public speaking through the study of jurisprudence.

So, as the train ground to a halt in the station at Oakland, the eager, lanky young man from Bakersfield got up out of his passenger seat and hefted a suitcase from the overhead rack. He was fortunate, he knew, to be off on his adventure. Few people back then could afford to send their children to college. The census of 1900 reported that a scant 86,000 of the 687,000 people still in school at the age of eighteen had one or more foreign-born parents—unlikely candidates to treat their children to a college education. Methias and Chrystal Warren's thrift had helped their son beat the odds.

Walking through the station, Earl felt his apprehension swell. With each step, he realized how far he'd traveled from home and his family—and how alone he was. But as he stepped outside and felt the bracing crispness of the fresh bay air, he took a long look around: the lights in the distance, the twinkling of the stars reflected in the water, the moon dancing overhead. In a matter of moments, his fears washed away. In their place rose an incredible sense of freedom. Freedom! He realized all at once that he would make a go of it at Berkeley. He would make it happen. Despite any problems he'd experienced with his schooling in the past, he would fit in, and he would succeed—because he fit into his new environment, and he longed to succeed.

The pocketful of money Earl had brought with him from home helped; he wouldn't have felt so comfortable if he'd been penniless. But he had managed to save eight hundred dollars from his part-time jobs over the years, a small fortune when an oil field roustabout averaged only twelve dollars a week. Better yet, the money was his to do with as he wished. His father had managed over the years to salt away enough to pay his son's college tuition, room, and board.

So young Warren walked to the end of the pier, not a worry in the world, where a ferry waited to take passengers across the icy waters of San Francisco Bay to the city beyond. Except for a weekend trip he had made with his friend Albert in 1907, Warren was about to spend his first night away from home in the largest metropolis in the state.

Climbing the gangplank to the boat on that crisp August evening, Warren worked his way forward: "As I stood on the bow of the ferryboat, surveying the beautiful land looking over to the Golden Gate, I filled my lungs with refreshing air and said to myself, 'I never want to live anywhere else the rest of my life.'"[26]

Looking back today, it's hard to imagine what inspired his appetite for the area, for the city itself was little more than an empty shell. It still clung to the wreckage of the great earthquake and fire of April 1906. A few buildings rose from the ashes like the great Phoenix along Market Street and elsewhere, sprouting from cleared lots and mounds of shattered bricks. But mostly the area lay in shambles.

Regardless, an undeniable sense of optimism exhumed itself from the rubble, a feeling of new life and a renewed spirit that the seventeen-year-old couldn't help but embrace. For a boy fresh off the turnip truck from a small farming and railroad community in the middle of nowhere, the romance and overwhelming grandeur of the city—even in tatters—was breathtaking.

The next morning, Warren took the ferry from the city back to Oakland, where he boarded an interurban train to Berkeley, home of the University of California. He was one of fewer than one thousand incoming freshmen on a campus of more than three thousand students and three hundred faculty.

After stopping off for a quick breakfast, he walked across the commons with its comforting combination of dense oak groves and sprawling eucalyptus stands. He marveled at the size of the ivy-covered buildings as he wandered on past the tropical trees and wild grasses beyond the newly opened Hearst Memorial Mining Building. He passed the bare steel frame of the soaring campanile destined to tower over the campus and its new library for decades to come. As he uncovered one visual treat after another, he vowed to do his best to become one of the school's most devoted alumni.

Warren checked out the rooms at the fraternity house of La Junta Club, which had been recommended by a trusted family friend. At that moment, he made another life-changing decision: He would move in, make the club his home, and flourish. He'd already heard about the La Junta members, all renowned for the seriousness with which they approached college life, standing for everything that Earl hoped to be but had failed to accomplish in his past. But now his past was gone, and his future beckoned.

The club's upperclassmen had a history of appraising and apprising incoming freshmen of campus happenings. Warren recalled in his memoirs that one upperclassman asked him in a meeting about his high school days. Hoping to impress the club member that he was just "one of the boys," Earl boasted of the cat-and-mouse relationship he and the other students at Kern County High had maintained with its principal, C. C. Childress, who was always on the lookout for gold bricks. Since old "C-Cubed" penalized entire classes on even the mere suspicion of cheating, the boys, of course, did their best to outwit him at every turn.

Later that week, university senior Herbert Whiting invited the freshman from Bakersfield to dinner, during which he admonished Warren for such childish behavior. "This is not the way things are done at the university," Warren recalled Whiting saying. He added that the university operated on the honor system, insisting "that there was no spying; that students were entrusted with self-government, and that they were expected to be honorable in taking examinations as in all other things."[27]

Moreover, Whiting added, cheating merely hurt other students, since most professors graded on a class average. If someone artificially raised that average by cheating, the honest students would suffer the consequence of poorer grades.

The admonishment fell on receptive ears. Warren, touched by the young man's sincerity and integrity, made a vow never to violate the fraternity's code of honor—and he meant it.

Within a few weeks of his arrival on campus, Warren was invited by the La Junta Club to become a member. He remained a resident there for the next six years, cherishing the companionship of other like-minded young men and the friendships he made and becoming more comfortable speaking among his peers as well as the general public. This was not an inconsequential development.

Warren's membership in the club couldn't have come at a better time. The La Junta was a secure den in a university teeming with insecurity and bursting with radical concepts and people, an oasis for every ilk of radicalism under the sun. Earl was still a member four years later when La Junta was absorbed as a chapter into the older, longer established fraternity Sigma Phi.

But while young Warren had been serious about devoting himself to integrity, he fell into the same trap as before with his studies. The new political science major with an eye on one day matriculating to law school found the distractions of college life too tempting to resist. Before long, his devotion was geared more toward having a good time and learning about his suddenly vastly expanding universe than his academics. He had no burning zeal, he conceded later, for knowledge: "No book or professor had a profound influence on me."[28]

To his fellow students, Warren fit into campus life seamlessly. To fulfill a military training requirement, he joined the fifty-two-piece university band as one of three second clarinets, the only college student in the band who was unionized! Eventually, he worked his way up to first clarinet. He earned pocket money playing for campus proms and other special events. Most of the university occasions were grim affairs over which the university's Junior Prom Committee presided. On their watch, they banned the popular but socially inappropriate dances the Turkey Trot, the Grizzly Bear, and the Back-Walk.

Before long, the youngster known around La Junta as "The Freshman" slowly began the inevitable process of maturation. His features softened as he put on weight. He parted his hair on the left instead of the right. He spent so much time playing cards and drinking ten-cent beers at Gus Brause's tavern that he left himself little opportunity for the more traditional pursuit of academic excellence.

Still, his father's admonishment to work diligently at whatever he chose to do had not fallen on deaf ears. When Earl began exercising at the gym, he took his workouts seriously. When he met fellow student Walter Arthur Gordon, the grandson of a Southern slave, who happened to be shadow boxing, Warren asked to spar with him. After donning a pair of gloves, the two went several rounds. Remarkably, no one was killed, and their sparring became a regular ordeal. Their mutual respect eventually grew into a lifelong friendship, with Gordon going on to become a Berkeley police officer while attending law school at night.

But the gym and the classroom were hardly the same. In his studies, the son failed to take his father's admonitions to heart. He rarely cracked open a book and hardly ever prepared for a test. It wasn't that he was lazy, and it wasn't that he hadn't the intellect to become a straight-A student. He just couldn't muster the desire.

Outside the classroom, however—that was a different story. There, Warren tackled a wide range of literature, from Rudyard Kipling and Robert Louis Stevenson to Charles Dickens, Upton Sinclair, Jack London, and Frank Norris, all authors he had longed to read. Two of his favorite three American scribes were native Californians who, significantly, turned out to be progressive social reformers.

Shortly into his academic career, Warren acquired a nickname bestowed on him by a nurse at the university infirmary where he had gone to be treated for conjunctivitis, or "pink eye." Several friends overheard her say to him, "Come on, Pinky, it's time for your medicine." The moniker stuck, partly because of his fair complexion and partly for his tendency to broil beneath the burning sun.

None of it hurt Warren's popularity on campus. Before long, members of Oakland's secretive Gun Club, which gathered on Thursday nights at Pop Kessler's Rathskeller, invited Warren to join, and he leaped at the opportunity. He was particularly fond of drinking beer and reading aloud the poetry of Robert Service, Kipling, Gel Burgess, and Bret Harte. He, himself, was renowned for reciting "The Sinking of the Mary Gloucester" and "Leave the Lady Willie," although admittedly his own favorite was W. E. Henley's "Invictus":

> It matters not how strait the gate,
> How charged with punishments the scroll,
> I am the master of my fate;
> I am the captain of my soul.

Membership in the society, which was based more upon camaraderie than on social or academic prowess, nurtured Warren's sense of idealism. As a member, he strove to recognize within himself the value of "men who put virtue, honor, and loyalty above else," as one fellow member put it.[29]

At the Gun Club, too, Warren learned to honor the homily of the university's football coach, Andy Smith: "It is better to lose than to win at the sacrifice of ideal." Warren identified with the affirmation that "the only thing that matters to a man is character. Character is determined by refusal to lie."[30] It brought memories of his father's influences throughout his life. Increasingly popular on campus, Earl in his last year was invited to join the select honor society Skull and Keys.[31]

As if his social activities weren't broad enough, Warren often trooped down to the Oakland-Alameda Estuary with friends to listen to the tall tales of overwintering salmon fishermen or to hang out at the First and Last Chance Saloon, where writer Jack London spun outrageous yarns of adventure to anyone who would front him the price of a drink. At other times, Earl and his classmate John Quinn grabbed a ferry across the bay to savor the spiked punch and free lunches at the Waldorf Bar.

Despite all the socializing—or perhaps because of it—Warren viewed his undergraduate years at Berkeley as inanely uneventful. He found his studies neither too demanding nor particularly attractive. In the summers he returned to Bakersfield, where he worked as a mechanic's helper in the Southern Pacific roundhouse to earn extra money for his school activities. He commented years later that while no one political party or point of view made a lasting impression on him, Berkeley in the second decade of the new century burned with the fires of Progressive activism. When Harrison Reed joined the faculty, all hell broke loose, and Earl Warren found himself once again under the sorcerer's spell.

Reed, a dynamic young socialist, was a political science professor and speaker who lectured on campus on weekdays and from the pulpit of the local Congregational church on Sundays. His fervor flooded the university. For Warren, *reform* meant not only a change in the status quo but also a political reckoning. When it came to dishonest, crooked politicians, "Throw the rascals out" was more than a mandate; it was a moral imperative, suited as well to society as it was to the soul.

With activism engulfing him, Warren's interests turned increasingly to the comforting world of politics. He participated in elections for student government, promoting the candidacies of his friends. Although never quite outgoing enough to run for office himself, he attended rallies at San Francisco's Dreamland Rink for Progressive gubernatorial candidate Hiram W. Johnson, and he spent election night as a poll watcher in San Francisco's Mission District. As a junior, Warren cheered a student demonstration for Socialist John Stitt Wilson, later elected mayor of Berkeley.

Warren's budding Progressivism, in contrast to his own inherited conservatism, owed much of its existence to the native Californian's antagonism toward the Southern Pacific Railroad and his father's identification with the reform-minded small businessmen who had fought for a share of the prosperity the giant corporations had hoarded for decades.

But Warren didn't become a confirmed Progressive until 1912 when he cast his first presidential vote after traveling to Sacramento to hear Wisconsin senator Robert La Follette Sr. pour out his heart while campaigning futilely for the Republican presidential nomination.

As governor of Wisconsin, "Fighting Bob" had pushed through a succession of political, economic, and social reforms that made him a champion of the up-and-comer, the go-getter, the ambitious young man—in other words, Earl Warren.

Decades later, Warren could still quote the reform-minded senator: "The supreme issue, involving all others, is the encroachment of the powerful few upon the rights of the many."[32]

La Follette left a lasting impression on Warren: "He was called a radical, a disrupter, a socialist, a subverter, and perhaps the only reason he was not called a Communist was because that term had not then been popularized as a term of opprobrium. But he was a lifelong Republican, steeped in the tradition of that party. . . . He believed in the party system . . . and his party in particular as a party of the people—farmers, workmen, small-businessmen; not as an oligarchy of dominant interests."[33]

At the end of his third year at Berkeley, Warren entered the school's Department of Jurisprudence in the recently inaugurated Boalt Hall. He was, even by his own admission, the least promising of the seventy-nine-student field enrolled.

From the start, the school's rigid curriculum provoked quiet rebellion in the first-year student. Under the leadership of Dean William Carey Jones, Boalt had adopted the casebook method of study that had recently been pioneered at Harvard. The five members of the faculty presided over the required courses, slavishly following the Harvard model of contracts, torts, property, criminal law, and common-law pleading. All were read from casebooks that began with Old English law and plodded onward toward the twentieth century.

But Warren realized that there was no introductory course to the practice of law and no practical training, shortcomings that grated on him. The school prohibited students who might have sought a broader education from working in a law office; it tolerated nothing that might interfere with a student's indoctrination into law as it was taught "the Boalt way": "The law school made a fetish of discouraging the acquisition of practical knowledge," Warren said, "and they were so committed to the case system that they denied you opportunity of seeing things in perspective."[34]

Despite his disappointment in the school's inflexible policy, Warren held his tongue until the end of the first year when he received his bachelor of law degree, which was not exactly a given. In fact, at one point the law school's dean openly attempted to discourage Warren from continuing his studies. "You will never graduate," he said in clipped rebuke.

The young man asked, "Why? Haven't I passed all of my examinations?"

"You have, yes, but you have not once raised your hand to speak out in class."

"Is that obligatory?"

"No."

"Was the class ever informed they needed to speak out?"

"No."

"Well, then, Dean," Warren argued, "since I was never told and it is not obligatory and I am passing my examinations, I am going to graduate!"[35]

And he set out to prove it.

In defiance of the school's rules, the law student took an afternoon job at a Berkeley law firm, serving court papers, handling nontechnical matters, and studying the interminable casebooks whenever he had an opportunity. The position offered him an insight into the everyday practice of law that he felt had been missing from Boalt's curriculum.

But once again, far from being the perfect scholar, Warren found himself much nearer to the bottom of his class than the top. Remarkably, he managed to avoid making the law review staff even once, a feat rarely matched in the annals of American jurisprudence. He also managed to avoid receiving a single award or other coveted collegiate honor. He did succeed in maintaining a humbling C average throughout his studies, although he was far from being voted Lawyer Most Likely to Succeed.

Part of Warren's lackluster performance was due to his persistent fear of public speaking; part was a general ambivalence toward structured learning. Nonetheless, he submitted his thirty-four-page thesis, "The Personal Liability of Corporation Directors in the State of California," on time. By May 1914, he had met and passed the final requirement.

Even though he had proven himself academically undistinguished in all ways, Earl Warren had kept his promise and managed to be among the fifteen men and one woman to receive their doctor of jurisprudence degrees that year, although even in graduating, he was ignominiously identified in the Blue & Gold annual as "Carl Warren."

One week after graduation, the graduates were admitted to practice in California. But even that created something of a problem for Warren. His father had expected him to return to Bakersfield and set up shop after law school. That prospect, after six years at Berkeley, seemed to Earl a fate worse than death. How could he have spent the past few years of his life moving forward on his own only to spend the rest of them reliving the past?

Warren toyed with the notion of moving to Sacramento, thereby short-circuiting his father's expectations. The state capital had jobs available—lots of them—for hungry young lawyers. But explaining to his father why he chose to escape the heat of Bakersfield for the heat of Sacramento would be difficult at best.

Finally he reached a decision to remain in San Francisco to gain the practical training he had missed in law school. He joined the two-lawyer legal department of the Associated Oil Company in San Francisco. The pay was a mere $50 a month, but that was more money than he had ever made at one time before.

So at last, at the tender age of twenty-three, a light-blond man with even lighter whiskers—rawboned and stocky at 6-foot-1—stepped out of the classroom and into corporate America, although not without some trepidation. "I guess I must have looked awfully young to people," Warren conceded.[36]

Contrary to his expectations, Warren's disillusionment with the firm was evident from the start. The company's chief counsel, Edmund Tauske, was by turns irascible and demeaning. He issued peremptory orders, gruffly dispatching Warren to fetch half a dozen Coronas from the cigar store downstairs while verbally dismissing his newest assistant's legal research as "inadequate" before adopting it word for word when advising management on specific points of law. A rasher man would have been pushed to the limit and quit, except for not wanting to embarrass the friends he had used as references. But Warren was not a rasher man, so he balked at the notion of quitting—up to a point.

But, as time crept by, Warren's job grew worse, and so did his outlook. His spirits fell even further when he recognized to what depths of inadequacy the practice of law had sunk in San Francisco. On one of his numerous visits to the temporary county courthouse to observe the day-to-day workings of the legal system, he realized that the majority of judges and prosecutors were hacks, mere creatures created by and for the Southern Pacific Railroad and the city's political bosses—bought and paid for to maintain the status quo.

"The atmosphere surrounding them was anything but inspiring," Warren wrote later.[37]

In fact, it was so uninspiring that the young lawyer began contemplating the genuine possibility of leaving the law altogether and going out to look for other employment.

His only question, he soon realized, was: doing what?

2

LONG AND WINDING ROAD

Warren's decision to set down roots in Northern California posi-
tioned him firmly in conflict with the geopolitical/social traditions of Los Angeles and Bakersfield. Southern California had sprouted
from the faded Mexican land grants and the steely-eyed businessmen who
snapped them up for obscene profits, while San Francisco was built upon
gold: The strike in 1848 had uncovered rich mother lodes ranging from
Sacramento to the western Sierra Nevada. Where the San Joaquin Valley
of Warren's youth had been founded on oil, agriculture, and ranching,
midcentury San Francisco was built upon the backs of teeming throngs
lured by precious metals and the easy money that poured from their veins:
the hangers-on who followed one strike after another, the gamblers and
dance-hall girls and prostitutes and speculators—and the gunslingers,
thieves, and other dregs of society, too, of course.

Gold helped to build California—white California, *Northern* California—providing it with its first and longest-lasting identity. In 1849 California's population stood at barely one hundred thousand; within three years,
it had leapfrogged to three times that size. It possessed what local historian
Hubert Howe Bancroft referred to as its two remarkable features ... youth-
fulness and paucity of women.[1] In 1850, under the weight of fortune seek-
ers pouring in from the east, California was more than 92 percent male, an
imbalance that corrected itself ever so slowly. Not until 1880 would women
comprise nearly one-third of the state's population.

Only a negligible number of those rushing to the goldfields actually
made their fortunes there; the vast majority who ended up staying out west
turned to trading, farming, hunting, trapping, fishing, or working for the
railroads, which by then were undergoing "furious construction," as author

Jim Newton put it.[2] Others manned the docks at one of the world's best natural ports—San Francisco.

Built upon the backs of frenetic young men, San Francisco was from the outset a volatile and unruly city. It was California's first great metropolis and its most decadent one. Money barons dominated society, such as it was. Industrialist Leland Stanford, along with fellow railroad tycoons Charles Crocker, Collis Huntington, and Mark Hopkins, built opulent mansions on Nob Hill from which they looked down upon their minions of the railroading and trading empires. Beyond the spectacle they oversaw, the Chinese ghetto and the burgeoning red-light district meandered like a river's backwaters onward toward infinity. The city's twenty-block central core gave way to streets bursting with brothels and saloons. With only one school and three churches, it hardly seemed a beckoning oasis for the slowly growing middle class of citizens—both devout and somber—every city requires to prosper.

It was no coincidence that a unique Northern California lifestyle sprang from "The City," as generations of Californians came to call it. Instead of men and women in dungarees and cowboy hats, San Francisco's elite turned out in high collars and stiff suits as they watched over all of the town's bustle and pretense: its docks, powerful unions, and ruthless political bosses. Horses clattered across glass-gilded cobble streets, and a battle-tested working class, mostly Catholic and liberal, engaged in escalating conflict with corrupt politicians and their vigilante allies.

The Communist Manifesto, published in 1848, had given a new structure to working-class grievances, after which Germany, France, and England were forever gripped by Communism and the rise of Lenin's First Congress of the Communist International. San Franciscans even back then grappled with the steady if tenuous pull of radicalization. In winter 1849, carpenters and joiners in San Francisco waged the first strike in the state's long prehistory. With that, The City embarked upon an unfolding drama arising from union organizing, strikes, resistance, and violence that waxed and waned with the town's tumultuous economy.

When Warren arrived, the place was still struggling to right itself from its greatest crisis and was confronting yet another. At 5:12 a.m. on April 18, 1906, California's preeminent city, its cultural and economic jewel, had fallen into a heap. Some locals called it the "ground shake," forty-seven seconds of a ruinous earthquake. South of Market Street, San Francisco's main thoroughfare, cheaply built tenements crumbled like cards atop one another; hundreds of people died in the first wave alone. Gazing out on the wreckage in the moments immediately following the first devastating blow, John Barrett, the city desk news editor of the *San Francisco Examiner*, described the earth as "slipping quietly away from under our feet. There was a sickening sway, and we were all flat on our faces."

Outside, pandemonium reigned. Trolley tracks were twisted, their electrical wires down, wriggling like serpents, flashing blue-and-yellow sparks in the dust. The street bore gashes in any number of places. Water spurted from some of the holes; gas, from others. Barrett turned to two of the paper's reporters and remarked, "This is going to be a hell of a day."[3]

It was, in fact, a hell of a *week*. With Act One played out, Act Two unfolded. Fires erupted with uncontrollable fury. Fire crews, hindered by the death of their chief, were overwhelmed and forced to resort to dynamiting the wooden buildings to deprive the fire of fuel. Block after block of The City was leveled.

The damage to San Francisco was staggering, and the reconstruction dragged on forever. For more than a year, the grand clock above the city's Ferry Building, one of few prominent edifices to survive, stood stuck at 5:16, the moment at which the trembling of the earth had begun. Even by 1908, when Warren arrived, the city remained in tatters. It was, he said, a "sad sight to behold. . . . Downtown, the place was a mass of rubble, with the frames of a few buildings, gutted by fire, standing skeleton-like in the midst."[4]

Then, from the very bowels of the debris and the detritus of the fire, came the great reckoning. San Francisco politics were catapulted by Progressivism into the future of California and the life of Earl Warren.

In the early twentieth century, San Francisco's blood ran red with corruption. Bribery dominated the backroom halls, and political candidates seeking office for personal gain were the norm. At the root of the worst corruption of all was a dapperly dressed dandy named Abraham Ruef, who had gained notoriety as the corrupt political boss behind the even more corrupt political machine of Mayor Eugene Schmitz before and after the 1906 earthquake.

Ruef's parents were of French-Jewish background. Their son was a bright student who gained admittance to the University of California at the age of fourteen. There, he majored in classical studies and developed an interest in fighting the rampant corruption that was endemic to not only local but also national politics. With a few fellow students, he founded the Municipal Reform League. He corresponded with like-minded individuals across the nation, including a young New Yorker by the name of Theodore Roosevelt. At eighteen, Ruef graduated with highest honors, after which he enrolled at the Hastings College of Law in San Francisco. He graduated less than three years later and was accepted to the California State Bar when he was twenty-one, the minimum age for admittance.[5]

At the time, California was the undisputed hub of the corruption that sprang from the weight of the Southern Pacific Railroad, which controlled both of the state's political parties. Party members and other well-funded individuals and special-interest groups used their economic leverage and influence to form trusts and monopolies that guaranteed their power. Many of the wealthiest of these people lived in San Francisco, where they reinforced their hold on government through their support of corrupt politicians and city bosses.[6]

Although Ruef had once been a Republican, he craved more power than the party could afford him, so in 1901 he founded the Union Labor Party. Using his newly gained authority, he maneuvered himself into a position of even more power.

Ruef selected the relatively unknown Schmitz, a violinist and amateur composer who was president of the Musicians Union, to run for mayor on the Union Labor Party ticket. Schmitz had no scandals in his past; tall and handsome, he was a commanding speaker with a friendly nature. The married father of two was just the man Ruef hoped would be both electable and conducive to influencing others along Ruef's journey to the governor's mansion in years to come. Behind the scenes, Ruef wrote Schmitz's speeches, planned his public appearances, and ran his campaign. Schmitz, who had become Ruef's puppet, was elected mayor in 1902.[7]

Through secretive appointments and rigged races, Ruef's political machine gradually gained control over the chief of police, the Board of Supervisors, and several prominent judges. But shortly after the 1905 election, his choice for district attorney, William L. Langton, began enforcing the vice laws that had been ignored up until then. Not everyone in the office was pleased. The Barbary Coast's infamous dance halls, brothels, and flagrantly operating gambling dens attracted money and people from across the West. The City's politicians were determined to keep the meter running.

Reformers gained considerable sympathy, if not wholehearted support, from the general population, which was growing tired of the nonstop illicit and immoral activities surrounding them. Radical Puritans such as Anthony Comstock as well as newly awakened prohibitionists began gaining in political influence. The reformers, among whom Ruef had once counted himself, slowly garnered power as Langton threw the weight of his office behind new attacks on the brothels and gambling halls he had once tacitly endorsed. The *San Francisco Bulletin*'s editor, Fremont Older, backed Langton's actions, and the publisher persuaded millionaire Rudolph Spreckels to fund a federal investigation into corruption at city hall.

Meanwhile, Ruef and his cohorts grew increasingly brazen. Charles Boxton, the chairman of the city's Public Works Committee, minced few words in putting the bite on the president of the Parkside Realty Company before the city provided approval for trolley service to reach the company's development project along San Francisco's western dunes.

It was among all these political shenanigans, financial kickbacks, and dirty deals that Warren reached a decision to quit his job and seek employment elsewhere. Within a few days, he learned that the Oakland firm of Robinson and Robinson was seeking a junior associate. He applied for the position, was hired, and went right to work. He kept the calendar for the other attorneys, ran errands to the courthouse on minor matters, and researched cases for the senior member, Edward C. Robinson, whom Warren later recalled as "a kindly old gentleman who later became a respected judge of the Superior Court."[8]

Unlike his visits to the courthouse in San Francisco, Warren found working with the judges and the attaches in the Oakland County Clerk's Office a pleasure. Before long, he had befriended many young lawyers who decided to get together and found the Young Lawyers' Club of Alameda County. Its numbers totaled nearly one hundred. Since Warren had been instrumental in its founding, he was elected as its presiding officer. Although strictly social in nature, the group soon realized that since the bar association hadn't met for six or seven years, they needed to become more actively involved in its reinstitution. Warren recalled:

> Accordingly we submitted a petition signed by every member of the Young Lawyers' Club requesting a general meeting of the dormant [state bar] association for the purpose of electing officers and reactivating its affairs. . . . We young lawyers made several requests:
>
> That there be an annual meeting for the election of officers;
> That there be standing committees to study problems of the bench and bar;
> That there be occasional meetings for the general discussion of such matters;
> That the rules provide for a vice-president to function in the absence of the president.
>
> After much discussion, these suggestions were agreed to, and, much to my surprise and embarrassment, I was elected vice president at the

suggestion of the younger member . . . [so] there I was, a lawyer less than three years out of Law School, working for a clerk's salary, and yet vice-president of the third largest bar association in California.[9]

The group met several times over the coming year and threw a joint dinner meeting of the county medical and bar associations that the attorneys christened the "Sawbones and Jawbones" meeting. During Warren's nearly two years with Robinson and Robinson, the young attorney supplemented his meager salary by coaching a group of men for the bar examination. One of them passed the exams and went on to become a judge.

As his second year with Robinson and Robinson came to a close, Warren decided the time was right to build a practice of his own. He joined forces with two other young lawyers who had been classmates of his at the university, and the three approached Peter J. Crosby, an elder statesman and respected trial lawyer. He was agreeable to the idea of forming a partnership in which he would get the lion's share of the joint earnings while the others benefited from his prestige and experience.

The attorneys were searching for a suitable office for their new firm when yet another distraction reared its ugly head: the rapidly escalating conflict in Europe. On April 17, 1917, the United States declared war on Germany.

World War I had begun on July 28, 1914. Contemporaneously labeled the "war to end all wars,"[10] it led to the mobilization of more than seventy million military personnel, including sixty million Europeans, making it one of the largest wars in history. Military losses were exacerbated by new technological and industrial developments and the tactical stalemate caused by a grueling new tactic called trench warfare.

The conflict had begun following the destabilization of the Balkans caused by the quick succession of rulers in a weakened Ottoman Empire in which competing Russo-Austro-Hungarian objectives were at odds. The results were the Balkan Wars of 1912–1913, a conflict limited in nature, like so many others on the Continent. But on June 28, 1914, Gavrilo Princip, a Bosnian Serb and Yugoslavian nationalist, assassinated Austro-Hungarian heir Archduke Franz Ferdinand in Sarajevo, leading to a diplomatic crisis. On July 23, Austria-Hungary issued an ultimatum to Serbia; interwoven political alliances quickly drew upon all their major European players in a frantic effort to protect their wide-flung colonial empires until, finally, a universal conflict erupted.

After German submarines sank seven US merchant ships in the North Atlantic, word reached Washington that Germany was attempting to entice

Mexico into declaring war on the United States to prevent the nation from entering the European conflict. Contrary to Germany's goals, the United States, fueled by an incensed and indignant populace, declared war on Germany on April 6, 1917.

None of this went unnoticed by fledgling attorney Earl Warren. Still floundering in search of his place in the sun, he was moved by the news flooding America's papers daily; so, as soon as the first Officers' Training Corps opened its doors in San Francisco, Warren crossed the bay and sought admission. He was one of the thousands of eager young men to apply, but the army could handle only a few hundred, and he was rejected.

Hearing that there would be another group selected within a month or two, he began working out to get in better shape, and his efforts paid off. The second time around, he was accepted, only to be told by the examining doctor that he had hemorrhoids. Swallowing his disappointment, he rushed back to Oakland; by midafternoon, he was in the hospital being operated on, confident he'd be ready to go the following morning. Instead, he awakened with ether pneumonia and was confined to his bed for the next three weeks. By the time he got out of the hospital, he had learned that the Officers' Training Corps had been closed, and the first draftees were being pressed into service. Although Warren's number was fairly low on the call-up list, he waived his immunity and was quickly drafted.

"I was put in charge of the first ten per cent of draftees who left Oakland on September 5, 1917, for Camp Lewis, Washington," Warren later recalled, "which had officially opened only the day before."[11] It was the first time he had been given such responsibility of leadership.

Camp Lewis was the training ground for the 91st Division, which was recruited from the Western states. Its members were assigned to I Company of the 363rd Infantry. At the end of four weeks, Warren made the rank of first sergeant and was placed in charge of the administration of the company. He supervised the barracks, the mess, the supplies, and the equipment. In fact, he did everything "except soldier, as my time was spent in the orderly room while the others were drilling and receiving instruction."[12]

While at Camp Lewis, Warren met and befriended Leo Carrillo, the Mexican American actor, descended from Spanish California settlers, who later played the character of Pancho in the popular television series *The Cisco Kid*, starring Duncan Renaldo.

On January 5, 1918, after five months of service, Warren was given the opportunity he had missed twice before: He was admitted to officer training at Camp Lewis. On May 1, when his course was completed, he was sent back to his original I Company for three weeks and then on to

Petersburg, Virginia, where he was assigned to Camp Lee. When Camp Lee was turned into a training center, Warren, now a lieutenant, was kept busy training a steady influx of raw recruits. Warren worked his way up to second in command when, after a few weeks, he was enrolled in bayonet school, the last form of specialization that the peace-loving young man would have chosen for himself.

"They ran us until we dropped from exhaustion," Warren later said. With a sudden rash of spinal meningitis and measles sweeping the camp, Warren and one other recruit "were the only ones of the entire school who weren't hospitalized."[13] The men remained there throughout "a miserably hot, humid summer."[14]

Before long, with his bayonet classes completed, he thought he'd finally be sent overseas. Instead, he was dispatched to Camp MacArthur in Waco, Texas, to become a bayonet instructor in the Central Officers Training Camp. By then he'd been promoted to the rank of first lieutenant, but he was on the job only a few days before the armistice was signed, ending the war.

Warren later said, "The Army was damned hard work; there were always extra duties and extra training. I don't believe I got out of Camp Lewis more than twice, and Camp Lee more than three or four times."[15] Warren spent the next few weeks "with little to do, the first relaxation I had experienced since my induction."[16] The free time enabled him to think about what he wanted to do with his future once he mustered out.

He already knew what he *didn't* want to do, and that was to return to a position as a subordinate attorney. That left few options available to him short of opening his own law firm—which was exactly what he decided to do. His two previously tagged law partners had both joined the military and were likely still dispersed in some far-flung place courtesy of the US Armed Forces. There was no telling when, where, or even *if* either of them would return.

So, out of the service and no closer to a job than he'd been fifteen months earlier, Warren boarded a train for California and stopped to visit his parents and sister in Bakersfield. He later recalled, "Especially joyous was the chance to see my gentle mother, whose first letter to me in the Army had remained with me throughout my service days. In it she had written: 'Earl, I cannot tell you how badly I feel about the necessity of your being in the Army, but I would feel worse had you been unwilling to be there.'"[17]

Shortly after Christmas, Warren traveled to Sacramento, where he met Charles Kasch, a fraternity brother who had recently been elected to the state assembly from Mendocino County in the northern part of the state.

Kasch and another elected friend, Leon E. Gray, made arrangements for him to become clerk of the assembly's Judiciary Committee for six dollars a day: "No better job could have been found for me, and I was delighted. The Legislature convened the next day, and I immediately went on the payroll, little realizing that I would from that moment, be in public service without a break until my retirement fifty years later as chief justice of the United States."[18]

Through hard work and a friendly, pleasant demeanor, Warren soon caught the attention of a powerful Republican named Joseph R. Knowland, publisher of the *Oakland Tribune*. Knowland introduced him to other progressive state politicians, including California governor Hiram Johnson. He and other leaders of the Progressive Era appreciated in Warren his deep-rooted disdain for corruption and crime.

Warren's involvement in several fraternal, philanthropic, and benevolent associations beginning in 1919 opened up still more contacts for the budding young politico-in-the-making, landing him in good stead within the community. Appearing before small groups of friends and neighbors, he also learned to help control his reticence for public speaking. Before long, he had joined the Freemasons, the Independent Order of Odd Fellows, the Benevolent and Protective Order of Elks (BPOE), the Loyal Order of Moose (where he achieved the Pilgrim Degree of Merit, the highest award offered by the fraternity), and the American Legion. Every organization he joined introduced Warren to still more new friends and political connections.

In the Masons, Warren rose through the ranks, culminating with his 1935 election to the post of Grand Master of the Freemasons for the state of California. In *Justice for All: Earl Warren and the Nation He Made*, author Jim Newton wrote that Warren "thrived in the Masons because he shared their ideals, but those ideals also helped shape him, nurturing his commitment to service, deepening his conviction that society's problems were best addressed by small groups of enlightened, well-meaning citizens. Those ideals knitted together Warren's Progressivism, his Republicanism, and his Masonry."[19]

Newton went on to claim that Warren "could not have become the man he was had he been raised anywhere but in the time and place of his upbringing."[20] More appropriately, he would never have become Earl Warren without having sat at his father's knee, just as Methias had done before him. Like many accomplished men throughout history, Warren gained both knowledge and his personal discipline mostly by example from his father. Methias had a solid understanding of those characteristics and traits that he wanted to instill within his son: honesty, integrity, spirituality, devotion—the very same characteristics that Warren found enumerated within the Masonic Lodge.

So, with Warren's acceptance of the position of municipal committee clerk, the new legislature opened its 1919 session fully staffed. Warren's delegation from Alameda County, of which Oakland was the county seat, included four senators and eight assemblymen. Most of them lived at the small Sequoia Hotel on K Street, a block and a half from Capitol Park. Although Warren still dreamed of becoming a trial lawyer, he realized he still had progress to make at overcoming his fear of public speaking. When he mentioned his ambition to Assemblyman Frank Anderson of Alameda County, with whom Warren had formed a "very warm friendship," Anderson suggested he apply for a job in the District Attorney's Office. After conferring with several other delegates, Anderson agreed to introduce Warren to the DA. He wouldn't have long to wait.

When county district attorney Ezra Decoto traveled to Sacramento to petition the state legislature for an additional deputy, the delegation jumped at the chance to create the position—provided that Decoto was prepared to appoint Warren to fill it. Decoto told them that would be difficult because he had already promised the next opening to Charles Wade Snook, the son of a former county DA. When Warren heard about the arm twisting that ensued, he called on Decoto personally. He told the man that while he would have liked the job in the DA's office, he preferred to withdraw his name from consideration rather than put Decoto under such stress. Decoto thanked him, adding that he had heard about Warren from the younger men in his office and would be happy to have him on his staff as soon as another vacancy occurred.

Only days later, Decoto lived up to his word, and Warren entered Decoto's office as a deputy DA, becoming his principal assistant and then, with his blessing, successor to the position of district attorney. Snook remained with Warren for several years as one of his key assistants, and years later, then-Governor Warren appointed both Decoto and Snook to fill judicial vacancies on the Superior Court of Alameda County.

Although that year's legislative session was far from memorable, Warren nonetheless found it "very informative and, in some respects, exciting." His appointment to deputy DA couldn't have come at a better time. It enabled him to learn about both the legislative process and its relationship to the other branches of government. It also taught him an unanticipated lesson concerning "the individual conduct of many legislators, and about the lobbying system in both its enlightening and its more sinister forms. By and large, I would say I learned more things to avoid than to follow. . . . Logrolling and lobbying [in the California legislature] were not centralized in one dominant organization like that of the Southern Pacific, but there was a triumvirate consisting of Sheriff Tom Finn of San Francisco, Mike Kelly of Oakland [the "leader" or "boss" of Alameda County, depending on whom you talked to], and Kent Parrott of Los Angeles, a politician of somewhat ominous reputation."[21]

The rest of the delegates of the state's three largest counties paid tribute to the powerful triumvirate. So did the lobbyists who stopped by to peddle everything from influence and entertainment to money. All the big corporate interests were represented, and they often worked in mysterious ways. As Warren later recalled:

> There were some legislators who were regarded as "boodlers" and who, according to a swaggering lobbyist years later, could be bought with "a steak, a potato, or a girl." Some of [the legislators] would not rely entirely on lobbyists for supplementary benefits. They set up their own system through what were called "cinch bills." They would learn of the vulnerability of a certain business or profession because of public prejudice against it or because of its being on the borderline of illegality in its objectives or practices. They would then introduce a bill to outlaw or seriously handicap that business or profession in the future. There would be no serious intention to press the bill for final passage; merely an effort to make the object of the bill pay for its defeat.
>
> The next step in the procedure would be for the sponsor of the bill to let the victim of the shakedown know that he had no time to discuss the merits of the bill, but that he was relying on a Mr. X in determining how the bill should move. The implication was that if the bill were to be stopped, Mr. X must be satisfied. If the intended victim was gullible or if his operations were so sensitive that publicity would greatly hurt them, he would then contact Mr. X. The latter would state that he had almost enough votes to pass the bill and would demonstrate in devious ways the friendship existing between himself and certain other legislators. Eventually he would let it be known that for a given amount of money he would be able to kill the bill. If the payoff was made, the disposition of the money would never be known, but the bill would, of course, die quietly on file. If the victim did not pay off, it would die anyway because it was generally understood which of the bills were "cinch bills," and the authors could gather no basic [political] support for them. Many of these bills were perennials, and would be introduced year after year, either by the same author or by shuffling them around among the small group of established boodlers. Sometime after the 1919 session, the speaker of the Assembly,

deploring this practice, told me he could identify as many as seventy cinch bills in that session. Observing the proceedings of the Legislature as I was able to do for many years thereafter, I believed I could identify many of them, not seventy, but enough to convince me that there was a coterie of legislators who made their living through that practice.[22]

At the end of three months, when the legislature had completed its session, Warren returned to Oakland. With his Sacramento earnings, he bought the first civilian suit he'd owned since coming home from the army. And he had a surprise awaiting him. Leon Gray invited him to share a private office in the Bank of Italy building. Gray worked as a deputy city attorney for Oakland under a man named H. L. Hagan. Before a single client had managed to find his way to Warren's office, a vacancy arose in the office of the city attorney. Gray recommended Warren, and Hagan offered the young attorney the job at two hundred dollars a month plus the right to practice privately on the side.

"It didn't take me long to make up my mind," said Warren later. "I didn't want money. I only wanted the right kind of experience. For the past nine years, ever since I entered Boalt Hall, I had been looking for the chance to get practical experience; now at last the heavy gate was opening for me."[23]

Warren had what he later called "a good general experience in the City Attorney's Office, advising city boards and officers, writing legal opinions, and having a fair amount of contact with the courts. I was netting about one hundred and fifty dollars a month in private legal work with Gray, although I put little effort into building a practice. Still determined to become a trial lawyer, I looked forward to [gaining] experience some day in the District Attorney's Office."[24] The opportunity for an appointment came sooner than he expected.

Before Warren's appointment, the turnover in the DA's Office had been light. In spring 1920, however, Decoto called Warren to say he'd have a vacancy on May 1 and that Warren would be welcome to it if he wanted it. It was the lowest job on the staff, paying one hundred fifty dollars a month—half of what he'd been making working for the City of Oakland. But it offered him an opportunity to gain the experience and the background he felt were critical if he wanted to advance his legal career.

At the time, between fifteen and twenty deputies occupied the office. Most of them were old-timers who predated Decoto's service. They were comfortable working there because the office placed no restrictions on private practices, which most deputies had to supplement their meager government salaries.

But by the early 1920s, law practice in Oakland had grown so profitable that many of the older deputies were leaving public service and setting out on their own. That created an increased workload for Warren, although he never seemed to mind. He was ready to jump in and help out anyone, day or night, on any case that came along.

Three and a half years after Warren joined Decoto's staff, the DA made him head of the civil side of the office and assigned the thirty-three-year-old to be legal adviser to the county Board of Supervisors. Warren's position was the most important outside of the DA's. Until then, Warren had shown little interest in politics, although he had volunteered to be campaign manager for his friend Frank Anderson when Anderson decided to run for a sixth term in the assembly.

Anderson, a quiet, humble man who enjoyed public speaking even less than Warren, was known around the assembly as the only man never to have given a speech in the legislature. He knew of his shortcomings and accepted them. What he *didn't* know was that he was "gravely ill with tuberculosis."[25] In fact, the doctors told his parents that he wouldn't live to see the opening of the 1925 session.

Unsure of whether or not they should dash their son's hopes by revealing the news, his parents called for advice from the one man they felt they could trust—Earl Warren. He suggested that the family carry on as if nothing were wrong, and he would continue managing Anderson's campaign until he got well. Miracles, after all, did happen.

So Warren ran a low-key campaign against a field of seven opponents, releasing statements on his friend's behalf, calling occasional strategy meetings at Anderson's bedside, and admonishing the press to remain silent.

On election day, Warren went from one polling station to the next. The news was not good. His friend was running behind in the tally. By midnight, all his other friends had given up and gone home, but Earl was too heartbroken to follow. Plodding from one precinct to another, he looked for some sign of hope. Finally, in the wee hours of the morning, he came to the city's two most populous precincts.

As Warren peered over the teller's shoulder in the dim light of the smoking kerosene lamps, he saw that Frank was slowly biting into his opponent's lead. An hour later, he had grabbed the point. By dawn, Anderson emerged triumphant by a whopping margin of thirty-five votes!

No streetcars were running at that early hour, so Earl scurried the several miles to the Anderson household on foot, knocking on Frank's bedroom window just as the sun popped above the horizon. "The sick man was overjoyed at the news," author Irving Stone wrote later, "and the two friends sat for several hours over steaming cups of coffee, discussing politics and Earl Warren's first foray into the field of politics. Anderson was ecstatic at what his friend had managed to pull off."[26]

But Warren could not, in the end, work miracles. Frank Anderson passed away quietly the following morning.

As the days rolled into weeks and the weeks wound into months, Earl Warren proved himself a loyal Republican. His conservatism was beyond reproach, and his political instincts were spot-on. In the presidential election of 1924, Warren had dutifully supported Republican Calvin Coolidge against Democrat John W. Davis and Robert La Follette, the presidential nominee for the faltering Progressive Party. In the privacy of the voting booth, though, "Warren cast one last, sentimental ballot for the man who had so inspired him, 'Fighting Bob.'"[27]

While Warren slowly built a legacy for hard work and fair-mindedness with the local press, his earlier experience in the state legislature endeared him to the state's district attorneys, who had asked him to lobby for reform legislation during the 1923 legislative session. Warren "had a lot of friends in Sacramento," recalled Fletcher Bowron, then executive secretary of Governor Friend W. Richardson. "He didn't get all he wanted, but he did get some changes in old laws"[28] along with some new laws that helped prosecutors put away hardened criminals.

"His success as a lobbyist marked him as a comer in law enforcement circles," according to author Ed Cray, "a man to be watched." More importantly, Cray continued,

> Warren and Bowron became friends. It was Bowron who introduced the deputy district attorney to the governor.
>
> Former newspaper publisher Friend Richardson was from Alameda County, and naturally took a special interest in his political base. He was a conservative or regular Republican, anxious to hold the rival Hiram Johnson Progressives in check. And he knew that District Attorney Ezra Decoto, [who had managed to build] a $10,000-per-year private practice, had his eye on a less demanding . . . office.
>
> Young Warren just might be the man to replace Decoto—if they could maneuver it. Alameda County political boss Mike Kelly, holding court after Sunday mass in the lobby of the Hotel Oakland, had another candidate in mind.[29]

But for Warren, all that was political speculation. He was perfectly content in his position as deputy district attorney working for Decoto. And he was gaining exactly the kind of legal experience he felt he needed for a successful future

> I became a sort of Jack-of-all-trades on both the criminal and civil sides. I tried criminal cases, one after another, advised Boards of Education, assisted the chief deputy in advising the Board of Supervisors, and handled lawsuits against officers of the county. It was exciting for me, every day of it, and I made quick progress. Whenever one of the old-timers would leave, Mr. Decoto would ask the chief deputy, "Who knows anything about his cases?" and the deputy would often reply, "Warren has been helping him." The district attorney would then say, "Well, let's turn his work over to Warren." I worked practically every day of the week and ordinarily five nights. In about three years and a half, I occupied one of the two equal top assistantships and was assigned to what was considered the most important job in the office, that of adviser to the County Board of Supervisors. This later proved to be of inestimable value to me. While I did not realize it then, I now have little doubt that Mr. Decoto thought this might afford me the opportunity to succeed him if he should ever resign, as the Board fills such vacancies. I had a very satisfying experience with the Board, and they relied implicitly on my opinions as to the legality of their acts. There was no phase of the county government that I was not made familiar with, but, as I went along, my duties took me more and more into the field of governmental administration and away from the trial of criminal cases.[30]

In 1925 Warren, who had recently turned thirty-four, got his big political break when Decoto announced his retirement. The Bakersfield native was tagged to take over the position of district attorney to fill the Alameda County vacancy. He was as surprised as anyone when it happened:

> I do not believe I had much ambition for the position until the opportunity actually presented itself. . . . I had not taken a job in the DA's Office with the intention of remaining in public service or even being there for any great length of time. I wanted the trial experience the office afforded, and I believed that about a year-and-a-half or two years at most would equip me for the private practice I contemplated. . . . When I had been there a little more than four years, talk circulated that Mr. Decoto was about to accept a state office, and there was, of course, speculation about his successor as district attorney. Because I was one of his two top assistants, my name was mentioned as a possibility. However, I gave little thought to it even then because I was a relative newcomer to a county of a half million population, and had no real political experience or associations. Consequently, when people mentioned it to me, I brushed it

off as being improbable. But finally when it appeared imminent that Mr. Decoto would be appointed to the State Railroad Commission, Supervisor John F. Mullins came to me and said I should ask the five-person board of supervisors to appoint me to the resultant DA Office vacancy. He said he would vote for me and that Supervisor Charles W. Heyer would also, and that I needed only one more. I told him Mr. Decoto had never told me he was leaving; that I would not try to do anything for myself while he was still in office, and that I would not be interested at all if he had someone else in mind to be the new district attorney. . . . [Decoto] called me to his office and . . . told me he had decided to leave and would be happy to have me succeed him. He assured me I was free to take any action I desired to obtain the appointment. He suggested that I solicit the vote of Supervisor Ralph W. Richmond, a representative of the agricultural part of the county who was not beholden to the county machine headed by Mike Kelly. I was very grateful, and thanked him for his confidence in me. I then contacted Supervisor Richmond and, although it was difficult for me to do so, asked him if he would vote for me. He said he would like to because of his friendship for me; that he would inquire of some of his friends in the district, and if there was no serious objection from them, he would do so. In about a week, he said he had found no detractors and would vote to appoint me. In the meantime Supervisor Heyer, who was also an independent from an agricultural district, voluntarily told me he would vote in my favor. The word was soon around the city, and while one might think that would be the end of it, the fight was just commencing.[31]

Two other members of the board were supporters of the Mike Kelly machine, and rumors swirled that Supervisor Mullins, Warren's original sponsor, was ripe for a deal to help Kelly open up Oakland to unlawful activities. Within the railroad, waterfront, and industrial sections of the city lay the cancerous community of Emeryville with its three thousand people who pursued every vice imaginable, from gambling and prostitution to bootlegging and drugs. And it was all controlled by Kelly.

Although Mullins denied any support for the mobster, rumors persisted to the contrary: When the time came, Mullins would back Kelly. The other two votes pledged to Warren were solidly in the deputy's camp.

"But people who knew Mullins and his twenty-year allegiance to the Kelly organization," Warren later wrote in his memoirs, "could not believe that he could withstand its suasions. His district was thoroughly dominated by Kelly. Mullins said he would not change his vote for me even if it meant the loss of his seat on the board of supervisors. His perseverance was doubted until he arose in a board meeting on January 12, 1925, and proposed my name for the district attorneyship. The vote was unanimous in my favor, though I really only had three solid supporters."[32]

Mullins, as feared, lost his place on the board at the next election. After Warren was sworn in as DA, the displaced board member, an ardent Roman Catholic, choked back a tear. "Earl Warren," he said, "you owe allegiance to no one except your God and your conscience."[33]

As Warren looked over his meteoric rise in government service, he had no regrets. The fifteen-hour days—often extending to midnight and beyond—were a joy and a challenge rather than a burden. His only recreation was having dinner in downtown Oakland with one or two of his coworkers or his friends from Boalt Hall who by then had founded their own private practices. He was wise enough not to neglect his health, going down to Schmidt's Cottage Baths in Alameda in warm weather to enjoy a quick swim in the bay, then grab a milkshake and sandwich before returning to the office at the end of his lunch hour. On Sunday afternoons, he played baseball with a group of amateurs, mostly old friends from college, at the Municipal Playgrounds. If he had a particularly grueling night's work ahead, he instead played handball for half an hour at the Athens Athletic Club or the Elks Club.

He went to the occasional weekend party, dance, or picnic and met attractive young women, but Warren was still a long way from getting serious about love or marriage. He wanted to establish himself and be sure of what he was going to do with his future before he undertook planning a family of his own. Being a bachelor was considerably simplified by the fact that he shared a solid family environment with his sister and brother-in-law, Ethel and Vernon Plank. Although not himself ready to settle down, he was nonetheless devoted to his young niece and nephew. They helped him realize how important children were in the life of a Warren. Once he finally did decide to start a family of his own, he knew he'd want children just like his sister's—except more of them, at least half a dozen, preferably three boys and three girls. Until then, his "adoption" into the Planks' rambling home removed the traditional inconveniences that might have driven a single man to look toward a serious relationship: the monotonous restaurant food, the buttons missing from his shirts, the loneliness of a hotel room when the need for conversation struck. For Earl, his life with the Plank family suited him just right. He could always count on a good dinner from his sister, who had settled in Oakland after her marriage to Vernon, a Southern Pacific storekeeper. Ethel loved her brother, of course, and Vernon was immensely fond of his brother-in-law, even if he was amused by the man's indifference to clothes. Earl didn't care what he wore as long as it was blue, double-breasted, and a suit. When it got too shiny, he threw the old one out and bought another one just like it. It developed into a family joke.

Ethel later recalled, "My husband used to kid him about it, and so he decided to buy something different. He came home one day with a black-and-white checked suit. My goodness, you never saw such a thing in your life. I think he went into the Army to avoid having to wear it. While he was gone, we gave it away."[34]

His taste in clothes notwithstanding, things were going well for Earl Warren. The world was his oyster, and he couldn't have been happier.

And then, one gentle spring morning, life threw him a curve. He showed up at a Sunday birthday breakfast thrown by a young married couple he knew. The guests met at nine o'clock for a prebreakfast swim at the Piedmont Baths. Earl got into his suit, walked from the locker room to the deep end of the pool, and greeted a number of his friends before looking out over a group of folks all laughing and splashing at the far end of the enclave. His world ground to a halt.

There she was. The young woman in water up to her shoulders, a bathing cap covering all but the radiant oval of her face. He couldn't tear his gaze from her. Fair skin, rosy cheeks, full mouth, all framed beneath two large, vibrant eyes. She was exquisitely sculpted, a model worthy of Rembrandt. And when this angelic apparition emerged from the water and turned in his direction, he spun around to address his hostess.

He asked if she would introduce him.

Nina Palmquist Meyers had looked up from the water and seen Earl at the very instant that he had caught sight of her. The hostess, somewhat hesitantly, nonetheless made the introductions, and as Earl took Nina's hand, he noticed her eyes were not merely expressive but alive. With their first murmured words of greeting, their first handclasp, their first swift and deep probing into one another's eyes, Earl Warren's life as he'd known it came to a screeching halt.

A new life had begun.

The story of Nina Palmquist's family was uncanny in its similarity to that of Warren's clan. She was born in Sweden and brought to Iowa when she was an infant, just as Chrystal Warren had been. Her parents had traveled west to San Diego searching for a warm, dry climate because of her mother's delicate health. There, when Nina was only three, her mother died in childbirth. Brokenhearted, her father took his three young daughters, Eva, Nina, and Hannah, and moved them to Oakland, hoping to flush out the pain and find a new life. But he was not the kind of man who could begin life over again; instead, he married an older woman so that his children might be cared for. The stepmother performed all the duties her husband expected of her, but the father never found health or happiness again. He died of tuberculosis when Nina was thirteen, leaving the family penniless.

Nina's older sister, Eva, immediately went to work for the sprawling plumbing supply house of Willis B. George. Nina occasionally stopped by to visit her there, and Eva devoted a few spare moments to showing the younger girl how she kept the company's books. When Nina finished high school, she enrolled in classes at Heald's Business College.

Meanwhile, the plumbing fixture salesman who handled the Willis B. George account had watched Eva manage the office and offered her a far better job working with him at the Crane Company. Eva went to her employer and told him of her opportunity. Mr. George said, "All right, I won't stand in your way, but I've seen you showing the ropes to that young sister of yours, so suppose you train her to take over before you leave."

So Nina went to work as a cashier and bookkeeper for the George company while she continued her stenographic course at Heald's at night. Since there were several short periods during the day when she wasn't busy, she asked her boss if she could study her shorthand during her slack time. George snapped, "Certainly not!" If she had any spare time, it would be much better if she went back into the stockroom and acquainted herself with the fittings. Instead of being offended, Nina did as she was told; to her surprise, she later said, she found that she was "fascinated by all the thousands of different small items, each in its cubbyhole, just as neat and tidy as possible. I went back to the storeroom so often that after a while I learned the business very well, and that was good for me."[35]

A short time later, the Crane salesman once again raided Willis B. George, saying to Nina, "How would you like to work with Eva in our Oakland office?" In the meantime, young Hannah had been stopping by on her way home to visit with Nina, and Nina had continued the family tradition. When she went to her boss to tell him that she, too, had been offered a better opportunity at Crane, the gentleman sighed and shook his head. "All right, but bring that young sister of yours in here and teach her to take over the job."[36]

Nina had completed her course at Heald's, and she and Eva had given young Hannah a thorough education in running the business. But, as with her two sisters before her, Hannah didn't last long at Willis B. George, and before long the three Palmquist girls were managing the Crane offices in Oakland and San Francisco, moving about interchangeably, earning good salaries, and garnering respect throughout the business community.

Eva eventually met and married a graduate from the Christian Bible Institute and accompanied him to China, where they served as missionaries for twenty years. Nina married a musician, Grover Meyers, and quit her job to become a housewife. Shortly after, Hannah married a railroad engineer.

But the dreaded curse of tuberculosis soon turned the bright and fun-loving young Nina's life to tragedy: Her husband came down with the incurable disease and died when the couple's son was only three weeks old. These were difficult times for the young mother, but she faced them with determination. She went back to live with her stepmother, knowing that she would have to find employment to support her boy. A few weeks later, when she was wheeling young Jim in his baby carriage, a sympathetic neighbor stopped to talk, asking what she intended to do. Nina said she hadn't yet decided. The woman, who owned a specialty shop that featured a luxurious line of women's clothing, lingerie, and hosiery, offered Nina a job, saying, "You will owe me money at first, but I'm willing to take a chance on you."[37]

Nina wanted to prove her boss's intuition correct. After only a few weeks, she had shown herself so capable that the owner raised her salary. A few months later, the woman bought a second shop and made Nina manager of the first. By the end of the year, the owner had acquired a third shop and Nina had done so well that she was made manager of the chain.

Nina worked hard, not only because she had to earn money to pay for Jim's keep and for insurance so that he'd be protected in the event of a catastrophe, but also because she loved merchandising; it provided her with an ever-changing challenge and a new outlook on life. The owner didn't want her waiting on customers, believing this was beneath her manager's dignity, but Nina loved to meet people, so she opened the street doors promptly at eight o'clock each morning. She often wrote up a full book of sales before the actual salespeople arrived an hour later. At six o'clock she went home to have dinner with Jim, play with him for an hour, read him a story, and tuck him into bed. With the child asleep, she went back to the store to work until midnight. She hoped that within a few years, she would have saved enough to be able to open a shop of her own.

So young Nina Palmquist Meyers was the thunderbolt out of the blue that Earl Warren never saw coming—a woman with courage and character, sensitivity and beauty, all discernible in the most stunning smile he'd ever seen. And her shapely figure didn't hurt, either!

As Nina felt her hand in Warren's, she sensed the warmth behind his smile and the openness and realness of his personality. She, too, knew at once that her past was irretrievably gone and her future called out to her, bright and beautiful.

"I spotted him just as quickly as he spotted me," she later said.[38]

Though there were twenty guests at the party, Warren managed to wrangle a seat next to Nina at breakfast. She wore a black dress that set off her blonde hair to its best advantage. They talked and laughed throughout the meal, and when they parted, he asked if he could see her the following Saturday. He took her to the Fulton Stock Company in Oakland, where they watched *Smilin' Through* and, later, *Rose of the Rancho*. After that, they went out together every Saturday evening, their date night. They had little time for each other during the week because, as Nina said, "I was as busy at my job as he was at his."[39] Sundays she devoted to her son. She and Earl kept nearly constant company for the next two years, when the couple got engaged.

Years later, Nina reminisced over the couple's initial meeting:

> My first husband, Grover Cleveland Meyers, a pianist of note, died of the incurable disease of tuberculosis, and I was left with a very young baby, Jim. This illness used up the resources of the family and I was compelled to return to work. I took a position in the office of a woman's Specialty Shop in Oakland, which I later managed. Jim was 6 years old when I married Earl.
>
> I met Earl at a birthday breakfast party (swimming) on a Sunday morning given by mutual friends. During the period of our engagement, both of us were very busy—Earl as Chief deputy district attorney, and I at the Specialty Shop. After Earl was selected by the Board of Supervisors to succeed . . . Ezra Decota, who was appointed to the Railroad Commission, we were married in the First Baptist Church in Oakland, by Dr. John Snape on October 11 [*sic*], 1925. (Earl was then District Attorney).[40]

Warren's recollection was slightly different. Until he met Nina, he'd never dated much and considered love and marriage something for the future, after he'd become an established trial lawyer. But he changed his mind when he attended a swimming party that fateful Sunday morning at Oakland's Piedmont Baths. He was immediately attracted to her. He later wrote:

> Her name was Nina Elisabeth Meyers. She was a young widow who was living with and supporting her little boy Jim and her widowed stepmother. Her father, deceased, was a Swedish Baptist minister named Nils Peter Palmquist. She had herself been born in Sweden, and had come to this country, like my parents, as a babe in arms. At the time of my meeting her, she was the manager of a woman's specialty shop in Oakland. She was as busy as I was, but we found time to become acquainted and often went to dinner and the theater on Saturday evenings. We also spent a part of our Sundays together whenever possible. It wasn't long until we were thinking in terms of marriage, but we decided to wait until my

income was sufficient to properly maintain a home. We were each then making about $250 per month and had no other resources to fall back on. Social patterns were different then, and I would have felt humiliated if my wife had been compelled to work.[41]

When he was appointed district attorney on January 12, 1925, the couple decided the time was right to get married, but a series of eye operations on Warren's mother, who was staying at his sister's home while recuperating, delayed them. His mother also incurred a severe internal illness and was forced to undergo an abdominal operation after which she was gravely ill for weeks.

When she was at last well enough to attend the wedding, the couple went through with their plans, marrying in the First Baptist Church at a quiet family service on October 14. The only outsiders present were two longtime friends who had inside information about their application for a marriage license.

Warren later recalled,

When we arrived at the church, these friends, Oliver D. Hamlin, the lawyer whose position as a deputy district attorney I had succeeded to, and George C. Feldman, the manager of the county garage, were in a car across the street. They had surreptitiously assembled the entire highway patrol of the county at a discreet distance to usher us noisily wherever we were going. Seeing them in the car, I said, "All right, come on in [to the church]." They did, and to this day they occasionally kid me about the "engraved invitations" they received for our wedding.[42]

Following the ceremony, the highway patrol fell into lockstep, a meandering line of police vehicles escorting the Warrens' car to the county line after which the newlyweds caught a train for British Columbia and a two-week honeymoon.

Warren's marriage to his dream wife was the cap to his budding young career. Feeling suddenly mature and settled in, he made the decision to run for election to his own full four-year term as DA, which he did the following year. And he won. As it turned out, he was fortunate to have taken two weeks off with his new bride to rekindle his energy. As time would tell, he was going to need it.

Within days of taking office, the new district attorney found himself deeply embroiled in prosecuting a wide range of lawbreakers—oil stock swindlers, unscrupulous health-insurance promoters, school board embezzlers, cleaning-and-dyeing racketeers, fraudulent building-and-loan sharks, lawyers and stockbrokers who had stolen funds from the estates entrusted to them, and a vast array of other twenties-era con artists and swindlers.

Warren also launched a no-holds-barred investigation into allegations that a deputy sheriff was taking bribes in connection with city street-paving contracts. He cracked down on bootlegging and took a hard stance against labor in the buildup to the San Francisco General Strike as well as in *Whitney v. California* (1927), in which he prosecuted a woman under the California Criminal Syndicalism Act for attending a Communist meeting in Oakland. When in 1936 the killer of a ship's officer managed to evade capture, Warren successfully prosecuted union organizers for their role in inciting the murder and aiding in the commission of the crime.

Warren also indicted an aircraft manufacturer for manufacturing a faulty wing on an airplane, resulting in the pilot's death. He convicted dope peddlers and reached into a sheriff's office to break up a slot-machine and prostitution-protection ring. The days never seemed quite long enough—or the list of crimes short enough—to allow him time to breathe.

By the turn of the decade, Warren had gained a statewide reputation as a tough, no-nonsense district attorney who fought corruption in government: In a 1931 survey, voters listed him as the best DA in the nation. Their support was based on Warren's running his office in a nonpartisan manner while vigorously supporting the autonomy of various law enforcement agencies. Even his courtroom archnemesis, the public defender, admitted publicly that Warren never brought people into court unless he could prove their guilt.

But winning wasn't everything for the new DA. Warren believed that *both* cops and prosecutors had a responsibility to act impartially. Nothing troubled him more than the possibility that he might be sending an innocent person to jail. His instructions to his staff were clear: "Get the facts honestly and don't color them. If the facts are there, you can proceed. If they're not, we don't want them."[43]

His approach paid off. Before long, the district attorney's conviction rate had soared to an astonishing 86 percent, far higher than that of any other DA in the state. One of the reasons for Warren's success rate was that he kept his office free of politics, something too many other DAs failed to do. As a result, despite his fourteen years in office and the thousands of cases he prosecuted, ranging from murder to window breaking, he never had a conviction overturned by a higher court.

Professor Raymond Moley of Columbia University described Warren in 1931 as "the most intelligent and politically independent district attorney in the United States."[44] Several years later, as Warren was rounding out his first year as governor, Moley explained his remarks: "The reason I spoke of him as a district attorney as I did was the calm and efficient way in which he organized his office, carried on the critical business of law enforcement without thought of immediate political considerations, stayed by it a long time, built up a fine organization, and when he moved on . . . left the office in good hands."[45]

Although a registered Republican, Warren had broad bipartisan support for his centrist-to-liberal views, a surprising fact that paid dividends in 1932. That year, Warren was named a delegate from California to the Republican National Convention that ultimately nominated candidate Herbert Hoover for president. For Earl Warren—riding on the high of his own populist perseverance—life couldn't have looked sweeter. The sky was the limit. There was nowhere else to go but up.

But then, just as the reputation of the office of the district attorney was soaring, everything came to a screaming halt.

It was a disaster that rattled the bones of every citizen in California. But nowhere did it hit harder than in the Warren household. It was a freak encounter that would help define the young DA's philosophy on life for the rest of his days.

On a warm Saturday evening in May 1938, seventy-three-year-old Methias Warren sat in the living room of his small frame house at 709 Miles Street in Bakersfield, where he had lived for forty-two years. The cluttered building was crammed with old unused furniture that he periodically cleaned up and gave to the renters of the hundred-some cottages he had built over the years and rented out in East Bakersfield. Methias was reading the same local evening newspaper his son used to deliver as a boy, the *Bakersfield Californian*, when he drifted off to sleep. His wife was in Oakland convalescing from a cataract operation.

The screen doors and windows were all open wide. A tenant came in at 8:00 p.m. to pay Warren fifteen dollars rent. He was most likely the last person to see Methias alive.

The following morning, as Earl was about to deliver a speech at a Sunday Masonic breakfast meeting at a Berkeley hotel, he was interrupted by an urgent telephone call from the Bakersfield police. His father had been savagely bludgeoned to death by an unknown assailant with a foot-long iron pipe taken from his backyard. The motive appeared to be robbery. The implement had been found in a neighbor's yard; the victim's broken glasses were on the kitchen floor and his empty wallet was found in a nearby schoolyard, the rest of its contents scattered on the street. Two pennies were found in the slain man's pockets.

Rumors were rife that the murder was politically motivated, aimed at Methias's ruthless crime-busting son. The DA of Alameda County had no jurisdiction in Kern County, but he immediately dispatched several aides to cooperate with the Bakersfield authorities. On Sunday evening, before boarding a plane for Bakersfield, Warren told reporters: "This is a terrible reason to have to make a trip home."[46]

In his Bakersfield hotel room, Warren later held a press conference. Reporters flocked there from all over the state. Speaking honestly and emotionally about his father, he broke down and sobbed while sitting on the bed. Everyone there was moved. Only one photographer snapped a photo. Shocked at such insensitivity, the other reporters reproached him and made him remove the sheet film from his Speed Graphic camera and hold it up to the light, destroying the image. No photograph of that scene remains. One photojournalist said that they all felt that Warren was such a decent guy that even all of those bastards wanted to protect him.[47]

More than a hundred suspects were questioned in the Warren murder case, and several were held, but all were later released due to lack of evidence.

After months of daunting police work, Warren's chief investigator, Oscar Jahnsen, was convinced that he had identified the murderer, a man who had been involved in business dealings with Methias Warren. But before Jahnsen could wrap up the case, overeager local authorities began giving the suspect the third degree without first informing him of his rights. When the man's attorney found out, he advised his client to remain silent, and no conclusive evidence was found to link him to the murder.

"I blew my top when they blew the case," Jahnsen recalled, still bitter years after the fact. "The Chief wanted his father's murderer apprehended, but he refused to break any of his [own] rules or use his own office to convict a guilty man without solid, legally secured evidence. He warned us that we had to follow our strict office rules in investigating *any* murder. He even said to me later, 'Oscar, you did the right thing.'"[48]

Bakersfield chief of police Robert B. Powers, who supervised twenty-five men working full-time on the case, believed that the culprit was an itinerant prowler. "The motive was robbery, and murder was not deliberately intended," he insisted for years. Warren reluctantly accepted his opinion. Among the suspects was a San Quentin prisoner convicted of another crime who may have been in Bakersfield at the time.

"I wanted to put a stool pigeon in his cell and plant a Dictaphone there," Chief Powers later admitted. But when informed of the plan, Warren flatly rejected it.

"We don't break the law when trying to enforce the law," he told them.[49]

And that was all he needed to say.

3

MR. ATTORNEY GENERAL

As painful as it was to get past the heartbreak of his father's murder, Warren knew the best way to put the past behind him was to immerse himself in politics. And the best way to do that, he reasoned, was to file for candidacy of the office of attorney general of the state of California on the Republican ticket, which he did. And then he filed as a candidate on the *Democratic* ticket. And, for good measure, he followed suit on the *Progressive* ticket. Meanwhile, support for his candidacy was growing.

On one evening in late spring 1938, as Judge Robert W. Kenny drove home with Judge Fletcher Bowron, a superior court colleague, the two men talked politics. Bowron, a Republican, asked Kenny, a Democrat, if he would cross party lines to support Earl Warren for attorney general. Although Kenny was raising money for the state ticket headed by Culbert L. Olson and was a candidate for his seat in the state senate, he agreed to endorse the Alameda County Republican.

"I was probably the only active Democrat in Southern California that [Warren] knew personally," Kenny later recalled. "I'd met him some years earlier when we were both in Sacramento lobbying against a bill that would have had the effect of granting a ninety-day leave of absence for bail-bond jumpers. He came down to Los Angeles and we had lunch together. I told him it would be a lot easier for me if he'd make some kind of statement on civil rights."[1]

Warren made his statement on July 20 in a handwritten letter to Kenny, who endorsed him three days later as "the only candidate I can support for attorney general."[2]

"I believe," Warren wrote, "that the American concept of civil rights should include not only an observance of our Constitutional Bill of Rights, but also the absence of arbitrary action by government in every field and the existence of a spirit of fair play on the part of public officials toward all that will prevent government from using ever present opportunities to abuse power through the harassment of the individual."[3]

That November the Democrats tried posting a write-in candidate, but Warren captured a million and a half more votes than his nearest contender. He became the only primary Republican to survive the 1938 California Democratic purge that swept Culbert Olson, an outspoken New Dealer riding on the coattails of Democrat Franklin Delano Roosevelt, into the governor's mansion. Olson was elected California's first Democratic governor in more than four decades.

Warren's knack for filing on all three parties' tickets was somewhat unusual but entirely legal. The move, called *cross-filing*, proved to be a stroke of genius that paid off big. Warren won the majority of votes cast in the August 1938 primary for not one but *all three* parties. He went on to win the general election that November. Earl Warren's political career was off and running.

In January 1939, two months after his impressive victory, Warren arrived early for his first day of work as California's attorney general. With him were three of his most trusted allies. Flanking him as he entered his Sacramento quarters were Oscar Jahnsen, a renowned and resourceful investigator; Charles Wehr, a hard-nosed prosecuting attorney; and Helen R. MacGregor, the petite librarian-like lawyer who had served as Warren's personal chief of staff. Of the three, MacGregor seemed the most out of place, and she was. A ferocious bulldog with a steel-trap mind, a stickler for details, and a relentless devotee to her job, she quickly became the no-nonsense, soft-spoken cog that made the wheels of the attorney general's office turn. Years later, after he was named chief justice of the Supreme Court, Warren extolled MacGregor's virtues in a speech commemorating her nearly two decades of service to him.

> [A] word about Helen MacGregor. I can never repay her for the service she rendered to the state during her many years in my various offices nor for her helpfulness to me and my family. She was with me almost twenty years, and in that length of time performed at least forty years of service. No hours were too long for her. No work too exacting. And, nothing disturbed her gentle disposition.
>
> I am sure all of us imposed on her. I know I did. She served with me in the district attorney's office, in the office of attorney general and for almost eleven years while I was governor. I am certain that no one contributed more to whatever success we achieved in those offices than she did.[4]

Each of Warren's three deputies had a specific assignment designed to reshape the corpulent if somnolent office that former attorney general Ulysses S. Webb had left behind. As chief investigator, Jahnsen was to infuse the policing arm of the office of criminal investigation and identification with Warren's strict standards. Wehr, as chief of criminal prosecutions, was to do the same with the thirty-six deputy attorneys general scattered around Los Angeles, Sacramento, and the central office in San Francisco. MacGregor received full latitude for administering the office, the first duty toward which proved to be clearing the attorney general's calendar of cases left behind to languish during the Webb years.

The largest share of the workload, of course, fell to Warren as he prepared to implement the reforms envisioned in the statewide ballot propositions adopted in 1934. He was particularly interested in coordinating the law enforcement agencies across the state to prevent the spread of organized crime that had sprouted throughout the eastern and midwestern United States from reaching California.

As he opened the door to his private office that first morning on the job, he found two telephone messages on his desk. One was from Walter P. Jones, the editor of the *Sacramento Bee*, and the other was from Joseph Stephens, a member of the state Board of Prison Terms and Paroles.

"Here are two friendly calls," he thought out loud, "so I'll show them I am already in business."[5]

He first telephoned Jones, who was frantic to know if Warren had yet talked to Stephens, who had something important to tell him. Warren hung up and immediately dialed the second number. Within minutes, Stephens was at the AG's office, where he laid Warren's first problem out before him. Stevens said that outgoing governor Frank Merriam's private secretary, who had received a midnight appointment to the superior court in Alameda, had peddled last-chance pardons to prisoners. The chairman of the parole board, he said, confirmed the story.

Warren called Senator David Bush, a respected legislator and ardent supporter of the governor. Bush admitted that he'd heard information he thought corroborated the charges of corruption.

Warren then called Jahnsen and instructed him to go to the governor's office and ask secretary Mark Megladdery to see him on a matter of urgency.

When Megladdery arrived, Warren put it to him bluntly: "Mark, you have been accused of selling pardons, and I would like to talk to you about it. Are you willing to talk to me?"

"Of course, Earl," he said.[6]

Warren summoned a stenographer and interrogated the judge for more than an hour. Warren later recalled:

> He answered glibly but not truthfully, and his statements led to his ulti-
> mate undoing. He was very cocky because, at midnight the night before,
> the last act of out-going Governor Frank Merriam had been to appoint
> him a superior court judge of Alameda County. I called the venerable
> chief judge of our Superior Court, T. W. Harris, and told him the story
> as I had heard it from Jones, Stephens, and Megladdery. The entire mat-
> ter, I said, would be submitted to a grand jury. When Megladdery later
> came into the Alameda County Courthouse to report for duty, Judge
> Harris said to him, "I know of your appointment, and having taken the
> oath you are now a Superior Court judge, but I have been told by the
> attorney general about the prison scandal, and you will be assigned no
> judicial work until that matter is cleared up. You may have an office but
> no duties to perform."[7]

Warren called the district attorney of Sacramento County, but since the matter involved not only the governor's office but also some of the legislators, the DA wanted no part in prosecuting. Fortunately, Megladdery lived in Alameda County, where some peripheral aspects of the matter were centered—enough to establish jurisdiction. So Warren called the county's new district attorney, formerly his chief assistant, Ralph E. Hoyt, who eventually took the case to the grand jury. Megladdery was indicted, tried, convicted, and sentenced to jail. To the great relief of the superior court judges of the county, all of whom had reputations for impeccable morals and integrity, he never sat as a judge in a case.

Although Warren hadn't displaced any of his predecessor's appointees in the attorney general's office, some of the senior attorneys soon retired as the rules governing moonlighting in private practice became stricter. With the dwindling opportunity to conduct private practice while using state facilities, the number of governmental vacancies increased, and Warren eventually filled those openings with what he termed a more "manageable unit."[8] The move was badly needed.

Before Warren, the AG's office had "no central filing system; no good system of fiscal accountability; no calendar control of litigation, and very little supervision of the work of the deputies. Each of them performed his duties almost as an independent official. I do not say this in derogation of my predecessor of thirty-six years, who was an honest man, but rather as an indication of the parsimonious manner in which the office was treated by the Legislature. More and more responsibilities were thrust on the Office with only infrequent additional deputies at paltry salaries to help with the increased workload. Things had grown in this manner through the years without a real chance to reorganize on an efficient basis."[9]

Warren knew that there were many places where the law was being flagrantly flouted, so he decided to tackle the violators one at a time until they were all removed. He theorized that, while some violators could defeat the law for a while, none of them could defy it forever. First on the new AG's hit list of habitual offenders were the slot machine and lottery parlors where Warren intended to prove his theory.

Although illegal in Alameda County, the gaming syndicates operated openly around the state just beyond the reach of county lines. Warren thought about the best way of handling the problem short of opening up several hundred lengthy and costly lawsuits. Finally, it struck him. In a letter to every district attorney and sheriff in the state of California, he discreetly offered to indict "any slot-machine operator . . . too solidly entrenched in any community to be prosecuted successfully by local authorities."[10] The warning was both implicit and unmistakable.

Within weeks, many of the gambling dens had closed voluntarily, while the slots that resisted became the subject of clandestine but highly publicized ax-wielding raids. Before long, the state had rid itself of the one-armed bandits. Bolstered by his handling of the parole-selling scandal and the proliferation of slots, Warren primed himself for his next big attack.

Dog tracks at the time were run by organized crime, which Warren viewed as the most corruptive influence in local government. The fact that they flourished throughout the state was due mainly to the police and sheriffs' departments openly tolerating them. As the chief law officer of the state, Warren had the authority to step in whenever local police, sheriffs, or district attorneys failed to enforce the law. And that's what he did.

Even before assuming office, Warren had received several letters complaining about illegal dog tracks operating in the South San Francisco towns of Tracy and Susanville; of bookie and gambling parlors in Santa Ana and Yreka, and of slot machines scattered across San Diego County. Their very existence offended Warren's ingrained bias against the organized gambling and brothels that plucked the workingman's dollar from his pockets at the expense of his wife and children.

Dog tracks in California had long been illegal because their operators employed a virtually foolproof method for swindling the public. There were only eight counties in the state where they were permitted by local authorities. Alameda wasn't one of them, even though the county was ringed by tracks in Contra Costa County to the north, San Mateo County to the west, and San Joaquin County to the east. A few more tracks ranged off toward the southern part of the state. They all worked together like one giant conglomerate, allocating different racing seasons so they wouldn't run at the same time, funneling profits from one another.

Three months after taking office, Warren moved against the Contra Costa County track adjacent to Alameda County. The operation was run by John J. Jerome, nicknamed "Black Jack" for his unsavory activities as a professional strikebreaker. Warren sent Wehr, his newly appointed chief criminal deputy, out to prepare a case for action. Within a couple of weeks, he reported back that everything was set to go.

Warren issued an invitation for Jerome to come down to his office to advise him of some problems concerning his El Cerrito dog track. When Jerome showed up, Warren told him, "Mr. Jerome, you have been operating your track for several years, and I will give you credit for believing that you are in a lawful business because the authorities in your county have permitted you to run, but I must inform you that dog track gambling is illegal and cannot continue. It must stop. I have prepared a case and am ready to act. If you choose to close down now, you may do so without any cost to you, but if we are obliged to proceed the hard way, it will be very expensive for you, and I believe I can assure you that in the end your operation will be closed."

Jerome informed Warren that he believed he was operating legally and asked if he could consult with his lawyers for their opinion. Warren said he could, and Jerome telephoned an attorney, who showed up at the office within minutes. Thomas M. Carlson was an "able lawyer" against whom Warren had argued several times in the past. Carlson consulted with his client for several minutes before returning to Warren's office.

"Do you intend to treat all dog tracks the same?" Carlson asked the AG, "or are you closing Jerome's track because he is Jerome?"

Warren said that, since all dog tracks were illegal, he intended to close them all. The two men conferred once again before Carlson said to his client, "I have known this man for many years, and if he says everyone is to be treated the same, he will do just that."

Jerome thought for a few minutes and said, "Mr. Attorney General, will it be all right if we run until Saturday night?"

Warren thought for several seconds. "I cannot give you permission to continue an illegal activity, but I hardly think this office would be prepared to issue an order until Monday morning, so if you shut down Saturday night, we would have no reason to issue that complaint."[11]

Both Jerome and his attorney left in good spirits. And that Saturday night, the track's loudspeaker crackled with the news that the facility's owners, while believing they'd been operating legally, had recently been told by the attorney general that they'd been mistaken. Since they were not prepared to buck the laws of the state of California, they would be closing the track permanently following the end of racing that night.

They were true to their word, and before long, that word had spread to everyone in the industry. Once news circulated that Black Jack Jerome had capitulated to the laws of the state, every other track operator fell into place. And that was the end to illegal dog track operations in California.

Warren used that same firm, well-conceived approach wherever possible, and it worked with surprising effectiveness. Instead of doing battle in court the expensive and time-consuming way, he engaged his opponents in a battle of wits and, backed by the law, invariably won. On those rare occasions when a violator of the law was arrogant enough to refuse to believe that he could be shut down, Warren proceeded with the prescribed method of taking the business down through the courts—and won.

Warren's swift assault against the state's illegal dog tracks led the Democratic *Los Angeles Daily News* to crow that California was headed for a good scrubbing behind the ears.

And they were right.

Over his next four years in office, Warren succeeded not only in closing down all of the state's illegal dog tracks but also in driving the bookies and slot machine operators out of business. And, not insignificantly, he won the first "naval battle" ever fought by an attorney general in the state of California.

The most prolific open gambling operations that had ever functioned in the state were conducted by the gambling ships plying the waters off the coast of Southern California. Festooned with strings of garish lights, the gaming vessels had operated just offshore for more than a decade. Protected by a succession of court rulings finding that they were anchored in international waters, the ships thrived in the sheltered calm of Long Beach Harbor and Santa Monica Bay.

Four ships comprised the armada—the *Rex* and the *Texas* in Santa Monica and the *Tango* and the *Showboat* in Long Beach. The largest and most notorious of the four was the *Rex*, owned by Antonio Stralla, alias Tony Cornero, a notorious rumrunner and underworld czar who made his fortune during prohibition and was intent upon expanding it in any way possible. The local police had entertained notions of shutting down the gaming ships from time to time, but the *Rex* was backed by big money from Al Capone and the mob in Chicago. Rampant rumors persisted about the ownership of the other gaming facilities, but everyone was sure they were all backed by the underworld.

Over time, the ships became such fixtures in the area that even the Los Angeles newspapers succumbed to carrying full-page ads promoting their gaming, bringing hundreds of dollars a day into the papers' coffers, a mere pittance compared to what the illegal gambling operations raked in. "All the thrills of Biarritz, Riviera, Monte Carlo, Cannes—surpassed!" the ads promised.

In the crystalline blue skies over the city, skywriting planes urged the sporting crowd to "Play on the *Rex*," while muckraking columnists reveled in describing the ship's salon, dining room, and casino, refurbished at the cost of $250,000, as a "sumptuous pleasure dome."[12]

But the ships were anything but sumptuous in the eye of the attorney general, who said, "With things like this going on, nobody can take us seriously when we're talking about dog tracks and the gambling house on the shore."[13]

Cornero, commanding the fleet's flagship (he had lost his interest in one of the other ships, the *Tango*, on a single cut of the cards), had a different take on the matter: "This ship is operated by courageous, open-minded, fearless American citizens."

Los Angeles's new reform mayor, Fletcher Bowron, who had recently defeated the incumbent in a bitterly fought recall election, was vehemently opposed to the gambling ships, but they were beyond his jurisdiction. Warren listened to the mayor's laments before announcing that he nevertheless intended to shut down the floating palaces. The mayor promised that if the county's district attorney and sheriff refused to help, he would supply the necessary city police officers to do the job, although he hoped that wouldn't require posting them beyond city limits.

But that brought up an interesting technical point: Just what *were* the limits of the ships anchored offshore? Their owners made sure to keep the vessels anchored more than three miles from the cities of Santa Monica and Long Beach, and they relied on that fact to assert their freedom from California's jurisdiction.

The harbors of both cities were similar in configuration. Their shorelines were jagged and deeply indented in a way that permitted a ship to be anchored more than three miles from the shore of either city but to be well within a line drawn from between two headlands that extended farthest out into the sea.

Warren contended that the state's jurisdiction ran three miles seaward from a straight line drawn from headland to headland, meaning that, to be clear of the state's authority, the ships had to be anchored at least *ten miles* out to sea from the innermost docks where their water taxis were based, an impracticality for two reasons. First, such a long trip over open waters would have been too difficult for either the taxis or their passengers to make regularly. Second, the anchored ship in the open Pacific would experience such violent swells that most people would lose all desire to gamble—or do anything else!

But what, Jahnsen wondered, if their thinking was incorrect, and the ships actually *were* outside of the state's jurisdiction? Warren had a response to that theory, too.

"We maintained that the operation of these ships constituted a public nuisance to the state of California," Warren later wrote, "[that] they were a detrimental enticement to our people, that they were connected up with the mainland by their water taxis, and one, the *Rex,* had set up a telephone line from the shore to the ship without proper authorization. We contended this all gave us the right to summarily abate the nuisance in the same manner as if it were all on shore, regardless of how far seaward it was."[14]

Warren kept track of the ships' activities while hundreds and sometimes thousands of customers a day were taxied from shore to ship to play at the dice and blackjack tables, roulette wheels, and one-armed bandits. The floating sports palaces felt immune to prosecution and advertised everywhere—not only in newspapers and the skies overhead but also on radio and billboards. Cash-depleted customers often complained to authorities of roughneck treatment whenever they protested that the games were rigged, but the *Rex* and the other ships flourished, sucking millions of nontaxable dollars out of the state. Recalled Warren:

> I sent Oscar Jahnsen to see Tony Cornero on the *Rex* and tell him that he must close out his operation. Jahnsen knew him from earlier days when, as a federal officer, he had arrested Cornero in a rum-running affair. Cornero greeted him cordially and said, "Jahnsen, don't be silly. I have the best mouthpieces in the country, and they tell me I am legal. Come along with me, and I'll show you what we've got." Jahnsen went around the ship with him, recording everything he saw in his notebook.[15]

Jahnsen also visited the other three ships while Warren checked with Vice Admiral Stanley Parker of the US Coast Guard, stationed at San Francisco. The admiral, a lawyer, advised Warren that the government's planned actions broke no maritime laws of which he was aware. Afterward, Warren consulted with US Attorney Ben Harrison, who similarly advised him that what the state was doing didn't conflict with any federal laws, either.

The field was clear to proceed. Jahnsen recalled:

I'd had a little shooting scrape with Tony about 1922, '23. It was in Los Angeles, at Sunset and Fairfax. I was working for the Treasury then, and he was smuggling Scotch up from Mexico. Well, I took my wife and two schoolteacher friends out to the ship. We had a nice dinner, then I got to gambling. A crooked cop put the finger on me. Tony came up and tapped me on the shoulder. "Mr. Jahnsen," he said, "what can I do for you?" I said, "Tony, don't you remember Sunset and Fairfax?" and he said, "Oh yes, of course." He asked me what I was doing on the ship, and I told him. I said, "Tony, you're violating the law, you've got to stop."

He said, "No, I'm beyond the three-mile limit. You can't touch me." Then he took us all over the ship, all four of us. He was particularly proud of his ship-to-shore phone, and at one point he opened up a desk drawer and let me see a big .41 Colt. The Chief told me to tell Cornero he could have a safe escort for all of his gambling equipment, get it across California into Nevada, where it would be legal. Otherwise, he was going to put the ship out of business and the stuff would all get busted or dumped in the ocean.[16]

Finally, on Friday evening, July 28, after two days of conferences with the district attorney, the sheriff of Los Angeles County, and the police chiefs of Los Angeles, Long Beach, and Santa Monica, Warren made his move. "The time for talk has passed," he said. "Now is the time for action."[17]

In searching for a legal means of permanently enjoining the ships' operations, Warren, in addition to the "public nuisance" approach he'd discovered, unearthed a primordial US Supreme Court decision claiming that even though the *Rex* was three miles from shore, it was still anchored within an ancient bay over which California could claim jurisdiction. Another ruling had found that water taxis were "public conveyances" and, as such, required state licenses to operate, none of which the *Rex*'s launches had bothered to secure.

Finally convinced that he was sailing in legal waters, Warren secured a court order empowering him to raid the *Rex* and the three other ships simultaneously, a step he felt was necessary to prevent one ship's owner from claiming discrimination in favor of another's. Warren realized that such coordination would require a significant operation involving several boats and some three hundred officers—and lots of closed mouths.

On July 28, 1939, the attorney general's office served an injunction on the ships requiring them to abate a public nuisance. The order, according to author Ed Cray, thundered with biblical rectitude. Warren charged that the vessels induced people of limited means "to spend upon wagers the money necessary for the support and maintenance of their minor children and aged parents." They had contributed to the delinquency of minors "by openly glorifying, in their eyes, gambling and the evasion of the laws of the State, and by inducing them to lead idle and dissolute lives." Finally, they had caused the loss of jobs "by reason of the idle and dissolute habits encouraged and developed by gambling."[18]

Tony Cornero was vacationing in Texas when the lawmen were piped aboard the *Rex* at 7:45 p.m. Some eight hundred customers had taken water taxis out to the ship for an evening of cards, dice, roulette, and bingo. They went on playing as the head of the sheriff's vice squad descended to the lower deck and handed the skipper a five-page legal document ordering him to desist at once.

"We are law-abiding citizens," a man identified as the ship's "trustee" said before sending word back to Warren that the *Rex* intended to stay in business.[19]

The same orders were given at the same time to the men in charge of the other three ships. Attorneys for all four gambling ships insisted the vessels were anchored on the high seas outside of the territorial waters of California and beyond the reach of the state courts. All four chose to ignore Warren's orders of abatement.

"I do not care whether the four ships operate within or without the so-called three-mile limit," Warren replied. "We shall proceed against them regardless of this and regardless of what action is taken in Congress or elsewhere."[20] At about the same time, a bill outlawing gambling ships was getting a sympathetic hearing from the House Judiciary Committee in DC, but while the lawmakers discussed it in Washington, the lawbreakers continued their operations off the California coast. If anything, business had picked up over the weekend rather than fallen off. Warren called in Jahnsen and Warren Olney III, assistant attorney general in charge of the criminal division, to draw up a battle plan.

"It was like a military operation," Olney told Bill Davidson years later:

Since we had only five investigators in our office, we had to use deputy sheriffs from the county of Los Angeles. We knew that many of them were in the pay of the gamblers, so Earl ran the whole thing with the utmost secrecy to avoid a tip-off to the ships. On D-Day, we locked up forty cops and eight accountants in Patriotic Hall in Los Angeles, and the Chief briefed them. Then we transported them to the waterfront in sealed busses, and loaded them directly into waiting patrol boats from the state Fish and Game Authority. The raids went off like clockwork. I later became an officer in the Marine Corps, but I always remember my experience with Warren's Commandos as my first amphibious operation.[21]

In July 1939, Olney and Jahnsen set about organizing a fleet. In the end, they had employed four Fish and Game Commission patrol boats and arranged to rent sixteen water taxis for their "navy." They mustered some of the manpower from their own ranks, going so far as to press several lawyers into service. When their plans were as complete as possible, Warren went to Los Angeles and asked District Attorney Byron Fitts and Sheriff Eugene Biscailuz to meet him at his LA office, where he told them of his plan and asked for their help. Both men demurred, saying that such activities might subject them to charges of liability on their official bonds, overstepping the mandates of their offices. But Warren had already explored that possibility and told them that the argument was baseless. When they continued to balk, he said he was prepared to invoke the new powers of the attorney general and supplant them in making the arrests and resulting prosecutions. He also told them that Mayor Bowron had promised him enough police officers to do the job if they refused to help.

As the officials turned to each other, one read the other's mind: Either they could play ball and be part of a successful raid or they could sit on the bench and look feckless to their constituents. They asked how many men Warren needed.

"I told them it could be done with one hundred and fifty from the sheriff and fifty from the district attorney," Warren later wrote. "They agreed and asked when the officers would be needed. I said one o'clock that very afternoon. They balked at first, but finally agreed and were given the rendezvous points. Many of our own men had infiltrated the gambling ships incognito as 'customers' and about two hundred men from the sheriff's and district attorney's offices were put aboard our raiding fleet."[22]

So, with everything set, Warren prepared to launch his ramshackle armada, which by then had added eight seagoing state accountants and lawyers who would accompany law enforcement officers to examine the ships' books.

Promptly at 3:00 p.m. on the afternoon of August 1, 1939, Warren's navy launched. They first fell upon the unsuspecting gaming ships *Tango* and *Showboat*, off Long Beach, both of which surrendered at once. "My God, cops!" Olney heard someone shout. "And they're not ours!"[23] The *Texas* in Santa Monica Bay resisted briefly before the mariners boarded the ship, the raiding officers rounding up and throwing overboard $25,000 worth of slot machines, roulette wheels, and gaming tables as local news photographers snapped away from circling motorboats.

Warren recalled:

> Little resistance was offered on three of the ships, although there was some scuffling on the Texas when the raiding officers stayed aboard until after nightfall, and someone pulled a main light switch, causing a minor melee in the dark. But when our boats approached Cornero's Rex, fire hoses were turned on them to keep them away and the gangway was denied them. Our men communicated this predicament to me, and added that there were more than six hundred people aboard. I was not with the offshore raiders, but had taken some rooms at a Santa Monica beach club with Fitts and Biscailuz to watch the proceedings through field glasses.[24]

From his post, Warren observed the *Rex* through a telescope and binoculars, barking orders to his crew via shortwave radio. The chief had placed Captain George Contreras, head of Sheriff Biscailuz's vice squad, in charge of an all-out attack on the recalcitrant *Rex*. But Contreras, commander of the *Marlin*, suddenly hit a snag. Someone, most likely one of Warren's less reliable officers, had alerted Cornero of the plans. The *Rex*'s crew drove back the invaders with streaming fire hoses and improvised an iron gate to prevent anyone from boarding. Cornero, gloating as his defenses worked to perfection, picked up a megaphone and shouted in the general direction of the *Marlin*, "I won't give up the ship!"[25]

Receiving the news by radio, Warren remained undaunted. He realized that most of the customers on the *Rex* would want to leave shortly since they had wives, children, and husbands waiting for them at home. They wouldn't be able to explain to their bosses why they were late for work the next morning, either—if they made it in at all. Warren barked instructions for the armada to make fast near the *Rex*'s gangway area. If his men couldn't get aboard, at least no one on the ship would be able to leave. "In effect," Warren said, "we blockaded her."[26]

On the afternoon of the raid, Warren received word that a commander of the Coast Guard by the name of Greenwood had called his office and said, speaking of him, "You tell that blankety-blank to take those boats away from the *Rex* or he will land in jail." The chief later recalled:

> He left a telephone number to call. I thought it probably was a hoax, but found the number in the telephone book under that name. I called and asked for Commander Greenwood. After identifying myself, I repeated

the exact language he was said to have used. "Yes," he agreed, "that is exactly what I said."

I replied, "Commander, before you start putting anyone in jail I would suggest that you communicate with your admiral, because he helped us work out this program."

There was a brief silence, and then he said, "Well, I'm for you fellows, but you didn't tell me anything about it."

"Perhaps we forgot to do so," I said, and the conversation ended.[27]

Cornero, confident as his crew managed to hold off the officers until nearly three o'clock the following morning, suddenly realized that Olney and his navy weren't going away anytime soon, so he battened the hatches in preparation for the long haul. By the end of the fourth day, the men in the patrol boats were confident that Cornero would soon exhaust his food, his patience, or both. Word reached Warren that the House of Representatives had just passed the bill making the operation of a gambling ship off the coast of the United States a federal crime. When Cornero received word of the new law aboard the *Rex*, he moaned, "It ain't right. It's unconstitutional."[28]

"He is sitting out there," Olney told reporters on Saturday afternoon, as the fifth day of the blockade neared an end, "cut off from shore and unable to operate. As far as we're concerned, he might as well be in Alcatraz."[29]

Cornero managed to hold out for ten days in all before surrendering unconditionally. The attorney general clambered aboard a Fish and Game patrol boat and motored out to the *Rex*.

"It was like General Grant taking General Lee's sword," Olney said.[30]

Cornero was escorted to shore shortly before noon and booked at the Santa Monica police station. Asked to give his occupation, he replied, "Mariner, Goddam it."[31]

The officers took possession of the ship, and the patrons were allowed to leave. The lawmen confiscated several dozen bags of money that was deposited in the state treasury. Meanwhile, back at the office, Helen Mac-Gregor had been digging into the law books. In a lengthy, detailed memorandum, she called attention to the maritime law dating back to the early seventeenth century confirming that the ships could be argued to have been within California's territorial limits.

She also uncovered a Supreme Court ruling in *New Jersey v. City of New York* (1931) that a state had the power to abate a nuisance even when the act creating it had occurred at sea more than twenty miles from the state's shores.[32] A superior court judge in Los Angeles County cited that historic hassle between the state of New Jersey and the city of New York. For years, New York had been dumping "noxious, offensive and injurious materials—all of which are for brevity called garbage—into the ocean at points of from ten to twenty-two miles from the New Jersey shore, polluting adjacent waters and menacing public health."[33]

It was of no importance where the acts creating the nuisance took place, whether within or without the United States, the Supreme Court held when its jurisdiction was challenged by New York City's lawyers. What mattered was whether the damage caused by the nuisance lay within the state court's territorial jurisdiction, as was the case in New Jersey. Similarly, the courts of California had jurisdiction over the nuisance being inflicted on the state and its residents by the illegal acts taking place on the gambling ships.

"The waters off Santa Monica, between Point Dume and Point Vicente, constitute a bay," Judge Emmet H. Wilson ruled, echoing MacGregor's memorandum, "and the State's jurisdiction extends three miles to sea from a straight line drawn between the two headlands."[34]

On November 1, having obtained a court injunction putting an end to the offshore action, Warren added insult to injury by writing a letter to J. H. O'Connor, Los Angeles County counsel, and sending a carbon copy to his old friend and college classmate John R. Quinn, county assessor:

"Ordinarily," Warren wrote Quinn in a covering letter,

> I am not inclined to exact penalties but these people as you know are racketeers who have not only flouted the laws of the State but have beaten and oppressed citizens who visited the gambling ship and have even taken innumerable relief checks issued by the County of Los Angeles for the care of poor families in the operation of their illegal gambling games.
>
> I think this is an opportunity for the County of Los Angeles to recover some money which could be well used for the solution of your relief and other problems.[35]

Four weeks later, on advice of counsel, Cornero capitulated, agreeing to the destruction of all gambling paraphernalia aboard the *Rex*. As the final indignity, a court ordered Cornero to reimburse the state of California the $13,200 it had expended in raiding his ship, along with a $7,500 penalty to the State Railroad Commission for operating a fleet of unlicensed water-taxi "public conveyances." He was also forced to cough up $4,200 in state back taxes.

Since the gaming ships were actually little more than barges and didn't have enough power to navigate or even to raise their own anchors, "we had to cut the chains (attaching them to oil drum floats for later recovery)," Warren said, "and the ships were then towed into port."[36]

Jahnsen was given the honor of leading a demolition crew armed with crowbars and axes to destroy more than a hundred of the ship's dice and blackjack tables, slot machines, and roulette wheels.

Although Cornero was fined thousands of dollars and lost his ship and all of the revenue he'd taken in, his problems weren't over. The attorney general's office discovered in preparing for court that, during Cornero's rum-running days, the United States government had assessed taxes against him totaling more than $100,000 plus penalties. When Warren notified the federal government of Cornero's connection with the *Rex*, the feds immediately attached the ship for the amount due. When the taxes and penalties weren't paid, the vessel was sold to satisfy the claim, eventually becoming a troop carrier for the Allies in World War II.

After the Cornero matter was settled, the pending cases against the other three gambling-ship operators were resolved quickly and amicably. And that should have been the end to offshore gambling in California.

But it wasn't.

Seven years later, a young state assemblyman named Frederick Napoleon Howser was appointed district attorney of Los Angeles County, and he permitted Cornero, who had obtained possession of a vessel called the *Lux*, to retrofit it in Santa Monica Harbor as a gambling ship. Although Warren had by that time moved on from the attorney general's office to that of the governor, he relished the thought of going head-to-head with his bellicose nemesis once more and made a public announcement to that effect. Cornero publicly replied that anyone who interfered with his business would be treated as a common, everyday pirate. The implications were clear.

Since Governor Warren had no law enforcement agency mandated to tackle the job, he threatened to activate the National Guard to prevent the gamblers' water taxis from plying between ship and shore. In truth, he was reluctant to use the Guard for any phase of civilian law enforcement, and as things turned out, he never had to, thanks to friends in high places. Recalled Warren years later:

> My first step was to write a letter to President Harry Truman telling him of the situation and of the threat made by Cornero to deal with law enforcement as if it were piracy. I pointed out [that] the . . . federal government was somewhat responsible for the situation . . . because it had issued a license for the ship to operate in coastwide trade, in spite of the fact that the vessel had no engines on it and was permanently anchored in the harbor for the sole purpose of illegal gambling. I asked for his assistance. In a few days, I received a telephone call from Attorney General Tom C. Clark in Washington. He said, "Governor, in relation to the

letter you wrote to President Truman, give me a couple of weeks, and I believe I can do something for you." I thanked him and waited. Within that time, the federal government moved in on the Lux, cut the anchor chain, towed the ship into port, and auctioned it off for the fines assessed against it. The charge was flagrant violation of the navigation laws.

Shortly thereafter the [US] Congress passed an act prohibiting gambling ships in the coastal waters of the United States.[37]

President Truman signed the bill presented to him by Congress, putting an end once and for all to the career of Admiral Earl Warren and his Offshore Avenging Armada. As for Cornero, he returned to Las Vegas where, in July 1955, he dropped dead of coronary thrombosis after an all-night craps game. He died a loser, $10,000 in the hole.[38]

For the next several weeks, Earl Warren was prominently featured in the newspapers of populous Los Angeles County. If closing a popular form of public entertainment cast him as a spoiler to some, his sense of righteousness appealed to thousands of churchgoing folk who lamented the general decline in public morality. As much as he thrived on the publicity, Warren could not devote all his time to the pursuit of criminal antics. Less spectacular, if equally important, tasks demanded the AG's attention.

The legal agenda in the attorney general's office was far broader than Warren had dealt with in Oakland, as he had already learned. Additional issues he faced ranged from (appropriately enough) admiralty law to Native American rights, from the education code to fish and game laws. He was, in short, no longer a trial or even an appellate lawyer as much as the administrative head of a large law firm with its main office in San Francisco and vibrant branch offices in Sacramento and Los Angeles.

Fortunately, he brought to the job of attorney general all the most effective work habits he had developed as district attorney. He expected his deputies to put in a full week, which included their being present for meetings in the office on Saturday mornings. And they were no longer allowed to represent private clients before state agencies. They were told to keep their personal cases out of the office.

"As the chances of private practice while using state facilities diminished, more vacancies occurred, and I was able to reorganize the office into a manageable unit,"[39] Warren noted later.

The days filled with activity. Between trips from Warren's sixth-floor office to San Francisco's Civic Center, he took to dictating correspondence to Helen MacGregor or revising her drafts of his speeches while a state policeman drove him around in the spacious black Buick that was Warren's favorite.

The woman he invariably addressed as "Miss MacGregor" lifted the routine burdens from the "general." His time ever more in demand, she repeatedly cautioned staff members, "He doesn't want you to reflect what he thinks. He wants you to give him your best advice, and he will make up his mind whether or not he will follow it."

Quite as capable and confident as the general himself, the forty-two-year-old MacGregor had attended the University of California Law School. She passed the bar in 1922 but was unable to land a job in a law office. "I think they weren't making any efforts to accommodate a woman,"[40] she said later. MacGregor, who "looked like everybody's idea of a librarian," according to Earl Jr., eventually found work as a secretary and law clerk to an appellate court judge. When her employer died thirteen years later, MacGregor joined the Warren office in Oakland as his personal secretary.

She soon made herself invaluable. "She was an immensely important person in the family," Earl Jr. recalled. "Dad could not have done many of the things he did in the political arena without her."[41]

In addition to MacGregor, two other political heavyweights figured in the administration of the office, one on the criminal side and the other, the civil, both unexpectedly.

With Charles Wehr stricken by leukemia, which would soon claim his life, Warren asked another of his former Oakland deputies to take charge of the criminal docket. Warren Olney III brought to the AG's office a commitment to public service as resolute as the general's own.

Son of a former state Supreme Court justice, the soft-spoken, dapper Olney had struck first a professional and then a personal relationship with Warren. With their shared values, they complemented one another—Warren the public figure, Olney content to work in the background, "the consummate gentleman, a courteous man, just a fine human being."[42]

In 1937 Olney's father resigned from the state court and asked his son to join him in private practice. Then-District Attorney Warren urged the younger man to accept: "It is a great tribute to you. You can never tell how long your father has to live, and if anything happened to him, you'd never forgive yourself."[43] There would be a job waiting for Olney when he returned, Warren promised. Olney thanked him.

Not long after, his partner/father died, and the younger Olney closed the firm in favor of public service. He rejoined Warren in May 1939 for the $5,000 annual salary of the assistant attorney general.

Nine months later, Warren made the last of his critical appointments when he persuaded his former campaign adviser, William T. Sweigert, to take charge of civil litigation in the attorney general's office.

Depressed by the death of his wife, Sweigert had resisted Warren's previous overtures. Finally, the thirty-nine-year-old relented, discovering renewed energy and commitment in his new environment. Within weeks, several other longtime deputies had resigned to devote more time to their private practices; others followed, allowing Sweigert to reshape the staff in Warren's image.

As willing to delegate authority as he was, there was no doubt that Earl Warren remained the boss. James Walsh, doubling as a clerk while he attended law school, recalled the Warren of those years as "rather intimidating. He had presence with a capital 'P.'"

To the men and women in the office, Warren "was polite, and somewhat courtly"—friendly but reserved, Walsh added. "He always held something back. I don't think he calculated everything; I just think it was half natural, the mask of the professional politician."[44]

As most politicians do, Warren compartmentalized his life into professional and personal spheres. He made professional acquaintances easily, but few of those became personal friends. On a succession of visits to Sacramento, he did strike up a friendship of sorts with a state police officer, a young black man who always seemed to be reading at his desk. Edgar "Pat" Patterson, who had been detailed to the governor's mansion, explained that he alternated reading the state penal code and the Bible. He was trying to resolve the apparent conflicts between the two.

On various visits, the attorney general stopped to chat with the young man, often to discuss those very conflicts between scripture and law. Over the next three years, "we got to be very, very close," Patterson said.[45]

The personable cop was the rare exception. The men with whom Warren occasionally hunted or faithfully attended University of California football games were social companions, rarely more.

Along those lines, the attorney general discussed political problems with only a handful of tight-lipped men. They included Joe Knowland and, increasingly, Knowland's son, Bill; *Sacramento Bee* editor Walter P. Jones; attorney Jesse Steinhart, a fixture in San Francisco's influential Jewish community; and his old college friend Robert Gordon Sproul, who had risen to the rank of president of the University of California. These advisers spanned the political spectrum from conservative Republican to New Deal Democrat.

As attorney general, Warren was remarkably effective but less than perfect. He argued two cases before the United States Supreme Court, both of which posed significant questions regarding states' rights. In the first, he secured for California a $17 million judgment on behalf of California's Native Americans who had sued the federal government for failure to ratify solemn treaties with various tribes. It was a rare SCOTUS win for our Native Americans, merely one more victory for the attorney general.

The second case was less rewarding.

When crops in southern California were ripe, the landowners welcomed migrant workers. The workers came from all walks of life, like a man named Fred E. Edwards. When not earning money as a migrant field hand, he was an occasional preacher at the federal Farm Security Administration camp south of Marysville. Like all migrant workers, he was a boon to California's landowners. The more migrants available to work, the lower the wages the owners needed to pay. In the slack winter months, though, when most of the migrants applied for welfare, they found the welcome mat gone.

One day, by coincidence, Edwards was arrested and charged with a misdemeanor of transporting indigents into the state to file for unemployment benefits. The "indigents" were his sister, her husband, and their two children. Edwards was convicted and given a six-month suspended sentence. Concerned that the conviction would remain on the books forever and possibly come back to haunt him if he chose to apply for more lucrative employment in the booming national defense industry, Edwards accepted the American Civil Liberties Union's offer to appeal the decision.

Representing the state of California, Earl Warren had precedents on his side dating to the Elizabethan Poor Laws. He had a century of United States Supreme Court decisions in his favor. He had an amicus curiae, or friend of the court, brief from the attorneys general of twenty-seven states that similarly banned transporting indigents to obtain state aid.

With both precedent and necessity on his side, the steadfast son of Scandinavian immigrants asserted in his brief before the court that the state of California had the authority to keep "an influx of paupers" from joining overburdened relief rolls. Doing so was necessary for the state's very financial survival.

In its ruling, the Supreme Court disagreed with Warren's states' rights argument, the justices finding that the constitutional right of travel from one state to another is inalienable. A penalty—the denial of welfare—could not be imposed upon someone merely for exercising that right.

Warren took the loss with equanimity. California's pioneers, he reminded reporters, "came here to seek opportunity, and that is the reason the present migrants come."[46] Despite arguing against them, he had not forgotten his own roots.

Although the SCOTUS decision made headlines, Matt Warren's son continued to attract positive national attention. In 1940, he was elected president of the National Association of Attorneys General. Shortly after, disaffected New Dealer Raymond Moley, in an article promoting the presidential candidacy of New York Republican Thomas E. Dewey, opined, "Only Earl Warren of Oakland, Calif, now Attorney General of that state, has ever approached Dewey's achievement as DA."[47]

That year Warren made only two token political appearances in the Republican presidential campaign, in keeping with his pledge to remain a nonpartisan law enforcement official. But even a symbolic gesture was sufficient to provoke Democratic governor Culbert Olson into reacting.

The friction between Warren and Olson had begun almost with the governor's inauguration two years earlier. Both sons of immigrants, both stubborn, both progressive-minded reformers in their youth, they had since gone their separate ways. Warren favored individual entrepreneurship and the Republican Party; Olson, the New Deal's program of collective responsibility and the Democrats.

At sixty-two, Olson—tall, lean, and fair of complexion with bright blue eyes and snow-white hair—was "type cast for the role of governor," according to author Carey McWilliams.[48] Running against the discredited Frank Merriam, Olson was an easy victor. At the very cusp of his political career, he was riding high.

But Olson's first act as governor, while legal, was politically ill-advised: He freed Tom Mooney from state prison.

Mooney and fellow union organizer Warren K. Billings had been convicted of murder in San Francisco's Preparedness Day bombings in 1916; ten people had died in the blast of the suitcase bomb set off near the parade's starting point on Market Street.

Several people—Mooney, his wife Rena, Warren Billings, and two others—presented credible witnesses who placed the two a mile from the explosion at the time. Amid charges of a frame-up by a politically ambitious district attorney, Billings was sentenced to life imprisonment. Mooney's death sentence was eventually commuted to life.

Twenty-two years later, Number 31921 was easily the most celebrated prisoner at San Quentin. Labor unions, particularly the more radical ones, had transformed the crusade of "Free Mooney!" into a symbol of working-class solidarity.

Despite suggestions of perjury and suppressed evidence, a succession of Republican governors declined to issue pardons to the two labor martyrs. Eventually, the decision fell to Democrat Culbert Olson.

Attorney General Warren conceded that he had no knowledge of Mooney's guilt or innocence, expressing no bias against the man. However, as the highest law enforcement officer in the state, Warren asked that

Olson not criticize the prosecution of the case, which would only throw kerosene on the fire.

The governor disregarded Warren's request. Climaxing a tearful ceremony in the packed state assembly chamber, Olson proclaimed Mooney an innocent man convicted "on perjured testimony presented by representatives of the State of California." Mooney walked from the Capitol a free man twenty-two years, five months, and twelve days after his conviction for murder. Warren took out his anger on the hapless Billings.

Because Billings had been convicted of a prior felony for possession of dynamite, he couldn't be pardoned without a recommendation from a majority of the state supreme court. The court, in turn, was guided by a nonbinding statement from the state Pardon Advisory Board. As a duty of his office, Warren sat as one of the five members on that board.

In February 1939 the board voted three to two *not* to recommend a pardon. Warren; Folsom Prison warden Clyde I. Plummer, who was the former head of the San Diego Police Department's "Red Squad"; and Clarence Morrill, a Warren subordinate, voted against Billings. Olson's planned pardon was defeated.

But that wasn't Warren's only run-in with the meddling of the governor into prison affairs.

Years earlier, on Sunday morning, March 22, 1936, the Swain and Hoyt steamliner *Point Lobos* was preparing to sail when the ship's union-busting chief engineer, George Alberts, boarded the vessel and entered his stateroom. A short time later, his lifeless body was discovered in a pool of blood. He had multiple bruises from a beating with a blunt instrument and several knife wounds, including one in his rear thigh that severed a vein, causing him to bleed to death.

It had been prior to departure time, and no one else was supposed to be aboard. Investigators failed to identify the killers, although rumors ran rampant along the waterfront. Finally, some informants said that the murder had been arranged by Earl King, the secretary and principal officer of the Oilers, Wipers and Tenders Union, who dispatched a goon squad to teach Alberts a lesson about meddling in union affairs. King later bragged to his inner circle that he had sent the squad over from San Francisco to "tamp up" on Alberts, but they had gone too far.

Warren learned that another union member, George Wallace, was one of the members of the squad, but he had disappeared from California and wasn't heard from again until he was apprehended in Brownsville, Texas. He admitted that King had sent him to Alameda County but claimed he acted only as a lookout.

Another man, E. G. Ramsay, a union grievance adjuster, aided the squad by posting crewman Frank Conner at a post from which he directed the squad to Alberts's stateroom.

After an extensive investigation, Warren indicted King, Ramsay, Conner, George Wallace, and Ben Sakowitz for murder. Sakowitz was still at large at the time of the trial.

As the proceedings unfolded, from hundreds to more than a thousand union protesters gathered outside the courtroom; some sixty thousand union workers were on strike at the time, and this murder trial only further fueled their fury.

The trial lasted for three months, and when it concluded, the jury retired to deliberate. After slightly more than three hours, they returned a verdict: guilty of murder in the second degree for all defendants.[49] Several months later, when the advisory board took up the governor's actions in the *Point Lobos* case, Warren appeared partisan and self-serving. The Congress of Industrial Organizations unions (CIO) had supported Olson with the understanding that he would reexamine the convictions of King, Conner, and Ramsay, all of whom had five years of their sentences left to serve in San Quentin.

The King-Ramsay-Conner Defense Committee prepared a brief for the governor detailing the exculpatory evidence: in particular, new details of an intimate relationship between prosecutor Charles Wehr and juror Julia Vickerson tainted the government's case. Olson bucked the file to his Pardon Advisory Board. The board met on April 11, 1940, in Lieutenant Governor Ellis Patterson's cramped San Francisco office. As Patterson recounted the meeting, Warren announced that he was "convinced that any lessening of the sentences meted out to these criminals would subvert the ends of justice."[50]

Patterson told Warren he should not vote on the board when the prisoners' petitions came up. As district attorney, Warren had prosecuted them; as attorney general, he was not likely to approve their release, which made him partisan.

Warren didn't take the advice, and the board voted four to one against recommending the pardons.

Under increasing pressure from labor unions, Olson traveled to San Quentin to interview King, Conner, Ramsay, and Wallace. Four days later, he announced to reporters that he had found only "a very slim thread connecting the three men with the murder." (Wallace, who had confessed, was another matter.)

The trial evidence, Olson asserted, was "largely conflicting and impeached. I can't figure them out as the type of men who would deliberately participate in the murder of anyone."[51] Olson admitted that he was considering overriding the board's finding and pardoning King, Conner, and Ramsay.

Warren was livid. He denounced Olson's comment as "shocking. Every good citizen of California should resent it." Olson intended to "appease the revolutionary radicals by pardoning for this crime Earl King, leader of the most murderous element of the Communist radicals in San Francisco and his hirelings."[52]

As for the "slim thread," Warren continued, "I challenge the Governor to say on his honor that he has read the evidence in the case, which consists of 4,275 pages." Olson, after spending only half a day talking to the prisoners, hadn't even bothered to discuss the case with any of the prosecutors, Warren asserted.

"Heretofore, I have never said one word against the Governor or any of his official acts, but silence on my part in this matter would be cowardice. These men are assassins—proven to be so."[53]

In a surprise turn of events, a pardon turned out to be unnecessary: Olson's Prison Board of Terms and Paroles on November 28, 1941, voted four to one to grant King, Conner, and Ramsay parole. They had served four years and nine months. (Wallace, the admitted murderer, would stay on in San Quentin until his parole in 1949.)

Normally controlled, Attorney General Warren exploded with the release of the three unionists. "The murderers are free today," he raged in a prepared statement, "not because they are rehabilitated criminals, but because they are politically powerful Communistic radicals. Their parole is the culmination of a sinister program of subversive politics, attempted bribery, terrorism and intimidation which has evidenced itself in so many ways during the past three years."[54]

The furor with which the Maritime Union reacted to Warren's condemnation was like none ever seen before on the coast. The men who'd been convicted were called martyrs in the cause of labor, while Warren was labeled a reactionary, an enemy of organized labor whose sole purpose in arresting these persons was to smash the unions. Every day during the trial, Harry Bridges of the longshoremen's union sent thousands of pickets to march solidly in a mass line around the courthouse, carrying banners praising the virtues of King, Ramsay, Conner, and Wallace while vilifying Warren. Pickets surrounded the Warren home to intimidate the family.

Yet, while the radical press of San Francisco was filling the air with its poison-pen diatribes, Wallace confessed to having acted as a guard while Sakowitz murdered the engineer, and Conner confessed that he, King, and

Ramsay had sent Wallace and Sakowitz to "tamp up" the engineer for his antiunion activities. King never denied his guilt.

When it became obvious that the four had not been guiltless, the tactic shifted to blaming Earl Warren for malfeasance in office. He was accused of assigning the case to one judge and then, without explanation, transferring it to another who had been handpicked for the bench on Warren's recommendation. Little did the union care that Warren had asked for a second-degree verdict rather than the death sentence. His role in the King-Conner-Ramsay case continued to alienate California's small, politically impotent radical Left. The extreme left-wing clique of the CIO would never forgive the attorney general for the case, even though Warren continued to carry every American Federation of Labor (AFL) and CIO stronghold in the state, proving that the rank-and-file union members cared no more for brutal political murders than did the district attorney. Joseph R. Knowland, editor and publisher of the *Oakland Tribune*, elaborated on Warren's code of honor:

> No one ever told Warren what to do in the line of duty, at least not more than once. I lost several friends who asked me to intervene in some important matter with Warren, and wouldn't believe me when I told them I couldn't influence Warren, and that if I tried to interfere it would only hurt them or their friends. He never tried to control politics in town; all he wanted was the best possible government. The only people who tried to attack him were those whom he had attacked for good and valid reasons. Our paper backed him all the way through, and so did all the other papers. He sought advice from his friends on every legitimate subject, but when he had a job to perform he went ahead on his own responsibility.[55]

In time the furor died down, but a second of Warren's personal feuds—this over the nomination of Max Radin to the state supreme court—soured his reputation with what remained of the Democratic New Dealers. Radin was considered a brilliant legal scholar, a superlative teacher, and an engaging popular lecturer. He took delight in challenging conventional wisdom or sniping at organizations such as the American Legion for their readiness to label any social criticism as "communistic." Frequently tarred as a Communist himself in the foreboding years of the 1930s, Radin briefly challenged his accusers to prove it. He was neither Communist nor Socialist, he claimed, but stood "left of center . . . the ideal position from which one may toss a few rocks at those too far right of it."[56]

Warren had once thought well of Radin, a professor of law at the University of California since 1919. In 1935, then–District Attorney Warren had declined to recommend Radin, "our old friend," for a seat on the federal bench only because Warren was the Republican national committeeman. "I am sure," Warren wrote a mutual friend, "that Max Radin would reflect honor on the bench, if he should receive the appointment."[57]

Olson's election three years later prompted rumors that Radin would be appointed to the state supreme court, "slated to be 'the Felix Frankfurter of California.'"[58]

When Olson did finally nominate Radin to the state's high court in June 1940, the outcry was clamorous. He was an "extreme leftist" and, worse, the author of an "atheistic" college textbook, according to one Christian fundamentalist organization.[59]

By the terms of a constitutional amendment that Warren had supported in 1934, all nominations to the bench were to be ratified by a Commission on Judicial Qualifications. The commission's three members included the chief justice of the state supreme court, the senior presiding judge of the courts of appeal, and the attorney general.

Chief Justice Phil Gibson had served as Olson's director of finance and had worked closely with Radin in the first year of the administration. He was a sure Radin vote. The senior presiding justice on the appellate court, conservative Republican John T. Nourse was just as adamant in his opposition to the nominee. The ballots were deadlocked. That meant Warren would have the deciding ballot.

Warren had challenged Olson's first appointment to the state supreme court, Jesse Carter, on narrow legal grounds and lost, with Radin defending Carter's appointment. Warren confirmed the second of Olson's nominees, Phil Gibson. The third nominee, Max Radin, was another matter.

Warren never publicly explained why he opposed the nomination of his old compadre. Privately, he told close associates that Radin lacked a "judicial temperament." As attorney general, Warren "couldn't go along with the appointment," he told a deputy. "The man was impractical, a visionary."[60]

While even Radin's acquaintances shared that opinion, Warren had another, unspoken reason for bucking his nomination: Democrat Radin had crossed Republican Warren one time too many in the past. Radin had publicly opposed Warren's assertion that a state legislative committee was entitled to subpoena lists of union members. The professor also contributed twenty dollars to the King-Ramsay-Conner Defense Committee and had stated publicly that he considered Conner innocent of murder. Moreover, Radin had defended Governor Olson's pardon in the Mooney case and supported Olson in opposing wide-ranging subpoena powers for state legislators. He had also defended Olson's first nomination to the supreme court.

But it was Radin himself who provided Warren the rationale the attorney general needed to vote against his appointment when, on June 3, 1940, eighteen employees of the Stockton office of the State Relief Administration refused to answer questions put to them by a state assembly committee. The committee was investigating the possibility of Communist infiltration of the agency. The eighteen were arrested for contempt of the committee and tried. Radin then wrote letters on law school stationery to two former students requesting that they "speak a word for a light sentence to the judge" if the eighteen were convicted.[61]

When the letters came to light, the chairman of the investigating committee objected. Radin's letters, Assemblyman Samuel W. Yorty proclaimed, were intended to corroborate testimony previously presented before "your committee in which he was named as a 'campus contact' of subversive groups."

Radin denied he had done anything improper in attempting to "soften the blow." Writing the letters was "a perfectly legal practice," he insisted.[62]

The Commission on Judicial Qualifications met behind closed doors on July 22 to consider Radin's nomination. The three members reviewed statements that Warren, as its secretary, had taken regarding Radin's fitness, a statement from Radin himself, and a sharply critical report from a three-member panel from the Board of Governors of the California State Bar.

After two hours, Warren emerged to announce Radin had been rejected, declining even to report the vote was two to one against the nomination. Warren gave no reasons for the rejection.

His coveted appointment lost, Radin blamed Warren, damning him as "a compound of Ku Klux, antisemitism, witch hunting, Republican partisanship, and . . . general cussedness." The attorney general, whatever his pretensions as a nonpartisan, was revealed as "a thoroughly unreliable and slippery politician," Radin charged.[63]

Some people found Warren's rejection of Max Radin as personal and visceral, perhaps for good reason: Warren was only human. Five months after the vote rejecting the professor for the court, he still fumed about Radin's nomination. In a private meeting with University of California president Robert Gordon Sproul, Warren "launched forth in a vigorous denunciation of Professor Radin, which very evidently contained a good deal of personal animus." According to Sproul's notes, the attorney general asserted that Radin's brother and daughter were both Communists, that Radin "constantly gives aid and comfort to Communists and other radicals, particularly free speech and civil liberties cases," and that Radin had sought lenient sentences for the state relief workers in Stockton.[64]

Warren was especially upset, Sproul noted, that such a man should have been appointed to the prestigious John Boalt Chair of Law. When Sproul asked his old friend what he proposed, Warren could only request that they stop favoring and glorifying Radin at every opportunity.

There the matter rested, "a black mark" on Warren's record, Warren's friend Robert Kenny concluded.[65] Radin continued as a member of the law school faculty. Warren moved on with the more pressing business of a crisis in a world gone mad. His relationship with the governor, Culbert L. Olson, a partisan Democrat, had been less than congenial as Olson thwarted his attorney general's every move. Throughout the war years, Olson was determined to run the state by decree from Sacramento. He bypassed consulting with his AG in legal matters and ignored the state's plans and programs for the law enforcement, health, and firefighting officials whom Warren had helped weld into an enthusiastic and cooperative organization for civilian defense. Olson went so far as to exclude his AG from the State Council of Defense, a group that Warren had labored for two long years to establish!

Around the same time, Warren—increasingly concerned about his state's vulnerability to a Japanese attack like the one ultimately suffered in Pearl Harbor—decided to take whatever steps necessary to protect his homeland from foreign invasion. He offered California as a laboratory to FBI director J. Edgar Hoover to use the state of California—the most vulnerable to potential attack—for any program he might decide to test in connection with ideas for the advancement of civil defense work. He wrote Hoover that he was particularly concerned about tracking subversive activities. Law enforcement files in that field were unverified and of questionable reliability.

By 1941, the relationship between Warren and Olson had deteriorated to the point of open warfare. Warren charged that Olson wasn't doing enough to promote the kinds of social changes that Olson's own Democratic president, Franklin Delano Roosevelt, was advocating. In doing so, Warren had thrown open the very gates to hell—something for which he later expressed remorse.

In February 1942, two months after the Japanese attack on Pearl Harbor, FDR issued Executive Order 9066, demanding the resettlement of Japanese Americans into concentration camps. Warren, attempting to play to both conservative Republicans and liberal Democrats with his support for the Democratic president's proclamation, quickly organized the state's civilian defense program on the heels of his earlier warning: "The Japanese situation as it exists in this state today may well be the Achilles heel of the entire civilian defense effort."[66]

In the anti-Japanese fervor surrounding the Second World War, Warren and others believed the concentration camps were necessary to protect the nation from subversive forces. The authorization for the camps was upheld by the 1944 Supreme Court decision in *Korematsu v. United States.*

Although Warren's tenure as California's attorney general from 1938 was marked by numerous successes, his most memorable "achievement" turned out to be the role he played in the Japanese evacuation in early 1942.

"No one person," according to Carey McWilliams, editor of the *Nation*, "had more to do with bringing about the removal of the West Coast Japanese during World War II—citizens and aliens alike; men, women, and children—than Mr. Warren."[67]

Shortly after Pearl Harbor, Warren issued his "Achilles heel" warning during testimony he provided to a House committee that came to California to investigate the situation. He said, "We believe that when we are dealing with the Caucasian race we have methods that will test the loyalty of them. . . . But when we deal with the Japanese we are in an entirely different field and we cannot form any opinion that we believe to be sound."[68] The next year, Warren, by then serving as governor, asserted at the governors' conference in Columbus, Ohio, "If the Japs are released no one will be able to tell a saboteur from any other Jap."[69]

Today, the statements sound as indefensible as a 1945 *Harper's* article characterizing the Japanese evacuation as "Our Worst Wartime Mistake."[70] But today, not all things are as they were.

Warren grew up in a city where Asians were nonpersons whose names weren't even included in the city directory. As McWilliams put it in an interview, Warren "was entrapped to a certain extent by . . . a kind of political environment out of which he came in California."[71] Like most California politicians, Warren was a member of the anti-Asian Native Sons of the Golden West. Not long before Pearl Harbor, he spoke to its members, saying, "It is at such times that we most need loyal and patriotic organizations like the Native Sons. . . . This is your order and mine."[72] He remained active in the Native Sons throughout his years as governor, despite its actions in urging exclusion of those of Japanese ancestry from US citizenship.

Also, the political situation on the West Coast at the beginning of 1942 was horrendous. The panic that arose from the Japanese attack on Pearl Harbor had an almost Alice-in-Wonderland air about it. "After Pearl Harbor," said former Los Angeles mayor Fletcher Bowron, "everything was in a state of confusion. We kept getting reports of Japanese spying and sabotage. . . .

There were reports they were in touch with the Japanese fleet . . . and we didn't have any way to tell who was loyal and who wasn't."[73]

In reality, there had been no actual cases of Japanese sabotage, but that failed to prevent the explosive fear of Japanese attacks on the mainland. Tom C. Clark, who was on the West Coast as a Department of Justice representative at the time, later recalled how "the papers had big headlines, 'Los Angeles Bombed' and 'LA Raided,' but it was pure hysteria." Clark asserted, "I think that you have to live it to understand the feeling Californians had about the people of Japanese descent after Pearl Harbor."[74]

If Warren was frightened to death of allowing the Japanese to go about their daily business along the coast, he wasn't alone. As McWilliams put it, "The sad truth of the matter is that you could count on the fingers of two hands the number of so-called public personages in California who opposed mass evacuation of the Japanese."[75]

Nearly every politician, labor leader, and newsman at the time supported the evacuation. Lieutenant General John L. DeWitt, commanding general of the Western Defense Command, strongly recommended the Japanese removal, claiming, "A Jap's a Jap. They are a dangerous element, whether loyal or not."[76] One of Warren's closest associates during the war years stressed the warnings of the military over personal sentiment: "Remember, we were civilians. We weren't about to contradict a three-star general."[77]

Years later, Warren, writing in his 1977 book *The Memoirs of Earl Warren*, said that he "deeply regretted the removal order and my own testimony advocating it, because it was not in keeping with our American concept of freedom and the rights of citizens. . . . Whenever I thought of the innocent little children who were torn from home, school friends, and congenial surroundings, I was conscience-stricken."[78]

Having resigned his Republican Party affiliation before running for the position of attorney general of California, Warren adopted a program of nonpartisan neutrality that he retained throughout his four-year term. He avoided participating in Republican politics—or, for that matter, politics of any sort. From fund-raisers to campaign endorsements, he deemed lying low to be in the best interest of the AG. He wanted to be the best attorney general in California's history, the best ever anywhere, and the surest way to do that, he believed, was to be totally nonpartisan and focus all his energies on enforcing the law. There was really nothing he would have preferred to do. As he elaborated in his *Memoirs*:

> I was intensely interested in my job and wanted nothing more than to be re-elected as attorney general in order to carry to fruition my plans

for making that office the outstanding one of its kind in America—a true instrument of justice and a model for civilian defense. Many people had urged me to run for governor, but I told them I had no interest in seeking that office. Which was the fact. I felt secure as attorney general because there was general praise for our efforts and no one likely to be a serious contender had appeared in the offing. I had no political organization or financial support to rely on, and no personal finances. The Democratic registration was by then almost two to one over the Republican. President Roosevelt was at the height of his prestige, having recently been elected over Republican candidate Wendell Willkie by winning in every state in the Union except Maine and Vermont. We were in a world war and in an atmosphere of "Don't change horses in the middle of the stream." I had a wife and six children and was obliged to remain in the law, for which I was trained, in order to support them. I felt that my opportunities in the legal field would be greater after holding the office of attorney general than after holding any other public position. There was little to attract me to a campaign for the governorship.[79]

Although he didn't realize it at the time, there was little to repel him, either.

4

NEW LIFE

With Governor Olson's meddling in the pardoning of King, Ramsay, and Conner after they served only four years for murder, Warren was nearing his limit. He later recalled, "The chasm between us was widening, and I could envision sitting in my office with nothing to do for four years in the event we were both re-elected to our respective jobs. All this was terribly disheartening, and it finally reached the point at which I could no longer stand it. Nobody of any substance signified an intention to run against the governor. I thought that Dr. Robert Gordon Sproul, president of the University of California, might be able to beat Governor Olson, and I urged him to try, but he was concerned about the effect it would have on the university, and so declined."[1]

From as early as May 1939, Warren's friend and close adviser Jesse Steinhart had drafted a plan to elect Warren governor. Steinhart's ploy was simple: portray the candidate as a reluctant entrant into the race.

"You [play] hard to get," as one man who had seen the confidential document paraphrased the advice.[2] The hesitant candidate would then yield to a "draft" by a preponderance of citizens anxious to see him run.

Because such drafts had to be carefully arranged, Joe Knowland convened a confidential meeting with Warren's Southern California political operative McIntyre Faries and two fund-raisers, San Francisco securities broker Charles Blyth and banker Jerd Sullivan. As Warren sat listening, Knowland methodically laid out his reasons for tapping the attorney general as their best candidate. First of all, Warren was reliable. "Nobody thought of him as in any way radical," Faries later explained.[3]

Secondly, Warren was a proven vote-getter, and publicity surrounding his crackdown on the gambling ships had only enhanced his reputation. No other Republican had Warren's broad political appeal.

Knowland proposed that he and the others raise enough seed money to promote a Warren candidacy. The northerners were prepared to put up $15,000 to launch a Warren campaign, an impressive amount at the time. Faries went on to sniff out a similar largesse in Southern California.

But Warren still had reservations about the campaign. "What do you want out of it, Charlie?" he asked Blyth outright.

"All I want out of it is honest government," the broker reportedly replied.

Warren could not have asked for more. By the end of the meeting, he had assented to a quiet exploratory campaign.[4]

Joe Knowland's son, Bill, was to be the point man. He traveled around the state, discreetly promoting Warren while reminding the general that, unless he ran, Californians would have to endure another four years of Olson.

The north fell into line. The south waited until May 1941, when the *Los Angeles Times*'s influential political editor, Kyle Palmer, signaled his consent: "Should Attorney General Earl Warren set aside his personal preferences, [he] would be one of the strongest challengers the Republicans could put up against any Democrat."[5]

Although Warren remained uncommitted, Knowland, ever the solicitous missionary, pressed on. "A large number of our friends in the south are champing at the bit," he reported on September 21, 1941.[6]

Later that year, a private poll identified Warren as the Republicans' most attractive candidate. The attorney general also led the critical independent and Democratic voters by a four-to-one margin.

When his advisers pressed him to announce his candidacy, Warren countered with a surprise announcement of his own. He intended to accept a commission as a colonel in the army.

Steinhart, stunned, urged him to reconsider: "What have you got to lose? If you run and lose, you can go in the army then; the war's going to last a long time. If you run and win, you could be a tremendous asset to the country as governor of this state."

Warren demurred. "Why, I couldn't afford to run for governor," he recalled, thinking back. "I had six children and they were all of school age."[7]

It was true. As attorney general, he was bringing home $11,000 a year; as governor, he would have made a constitutionally mandated $10,000. The family budget was already stretched to its limit; unlike other California officeholders, Warren had no "slush fund" contributed by supporters for his personal use.

As a counteroffer, Warren suggested the party draft a substitute, so they approached Los Angeles mayor Fletcher Bowron. But the mayor, afraid of a rising Democratic tide, joined with University of California president Robert Gordon Sproul in declining.

Finally, with no better plan immediately available, the tipping point was reached. Olson had designed a proposal outlining the roles of key administration officials—Democratic officials—in the event of an attack on California by Japan. Since Warren was the Republican Party's highest-ranking elected official, Olson made sure his DA had no role to play in the defense plan and, thus, no glory to grab should Warren have had plans for unseating the governor.

That action was the straw that broke the district attorney's back. During the state's efforts to organize the forced removal of "persons of Japanese heritage" from their homes, as Warren wrote in his *Memoirs*, he made the decision to run for governor:

> After much inner debate, I left my office one morning, went across the Bay to my home in Oakland, and told Nina to prepare herself for a shock. She inquired about the nature of it, and I told her that, as a last resort, I had made up my mind to run for governor. It was, indeed, a shock, and she asked if I thought I could win. I told her that was not the main consideration; that the governor [Olson] and I were at loggerheads; that he would not permit me to do the things that the Constitution and laws of the state required of me, and that I would not sit on the sidelines for a term as attorney general while we were in the midst of a war that threatened our very national existence. She said, "All right, if that is the way you feel, you should do it."[8]

So, with that resounding endorsement ringing in his ears, Warren called his staff together to announce, "Contrary to what I told you . . ."

It was true, the general had told his staff only two weeks earlier that he had decided not to run. Suddenly, the tides had changed. "I don't want to run," he told them. "I like this job, but I'm forced, as a citizen of this state, to accept the decision of others that it's the only way we can defeat Olson, and I'm running."[9]

His decision wasn't met with universal applause. As he recalled, "I told some of my close friends in the San Francisco Bay area of my decision, and they were aghast. They told me that, while they had wanted me to run for governor and had believed I could win, the war had changed their thinking. They now considered it most unwise for me to do so. They enumerated the obstacles that would confront me, all of which I conceded. But, I told them, the war had changed my mind also, and although I previously had been unwilling to run, I now believed I must do so if I was to perform any useful function in the war effort. Reluctantly they agreed to support me if that was my final decision. However, they said a poll had been taken in Southern California and it showed that only about twenty per cent of the voters there were of a mind to back me."[10]

Regardless, the attorney general announced his candidacy publicly on April 10, 1942. No one, he joked, could run the state any worse than Olson—not even him!

Taking his cue from his own prior successful bids for office, the attorney general paid the $250 filing fee and formally cross-filed for governor on both the Republican and the Democratic tickets. The race for governor had begun.

But the task before him was formidable. One survey taken for the Republican Finance Committee in late March 1942 showed Olson with a 29–19 percent lead, with 52 percent of the voters undecided. It was within that uncommitted 52 percent that Warren saw an opportunity. The vast majority of the undecideds had either a favorable impression of Warren or an unfavorable opinion of Olson. "I'm going after them," Warren told his advisers.[11]

So, six weeks after Olson pocket-vetoed an appropriation of $214,000 to meet the additional costs of running the attorney general's office as required by the war, Warren announced his candidacy for governor. In the statement he made to the press, the attorney general said the times called "for a unity of purpose and action that rises above every partisan consideration. They demand a nonpartisan administration of our state government. If elected, I will give such an administration."[12]

Olson's press conference the following day was expectedly nasty; the governor said, "His hypocrisy is only equaled by the fraudulent nonpartisanship of the Republican predatory interests and their newspapers, which sponsor and support him."[13] All through Olson's campaign, he chiseled away at his opponent in a similar vein: "Anyone who is so cowardly as to put on the cloak of nonpartisanship in an election like this either acknowledges that he is a political eunuch and does not know what it is all about or that he is a political hypocrite."[14]

But, as Warren had said from the outset, "I believe in the party system and have been identified with the Republican Party in matters of party concern, but I have never found that the broad questions of national party policy have application to the problems of state and local government in California."[15]

For more than thirty years, ever since the high tide of the Progressive Era, Warren reminded his electorate, Californians had lived with nonpartisan city and county officials, courts, and schools. During that period, he said, legislators and other elected officials had come to look at the state's needs without regard to party or partisanship.

Despite Warren's dogged determination to get into the fight, the "smart money" donors in the political wings remained unmoved. In a meeting at the exclusive California Club in Los Angeles, a group of sixty-five influential corporate executives decided to put their time, energy, and money into legislative campaigns rather than the governor's race. Realizing that Olson was vulnerable, they believed they would have greater success unseating the governor by electing a more conservative legislature.

Ironically, many of the same men had previously urged Warren to run for governor. Their loyalty, it turned out, was paper-thin. Among the executives there, only one spoke up on Warren's behalf. He was a junior partner in a large insurance firm who was filling in for his senior partner, who had been unable to attend. Warren later recalled:

> His name was Gordon Campbell, and he was best known as a fullback on the University of Southern California football team fifteen years or so earlier. He performed at this meeting as directly as he played football. He told the rest that they were a bunch of hypocrites; that he had heard many of them say I should make the race, and that it was a cowardly and dishonest thing for them to throw cold water on my candidacy in this manner. His words created some consternation but changed no votes, and the meeting adjourned on this 64-to-1 basis. I did not know Campbell at the time, but we soon became close friends.[16]

After Warren learned of the meeting, he worked up a list of a dozen businessmen who had been present and who at one time had urged him to enter the race. He visited each of them, telling them he had not come to induce them to change their minds but rather that he knew what had transpired. He reminded each that he had never asked for any financial backing and that their action would not change his plans. Warren wrote later:

> Their embarrassment was great, and they tried to explain; however, I told them I was not seeking an explanation. I only wanted them to know that I knew of the meeting.
>
> While I did not fully realize it at the time, this was one of the best things that ever happened to me politically. The first public reaction of Governor Olson to my candidacy was that the people of California would not want as their governor a district attorney who was the creature of the moneyed interests of the state. But my action had deprived him of one of his appraisals of me, and, what was far more important, it

had relieved me after my election of any pressure based upon campaign contributions from powerful southland interests.[17]

At superior court judge Fletcher Bowron's suggestion, Warren asked Raymond H. Haight, a young liberal Republican, to be his Southern California manager, and Haight agreed. Haight, too, had heard about the California Club meeting and suggested that the lone dissenter, Gordon Campbell, would make an excellent chairman of the Finance Committee. Warren agreed, "and by great diligence in seeking small amounts [Campbell] raised about $75,000, which in those days enabled me to make a fairly good primary campaign in that part of the state."[18]

Throughout his career in public service, Warren's independent convictions were crucial to his sense of self-worth, as Deputy Attorney General Adrien Kragen pointed out. Summoned once to Warren's office in the middle of the campaign, Kragen found himself confronting a group of lawyers representing several newspaper chains. They wanted Warren to drop a lawsuit that would have forced the publishers to pay a sales tax on newsprint.

Warren turned to Kragen. "Do you think it's an important case?"

"Yes, I think it's a very important case."

"Gentlemen," Warren said, turning to the publishers' representatives, "You have your answer." He advised Kragen to press on with the case regardless of the political costs.[19]

That kind of independence played well with the voters, particularly because Warren came across as a man who might actually make a nonpartisan governor. League of California Cities director Richard Graves commented that Warren "talked of the office as one where executive ability, not partisan philosophy, was needed. And he believed implicitly that a time of war forbade partisanship."[20]

And it was true. With Japan's December 7, 1941, attack on Pearl Harbor, Warren felt that abolishing party differences for the sake of national unity was imperative. "We are not Republicans now; we are not Democrats now. We are Americans. And we want the type of government in California that puts America first and all other things second."

After all, he continued, "we are fighting for freedom now, not just for Party." And he believed that with every fiber of his being. Over the next seven months, his campaign's theme was "Leadership, Not Politics."[21]

The concept had come out of a meeting of a small group of committee advisers made up of Steinhart, his outgoing law partner Ed Feigenbaum, San Francisco society figures J. Ward and Kate Mailliard, Joe and Bill Knowland,

Charles Blyth, *San Francisco Bulletin* editorial writer and lawyer Eustace Cullinan, and Assistant Attorney General Bill Sweigert.

Despite their sway with the candidate, they realized they were advisers only. They could only offer advice, not make him take it. In the end, Warren called the shots. "Warren was his own campaign manager when it came to setting the tone and philosophy of his campaigns," a veteran newspaper reporter declared. "It had to be a Warren-for-Governor campaign from start to finish."[22]

Warren did manage to agree to one significant suggestion by Joe Knowland, who feared his man was not getting sufficient attention in the press. The AG agreed to retain the services of San Francisco-based Campaigns, Inc. to handle his publicity and promotion.

Founded in 1933, Campaigns, Inc. was created by the husband-and-wife team of Clem Whitaker, a onetime newspaperman, and Leone Baxter, the former director of the Redding Chamber of Commerce. The PR team's first move was to "humanize Warren," as partisan critic Carey McWilliams put it.[23] Gone were the round, black-rimmed glasses that made previous campaign fliers and window cards appear as if they'd been defaced by a bunch of giddy teenagers. In their place: a pair of gold-rimmed glasses to add a cheerier touch to the trademark Warren smile.

Next, on a campaign trip to Los Angeles, the team arranged to have Warren visit the weathered two-story frame house at 457 Turner Street where he had been born fifty-one years earlier. The publicity shot of Warren nattily dressed in a suit and hat, smiling at neighborhood ragamuffins on the front walk, ran in every newspaper in the state. But Warren the campaigner was a man of integrity and dignity. After the photos appeared, he refused to pose for any more of the "gag" shots, as he called them, that most politicians lived for. No more kissing pretty girls; no more holding newborn babies. His Plumas County chairman recalled that, while Warren might occasionally don his American Legion cap, "he always seemed a little self-conscious wearing the thing."[24]

Leone Baxter and actor Leo Carrillo, Warren's friend from their days at Fort Lewis, did persuade Warren to use a photograph of the family they'd found in the *Oakland Tribune* morgue. Taken on the steps of 88 Vernon, the shot showing eight Warren family members appeared on hundreds of thousands of penny postcards mailed to Democratic women across the state—a touch that eventually paid dividends.

The critical decision in the campaign, though, came when Warren decided to run independently of any party label under the banner of the Warren-for-Governor Non-Partisan Campaign Committee. His goal was to campaign without seeking or offering other candidates' endorsements. He went so far as to refuse to appear with other Republicans at various campaign events. It was a radical notion whose time, Warren believed, had come.

Whitaker and Baxter assembled several independent committees that spotlighted occupational groups ranging from cosmetologists and insurance workers to pharmacists and women realtors. Carrillo himself chaired a Loyal Democrats for Warren Committee, while a Railroad Men's Non-Partisan League for Warren proudly announced that four of its members had known the candidate as a boy in the Southern Pacific yards—and liked him!

The PR team went so far as to create a campaign flyer directed at union members. The flyer heralded Warren's membership in the musicians' union along with his support of the right of union members to organize. The pamphlet made a virtue out of what had once been a handicap: "His father was a union man, and was blacklisted for fighting for union rights."

But Warren didn't stop there. On June 30, he announced that the attorney general's office would appear as a friend of the court in support of legislation to exclude the Japanese from the West Coast. A week later, Olson suggested that evacuees be used to bring in the vital San Joaquin harvest.

The agriculturist backing that Olson claimed for this proposal vanished under a press attack mounted by Whitaker and Baxter: "[T]he vast majority of farmers as well as other citizens of California have no sympathy for the Governor's program and want the Japanese evacuated from the Pacific Coast area."[25]

Throughout the exchange, Warren appeared resolute and patriotic while Olson came across as weak-willed and feckless; Warren stood with the vast majority; Olson, with a diminishing minority.

Three weeks later, Olson announced his opposition to an initiative to repeal the state income tax. Warren just as quickly endorsed the proposal. He appeared to be on the side of hard-pressed taxpayers while Olson's stand placed him squarely opposed to their plight.

Finally, Warren accused Olson of pandering to "communist radicals" by previously releasing King, Conner, and Ramsay from prison. Olson's attempted defense came across as politically motivated when he asserted the three had not personally killed George Alberts. Besides, he insisted, he hadn't pardoned them but merely commuted their sentences to time already served.

Throughout all, Warren continued asserting his nonpartisanship and independence. "[I]f elected, it is my intention to represent all of the people of the state of California. In this primary I have no running mates and I am not part of any ticket of candidates."

Throughout the campaign, the attorney general was careful to avoid wandering into troubling economic waters and making outlandish political promises. He insisted the night before the election that "I would rather be overwhelmingly defeated at tomorrow's election than to win an easy victory on false promises."[26]

Warren did issue a "pension pledge" intended to appeal to the swing voters of California's large and vocal senior citizens' lobby, who were subsisting on a forty-dollar-a-month state stipend. Need, he argued, should not be a requisite for a pension, nor should citizens be forced to sell their homes to qualify for one: "A system which arbitrarily freezes people out of industry and declares them to be obsolete, merely because they have lived a fixed number of years, must make honorable provision for their support during the years of their enforced idleness."[27]

Warren's platforms paid off. On the night of August 25, 1942, he and Nina celebrated with Joe Knowland as the returns chattered across the wires of Oakland's Tribune Building. In the end, Warren swept the Republican primary, gathering 404,000 votes, while Olson's Democratic primary bid netted him 513,000. The closeness of the numbers alarmed Olson, who picked up the tempo of his attacks against Warren in the lead-up to the general election. The governor referred to his opponent as a political eunuch and a hypocrite, little more than a pretender to the throne who was unfit to be governor. But Warren saw a growing split within the Democratic ranks: The people weren't buying it, and FDR offered Olson only tepid support from the White House.

Following his decisive primary win, the people from Southern California whom Warren called "the moneybags" offered to put together a finance committee "and give Olson a real licking." Warren demurred, saying he would stick with his finance chairman, Gordon Campbell, and if Campbell couldn't raise money, "then we won't have any to spend."[28]

As the gubernatorial campaign switched gears, a subtle intentional change overtook Warren's operation. According to a Whitaker and Baxter internal memorandum, Warren was going to "make the attack on Olsonism and not the Democratic Party."[29]

It was a shift in strategy that left Olson dumbfounded, dazed, and confused. He struck out at Warren for his "predatory interests," claiming he was nothing more than a bitter Republican partisan who had come from the most reactionary conservative faction of his party.

Olson's attacks played right into Earl Warren's hands as the attorney general replied piously that the governor's attacks were driven by "bitterness, prejudices and hatreds" at a time when wartime unity was required.

To back up his words, Warren had recently convinced the state GOP to incorporate into its public policy platform a pledge to halt partisan party politics "so that we may give [Democrat] President Roosevelt our unqualified support in prosecuting the war to a victorious conclusion no matter what the cost might be."[30]

Undaunted, Olson increased the intensity and frequency of his attacks. When the governor lambasted Warren for upholding the California law that required schoolchildren to salute the flag or be expelled as delinquents, Warren, nonplussed, countered that he would be happy to stop his defense of the law just as soon as the Supreme Court, which had mandated it, reversed itself.

As Olson felt his political star waning, he appeared as confident as possible, going to the radio to deliver one attack speech after another. Warren decided on a different tack. He began stumping the state, driving in an open car, often with Carrillo behind the wheel. The enigmatic, outgoing Carrillo, whose family had settled in California long before it became a state, was the perfect foil for the staid and stoic attorney general. The Hispanic American told jokes, related his own life's stories, and signed autographs. Warren, realizing that nothing appealed to a family of voters more than the family-man image Warren had carefully cultivated over the years, threw his three daughters into the race every chance he had.

Robert Kenny, then a state senator from Los Angeles County who would mount a losing campaign to unseat Warren as governor in 1946, summed it up best: "I'm not saying that Earl Warren capitalized on that large and beautiful family he has, but [they] always appeared in his campaign literature, and I complained to him once. I said, 'Are we running against each other for governor, or is this a fertility contest?'"[31]

Olson, finding himself fading in the polls, still had an ace in the hole. He telephoned the White House and asked President Roosevelt to come to California to stump for him. But Roosevelt knew better than anyone the role Warren had played in swinging the GOP to the president's wartime support. He flatly declined. The president realized that Olson, no longer able to unite the Democratic Party behind Roosevelt's New Deal rhetoric, had become a liability. Olson was a dinosaur whose time had passed. He was on his own.

Down but not out, the ever-flamboyant Olson pressed his campaign into Warren's very backyard, into every corner of the state, and Warren parried expertly, countering the governor's every thrust. Meanwhile, the state's electorate ignited. The race was turning out to be one of the most eagerly anticipated political contests in California history. With each passing week, Warren received new evidence that his campaign was on fire. Shortly before the general election, he told young capital patrolman Edgar "Pat" Patterson that he expected to be elected and would see that Patterson was detailed to the governor's mansion. "I want you to help take care of my kids," he said.

"I'll take care of you and your kids," Patterson replied.[32]

As the general election drew toward its conclusion, Olson lagged badly. Finally, with the dawn of election day 1942, Californians turned out in staggering numbers. By the end of the day, Warren had swept fifty-seven of fifty-eight counties, defeating his overconfident opponent by more than 342,000 votes (1,275,287 to 932,995). It was an upset stunning in its magnitude. Olson later commented about the victor: "Warren is the slickest politician I ever met."[33]

In keeping with the nation's wartime regulation prohibiting the assembly of large crowds, Warren took the oath of office privately before the state legislature. There was no Inaugural Ball, no massive celebration, no parades or other festivities—a change from the norm that Warren found so refreshing, he repeated the routine for his next two gubernatorial victories.

Following the ceremony in the assembly chambers, outgoing governor Olson joined Warren, his sister, and his wife in the elevator on the way down to the governor's office. Olson turned to the victor and said, "Warren, if you want to know what hell is really like, just wait until you have been governor for four years." Warren replied, "Governor, I hope it won't be that bad." Olson's rejoinder was, "Just wait and you will see."[34]

At the small reception following Warren's victory, newly elected Lieutenant Governor Fred Howser gave a three-minute speech that was followed by a forty-minute rambling oratory from the governor-elect. Afterward, Warren joined his wife and two boys to meet the press and field a few questions. Eager to win some points with California's newest exec, one of the reporters asked twelve-year-old Earl Jr. which speech he had liked best, expecting him to say his father's. After thinking it over for a few moments, "Ju-Ju" blurted out that he liked the lieutenant governor's speech because it was the shortest.

Another reporter asked seven-year-old Bobby what he had to say about all the excitement. Bobby calmly took out the wallet he had received at Christmas and pulled out an identification card. It listed his name and new address as "Governor's Mansion, 1526 H Street, Sacramento, California." He turned the card over and showed the reporters the Warrens' former address, remarking that the family would be moving back to their old home when their four years in office were up.

Four years. It was a good point. It reminded Warren that, up until then, only one governor in California's history had ever served out his four-year term and been reelected to a second. Four years, he reasoned, was all the time he could realistically expect to maintain the governorship. So, then and there, he made himself a promise not to get too attached to the real estate on H Street. As it turned out, it was one of few promises he made to himself that he would fail to keep.

Meanwhile, within hours of assuming office, Warren and his wife found themselves facing a family crisis. After Warren decided they needed to move into the governor's mansion in Sacramento to affirm its importance as the center of state government, Nina realized that the governor's house, which had been built as a private residence in 1878, had been kept up little ever since. Most previous governors chose to live elsewhere, eschewing the "Nightmare on H Street."

It was no exaggeration. Before the Warrens could move in, the mansion needed interior and exterior paint. The rotting porch had to be replaced. The tilting cupola needed to be righted, and the upper floor, which had been boarded off for safety, required reshoring and replacement. Nina thought that wasting what was once a perfectly beautiful home was a sin, so she launched a program of rehabilitation that finally succeeded in turning an empty shell into a fully functioning residence. Using only $4,000 of government funds, she restored the seventy-year-old, ten-room, gargoyle-studded relic to its former luster, inside and out.

Not long after, a reporter from *Life* came out to interview the family, writing: "The Warrens share happy dispositions, unselfconsciousness, and violently good health. The children adore their father and come running from what seems like all directions the moment he enters the house. Warren in turn is devoted to them. He has no intimate friends, and no real hobby except fishing, and his greatest relaxation is to teach Bobby how to use the new air pistol he bought for him in Chicago, or to help Ju-Ju in the victory garden."[35]

Despite all the bitter political machinations bubbling up around him, the governor remained the same committed, doting, loving father he had always been. His wife rounded out the familial esprit. Each year, she turned Christmas in the governor's mansion into an authentic Dickensian affair, complete with ribbons, bows, and bells, with candles in the window and carols at the spinet. The family, ever mindful of their many fortunes, enjoyed sharing their joy with others, including total strangers down on their luck.

But that esprit of the young Scandinavian wife and mother was apparent in everything she did: Christmas, the holidays, even her family's birthdays. Never did she overlook the natal day of a single Warren family member— with one notable exception: hers. That she refused to acknowledge even with a simple, basic cake. She never told anyone why she had such an aversion to celebrating her birthday until many years later when she had grown close to grandson Jimmy Lee, who occasionally traveled to Washington to visit his grandparents.

Jimmy Lee recalled the story told to him by Nina about her father's remarrying a woman known only—as he recalls the spelling of her name—as Nanapomp:

> She was a dreadful disciplinarian, in the words of Mama Warren. The family had very little money. They were really poor, [and] Nanapomp did things like . . . buy the three girls new shoes and, as the shoes started to wear out, she would make the girls wear them on the opposite feet so that they would wear more evenly. It would take a longer time for the soles to wear through. And, of course, she would put cardboard and tar paper or whatever else in them so she wouldn't have to buy new ones. Mama Warren had club feet, and she insists that was because she had to wear shoes on the wrong feet.[36]

Another story she shared with her grandson was that the girls, who were all very good seamstresses, worked in a shop where they made clothing for other people; Nanapomp made them bring the scraps from those clothes home and stitch them all together to make dresses for themselves.

"[The] girls," according to Warren, "were really ragamuffins. When you're growing up and have to go to school in rags—even though they were very nicely sewn, they were rags—[Nina] would talk about the humiliation" that left a scar on the girl that lasted her entire life.[37]

As if all that weren't bad enough, on Nina's eighth birthday, her brother Jim gave her a unique present—a porcelain statuette of a lamb that he had bought from a man down the road. Thrilled, the girl brought the present inside to show to her siblings. Nanapomp, who had only recently married Nina's widowed father and inherited his three girls and a boy, was unrelenting in her lack of love and understanding. When Nanapomp caught sight of Nina with the statue, she glowered at the child and demanded to know where she had gotten it. Her brother spoke up, admitting that he had bought it for a nickel to give as a present to his sister. The woman ripped the statue from Nina's arms and held it out to her stepson. "Return this to where you got it," she snapped, "and get your money back! We have no time for such foolishness around this house!"

When the boy came home after returning Nina's present, Jimmy Lee recalls, "Nanapomp beat Jim, really whipped him in front of Mama Warren.

She beat him to tears. Jim was so horribly maimed by that woman, he could barely walk."[38]

As a result, Nina vowed never again to revisit those memories on her birthday.

And she never did.

Yet, despite the pain she endured that day, she managed to grow past the disappointment and seek out the best in people. Like her husband, she was warm, gregarious, and totally open to public scrutiny—just the opposite of most public figures of the day (and since!). When a reporter once asked the governor why he'd elected to keep his home telephone number listed in the directory, he told him that, with three teenage daughters at home, he had no choice.

Warren had come a long way since his days as attorney general, but he never turned his back on his political roots. Former California governor Edmund G. "Pat" Brown said of Warren's years in the State House: "I've always felt that Warren grew from the days that he was a prosecutor and Attorney General, where he was primarily interested in law enforcement."

In those days, said Brown, Warren did not "evidence any great liberalism. As he stayed in the Governor's office and saw the need and the plight of the people, I think he gradually changed. And I would say that I as a Democrat and he as a Republican thought pretty much alike."[39] President Harry S Truman, commenting on Warren's liberal wolf-in-sheep's-clothing persona, said of the governor in 1948: "He's a Democrat and doesn't know it." When told of the president's comment, Warren smiled. "Yes, but with a small 'd.'"[40]

So life in the governor's mansion was comfortable for the Warren family. By the time 1944 arrived, so, too, had the maneuvering of the looming presidential election. Only two years into his term as governor, Warren began fielding calls from his national party's representatives asking him to run for office. As flattering as he found the notion, he took a hardened look at the possibility. He rationalized his chances of being nominated and, if so, elected.

He concluded that the timing was all wrong. His best opportunity for making a bid for the presidency, he felt, would come in 1948, by which time the war would be over, and he would have had a few more years in which to learn how to tackle the nation's problems from the experience of a battle-tested administrator. There would be other opportunities, and better ones. Until then, he would bide his time.

Author Robert Coughlan, writing in 1944, agreed: "Warren can complete his home course in foreign affairs. By 1948, too, he can come before the voters with a substantial record as governor of a great state."[41]

Suddenly, it appeared that less prominent candidates would be making their bids for office, and "it is possible that one of them may end up with the nomination," wrote Coughlan.

Still, the writer had to admit, "Warren, who stands four-square in the middle between the party's liberal and conservative wings, would be a logical choice."[42]

But even if Warren came up short and missed the party's presidential imprimatur, his national aspirations would be anything but dead. He'd still have an excellent chance at being tagged the vice presidential nominee by the man most likely to gain the presidential candidacy, New York governor Thomas Dewey. Coughlan felt that Warren, coming from the West, would have made an excellent veep. He explained:

> This is important because (a) he would thus balance a Dewey ticket geographically and (b) the West is politically nervous. Lacking representation in the Cabinet, the Supreme Court or the top strata of the big war agencies, and uneasy about its postwar future, [California] will be inclined to vote for whichever party can guarantee it an ambassador to Washington. The Republicans must carry California to win, and Warren has a demonstrated ability to carry it.[43]

But Warren wasn't biting. If he couldn't be president, why would he accept the lesser, mostly symbolic position of vice president? And why, particularly, would he want to be vice president under Dewey in 1944 when odds favored his winning the presidency in 1948?

So when Warren received a telephone call from presidential hopeful Wendell Willkie, who was canvassing potential running mates to find the strongest candidate possible for his own national run, Warren didn't take long to make up his mind. Willkie had long agonized over how to land the big fish who had become a political powerhouse on the West Coast. Willkie had run for president during the election in 1940 and lost in a landslide to Roosevelt. Now that the war was winding down, he felt he had a good chance to trade on the optimism of a nation returning once more to peace—and a better opportunity, still, of winning with Warren on the ticket.

But, as a seasoned politician, Warren sensed the direction of the growing political tides. He declined. FDR was running for an unprecedented fourth term, and Warren knew that—regardless of the state of the war—the popular Democratic incumbent was a shoo-in. As it turned out, he was. He defeated Dewey by more than 3 million votes.

Turning his attention from the presidential election back to his home state, Warren set about tackling California's most pressing problems. His nineteen years of service to the city of Oakland and Alameda County enabled him to step into the governor's office and dive into work. One of the first pressing problems facing him was the perennially elusive issue of public health.

At the time, many California counties had no health officer, and the state's own Board of Public Health was bogged down by a group of feuding physicians whose primary interest was keeping the public from meddling in their affairs. Warren took steps to correct the situation by hiring a new state director of public health, Dr. Wilton Halverson. Halverson and Warren began their work together by reviewing water samples taken at three Los Angeles–area beaches. The results weren't good. All three samples revealed dangerously high levels of bacteria. Upon further investigation, Warren discovered that the bacteria were coming from raw sewage being dumped into the ocean by the City of Angels itself! Warren asked Halverson what he thought the solution to the problem might be.

Halverson said that they had to close the beaches. That policy didn't sit well with the locals or their elected officials. But Warren's failure to act could have resulted in a deadly outbreak of infectious disease, so the beaches were ordered shuttered. Next, they had to find the money required to build an efficient waste-disposal plant. Only then would the beaches be reopened. The solution? The city held a bond election to raise the necessary funds. As public pressure mounted to clean up their coastline, the Angelinos secured the funds, constructed the treatment plant, and solved the problem.

But that was only the tip of the health-care issues Warren had inherited. He ran headfirst into a woeful dearth of health-care facilities, so he worked alongside the state legislature to establish the California Physicians Service, whose goal was to help the poor obtain medical treatment, particularly in the area of mental health. Before that, an Alameda County resident needing mental health care had to have a relative or someone else who knew the patient go to the district attorney's office, swear out a complaint charging the person with insanity, and testify that the person was a danger to him- or herself and the community.

If that person were ordered to submit voluntarily to the emergency room for examination and refused, a warrant would be delivered to the police, and the person would be picked up and taken to the hospital by force. Once there, the patient would be kept in a cell-like room until that person's case could be heard and a judgment made.

To rectify the situation, Warren joined Halverson in a tour of each of the state's ten mental health facilities. They found the conditions in all ten centers so deplorable that Warren couldn't sleep for a month. Some of the buildings they'd visited were little more than shacks; others were rat-infested firetraps.

Some had been built as temporary quarters for survivors of the San Francisco earthquake in 1906. Not one was suitable for use as a medical facility.

When faced with the question of what to do about the situation, Warren elicited suggestions from several friends and a group of prominent local physicians before deciding that the state had to condemn every one of the ten hospitals and build new ones. It took nearly eight years and $200 million to get the job done, but it was money well spent: California's state mental facilities were soon ranked among the best in the nation.

For the third health issue he faced, Warren came to realize that far too many Californians were situated far too distant from a suitable medical facility to be of any good, so he set about building new hospitals so that everyone in the state would reside within an hour's drive of quality medical care.

This was no easy task. California stretches out for nearly a thousand miles and is divided by two major mountain ranges; circumnavigating the state is a statistician's nightmare. But hospitals needed to be built, and Warren saw that they were. The program was subsidized partly by locally issued bonds with the rest coming from matching federal dollars. As new hospitals sprang up in rural communities around the state, they were staffed with young doctors fresh out of medical school and eager to begin practice. The results were improved medical facilities for everyone.[44]

Warren next supported Halverson in spearheading a drive to bring the state's related medical agencies together under one roof. The University of California conducted critical medical research. So Halverson had the university join forces with the state's Board of Public Health to create the University of California School of Public Health. By uniting various other government agencies under the common banner of better health care for everyone, Warren succeeded in bringing the state's medical services out of the Dark Ages and into the progressivism of the twentieth century.

Progressivism. It was an appropriate word for the first-term governor. Warren concentrated his focus next on petitioning the California state legislature to approve a comprehensive prepaid medical and hospital care program for all California workers and their families. It would have been the first in the nation, financed by a 3 percent payroll tax. But the bill ran into stiff opposition from the influential medical lobby, which termed the plan "socialism." The bill failed to pass. But that was only the beginning—not the end—of the governor's fight for social equality.

Following that defeat, Warren went to work tackling legislation designed to desegregate the California National Guard. Although facing dogged opposition from special interest groups and legislators who felt that enrollment in the Guard would fall off if the all-white units were forced to accept black enlistees, Warren felt otherwise. In a close vote, his supporters won, and a bill was passed opening up the Guard to males of every ethnic and racial group.

Warren next fought and won a battle to improve California highways by inaugurating a decade-long road-building program funded by a gasoline tax—a revolutionary concept only sporadically employed by a handful of other states in the past. In accomplishing these last two politically charged goals, the governor made some loyal friends as well as some powerful enemies.

The governor next decided to look into problems long facing California's penal system, a statewide embarrassment. The system had begun around 1850, when the state turned an abandoned sailing ship in San Francisco Bay into California's first prison. A few years later, San Quentin was built, followed in the 1880s by the construction of Folsom Prison.

Warren's investigations into the state's penal system identified several serious problems. One concerned some institutionalized prisoners who were regularly given front-office clerical jobs. That also gave them access to prisons records and printing presses. The result was a statewide ring of forgers who changed prisoners' records to look as though those who had been charged with serious crimes had been sentenced for less severe offenses. How many prisoners had been released before their actual jail time was served? Warren could only speculate.

To correct the situation, the governor hired a group of penologists to reform the rules and procedures for handling prisoners and for overseeing the running of the state's prisons. Within a few months, the prisoners were booted out of the front offices and back into their cells.

Not all the problems Warren faced were handled so expeditiously. Some dragged on for years. Others, like those encountered in everyday life, were overcome over time only through hard work and diligence.

One such issue emerged as California grew in population until it had become the most populous and most liberal state in the union. That meant it was also the most polluted. Warren soon realized the need to conserve California's natural resources. Long before the media focused national attention on the environmental issues of the late 1960s and early 1970s, Warren's common sense told him that, as California's population boomed, the government would need to respond to the growing responsibility for protecting the state's beaches, parks, mountains, streams, and forests.

With the help of Professor Emanuel Fritz of the Department of Forestry at Berkeley, Warren created a new State Forestry Board. Together, the men established comprehensive programs for eradicating damaging insects and replanting forests that had recently been logged.

But when Warren attempted to tackle the problem of smog and air pollution hanging over the Los Angeles basin on all but the windiest of days, he met fierce resistance from that city's vested officials. They told the governor that the smog was their problem, and they wouldn't have the state meddling in local affairs.

Despite independent studies that showed air pollution to be a severe threat to human health, Warren found himself powerless to fight the local bureaucracy. Another decade or more would pass before the same people who had resisted his attempts to clean up California's environment would clamor for federal aid to do so.

But environmental pollution, penal and health-care social reforms, and desegregation were only some of the issues that frustrated Warren during his tenure, which would last for three full terms. In the end, it would not be his inability to cope with the problems he faced as governor that would remove him from office, nor would it be illness, apathy, or a desire to move into national politics. Instead, it would be something much more momentous, much farther reaching for both Warren and the nation. It would be the Supreme Court of the United States of America.

But in April 1946, Warren had other things on his mind. He announced for a second gubernatorial run, in which he again won both the Republican and Democratic primaries and emerged as both parties' candidate before going on to win the general election. It was no surprise to the governor. Warren had won most of the political battles he'd fought over the years because the people were on his side—for a good reason.

He had cleaned up the corruption in the state government and secured significant reform legislation, including increasing old-age pensions and unemployment benefits. He proved to be an effective administrator. He balanced the budget and realized significant tax reductions while establishing a rainy day fund of nearly $75 million, all despite a broad expansion of statewide programs.

Pat Brown, the Democratic governor who served California several years after Warren, said of his predecessor: "He felt the people of the state were in his care, and he cared for them. . . . Earl Warren faced the problems of social responsibility and growth and met them head on."[45] In fact, growth was a genuine concern of Warren's.

"Gentlemen," he used to tell his Governor's Council, "we have to plan for a whole new city of ten thousand people every Monday morning."[46] In his later years, the chief justice recalled proudly that, during his tenure as governor, his state had been able to absorb five million new arrivals "without any confusion or discord whatsoever."[47]

Even his political opponents couldn't help being impressed by Warren's performance. Robert W. Kenny, a Democrat and unsuccessful opponent to Warren, told of how, on a visit to the White House, he was asked by President Roosevelt, "What kind of a fellow is your . . . Governor?"

"Well, Mr. President," Kenny replied, "I'm just a California booster. Everything we have out there is better than it is anywhere else. Even our Republicans are better than they are anywhere else."[48]

Indeed, the California voters agreed. In the process of being elected for three consecutive terms, Warren buried his opponents in his dust. He nearly won both the Republican and Democratic primaries in 1942 when he defeated incumbent Governor Olson in a landslide. He won both party primaries in 1946 and again in 1950 when he went up against Democratic candidate James Roosevelt, FDR's son. It didn't matter to Warren what party affiliation he identified with, and it certainly didn't matter to his electorate.

As a result of such progressive thinking, Warren's political success had garnered national renown. In 1946, shortly after winning his second term, the governor—in a rare example of partisan politics—threw his support behind Jerry Voorhis for reelection to Congress. Voorhis, LA's Twelfth Congressional District representative, had backed Warren on his health insurance proposal and the governor's ongoing fight with the oil and trucking industries. Voorhis's primary Republican opponent, a lawyer named Richard Nixon, asked for Warren's support. Warren, never very impressed by Nixon's sleazy reputation, declined. Voorhis's opponent went on to win an upset victory anyway by using his notorious smear tactics and demagoguery.

Suddenly, the antipathy between Warren and Nixon exploded into public disdain. It became a boiling cauldron of emotions that would last throughout both men's lifetimes, bubbling up more violently with each passing year.

During Warren's second term in office, a single word signified his tenure: *growth*. California grew in stature, increased the number of social programs instituted for the benefit of its people, and expanded its population, which by then had leapfrogged past that of any other state. Meanwhile, the governor's reputation was being noted three thousand miles away in an anteroom in Washington, DC.

On the heels of his 1942 gubernatorial sweep, Warren was already being touted as presidential-caliber material. Articles appeared about his work in the *Saturday Evening Post, Collier's, Life, Time, Newsweek, Look,* and *Better Homes and Gardens.* When the Republican National Committee invited him to be temporary chairman and keynote speaker at the National Convention in Chicago in 1944, he accepted, catapulting him overnight to become the consensus vice presidential candidate despite his continued assertions to the contrary. After Warren had presented his speech and the convention had elected Tom Dewey the Republican presidential nominee, all eyes fell once again upon Warren. The party—even his own California delegation—believed he would reconsider his stance and relent. On the day of the vice presidential nomination, Dewey spent the better part of an hour trying to convince Warren to accept the nomination, but the governor stuck to his guns, and Dewey eventually tagged Senator John Bricker of Ohio, who was formally nominated that evening.

Running against Dewey and Bricker were Franklin Delano Roosevelt, seeking an unprecedented fourth term as president, and his new vice presidential running mate, Harry S Truman. Roosevelt and Truman won.

Four years later, the 1948 Republican National Convention met again, this time in Philadelphia, to select presidential and vice presidential candidates. Their hopes for success ran high. Among the front-runners at the opening of the session were Speaker of the House of Representatives Joseph W. Martin of Massachusetts and his close associate, House majority leader Charles A. Halleck of Indiana. From the other side of the Capitol dome came leaders who felt confident that one of their members would receive the nomination. Senator Robert A. Taft of Ohio was the leading senatorial candidate, but Senators Arthur Vandenberg of Michigan, Edward Martin of Pennsylvania, and Raymond F. Baldwin of Connecticut were pressing him hard.

In addition to these three seasoned national candidates, four governors from across the nation were equally dedicated to campaigning for the top spot, including front-runner Thomas E. Dewey of New York, former governor Harold Stassen of Minnesota, Dwight H. Green of Illinois, and California's favorite son, Earl Warren.

The strength of the political machine of the governor of New York turned out to be unsurpassed by his opponents, and Dewey was nominated on the third ballot as candidate for president. As political analyst Charles H. Titus later wrote, "The opposition could not agree to unite."[49]

After winning the nomination, Dewey, in the darkness of a predawn Thursday, picked up the telephone and placed a call. Warren later wrote in his *Memoirs*:

> The night before the morning session that was to nominate a vice-president, I went to bed about midnight, and was awakened from a sound sleep about 2:30 a.m. by a ring of the telephone. Tom Dewey was on

the line. He asked me if I could come to his hotel headquarters. After dressing, I went directly there. He was waiting for me and told me that earlier he had gathered together a number of Republican leaders from distant parts of the nation. They were agreed that I should be his running mate, if I would accept, and he said that would please him also. He told me he could understand why I would not relish merely presiding over the Senate, and that, if I accepted and we were elected, he would make the job meaningful by having the vice-presidency play an important role in his administration. We talked the matter over for a half hour or so, and also some of the family problems involved in such a move. Finally I told him I would accept.[50]

Warren's was a shock. Political pundits for more than half a century since have pondered the question of why Warren was willing to be Dewey's running mate. If Dewey's invitation to the governor was a surprise, Warren's acceptance was even more so, because those close to the governor understood that, if Warren couldn't be first on the ticket, he'd pursue other plans. But such a request, as Titus wrote, was "a real temptation. Perhaps Warren remembered another Californian who refused a similar invitation and lived to regret it. Senator Hiram Johnson never forgave himself for declining the offer of Mr. Harding in 1920."[51]

As vice president, Warren would become titular leader of the Senate, an honor he never considered especially enticing. According to biographer Bernard Schwartz, Warren was alone with a man named Merrill H. "Top" Small, Warren's executive secretary, shortly after the governor received the vice presidential nomination. According to Small's account, "[Warren] turned to me, and he said, 'Top, I had to do it. I had to do it. If I hadn't taken it this time, they'd never consider me for anything again!'"[52]

The vice presidential candidate himself later reflected upon his decision:

Things [in 1948] were different for me than in 1944. I had fulfilled my commitment to the electorate after serving six years [as governor]. There were only two years left on my second term, and two four-year terms are normally all any governor serves. I did not wish to be a senator or a cabinet officer. There were no other public positions that I looked forward to, and, liking public service as I did, it seemed as though this might be a satisfactory way of topping off a public career. I was then fifty-eight years of age.[53]

After his meeting with Dewey, Warren recalled walking back to his hotel, waking up his wife, and telling her the news: "I am sure she was stunned, but characteristically she made no complaint, in keeping with her practice of not trying to direct or interfere with any of my political affairs. Her concern was always for my happiness. However, she doubted whether I could be happy with Tom Dewey directing my activities. She was as interested in my independence as I had been through the years, and she considered this a potential inroad on it."[54]

The next morning, when the nominations were to be announced, Nina and the three Warren girls left the hotel for the convention hall while Warren remained behind, monitoring the events over the radio. He remained in his room until he learned that Harold Stassen, whose name was also under consideration for the vice presidential nomination, withdrew. Earl Warren was nominated by acclamation. He rushed out of the hotel and down to the convention hall. He hadn't prepared a speech, but he recalls his opening statement:

"Now I know how it feels to get hit by a streetcar!"[55]

That evening, Warren telephoned home in Sacramento to talk to his sons. Bobby, twelve, answered.

"Hello, Bob," Warren said.

"Hello, Dad."

"How are you?"

"I'm fine. How are you?"

"Fine," the father replied. "Did you hear what happened here in Philadelphia today?"

"What?"

"I was nominated for the vice-presidency."

After a pause of several moments, Bobby replied, "Is that good?"[56]

Unlike most other political observers, Warren realized soon enough that he was heading for the first electoral defeat of his life. From the very start, he was disheartened with Dewey's virtual do-nothing campaign. Earl Warren Jr. recalls his father talking to Dewey on the phone numerous times during the campaign. "I can remember Dad saying, 'But Tom, you've got to go out and talk to the people.' 'Tom, you've got to tell them something.' 'Tom, you've got to talk about the issues.'"[57]

Dewey listened patiently but never fully comprehended. He was a well-educated, erudite politician with stars in his eyes. Warren, on the other hand, was a shrewd, hard-working politico and a loyal campaigner with politics in his veins. He was a blue-collar politician often more successful on the stump than his boss, who had arrogantly predicted a victory over political dark horse Truman.

Although Warren worked tirelessly, handling the job of both governor and vice presidential candidate, the campaign proved to be much tighter than Dewey was prepared to admit. Right up until the day after the election, as the results slowly funneled in from across the nation, Dewey was still bragging about "burying" the hapless Truman. Even the nation's newspapers had bought into the story. One—the *Chicago Tribune*—went so far as to declare Dewey the winner on its front-page headline. One of the most famous political photographs in history shows a jubilant Truman holding up a copy of the *Tribune* with its banner screaming, "DEWEY DEFEATS TRUMAN."

Of course, Dewey didn't defeat Truman, and, in fact, was crushed, his political career snuffed out overnight. It came as no surprise to his running mate. Well before the election, Warren knew that the Dewey-Warren ticket was doomed. A former member of his staff said, "He told us we were going to be licked. He said, 'Truman's gotten through to the people.'" When, after the defeat, reporters flocked around Warren to ask why Truman had won the upset victory, he smiled disarmingly and replied, "He got more votes than we did."[58]

The defeat—the only one Warren ever suffered at the polls—affected his future, too. But Warren was too ambitious and politically savvy to allow such a trivial matter as a failed presidential bid to get in his way.

The governor of California had met Truman in the 1930s at a national Masonic convention. The two later joined in several Senate hearings. They liked each other from the start, and Truman at least tacitly promised his support to the governor whenever possible.

And that, too, took some of the sting out of Truman's victory.

5

PRIME TIME

Shortly after the Warrens' marriage, Earl had told his young wife that he hoped they would have six children—three boys and three girls. He did just that, giving himself what rival political opponents termed the Warren "unbeatable family."

It was no overstatement. The importance of Warren's family formed the bedrock of his life. If, as Justice Potter Stewart said, Chief Justice Warren looked at cases in terms of "those eternal, rather bromidic platitudes" such as home, family, and country, it was only that they were "platitudes in which he sincerely believed." Warren's own home and family life furnished the foundation for his scale of values throughout his professional and political life. If there was something of the Babbitt in this, it was also, as Stewart put it, "a great source of strength, that he did have these foundations on which his thinking rested, regardless of whether you agreed with him."[1]

By the time he began the second year of his first term as governor, Warren had already grown to be one of the most towering political figures in America. Presidents came and went. Congressmen won and lost. But there was only one governor of the state of California; there was only one Earl Warren.

The press had not failed to take notice. The political successes and the power base building around this homegrown enigma shone clearly in the political sea that had been shrouded within state politics forever. As the accomplishments of the progressive governor of the largest state in the union grew, so too did Warren's notoriety. Soon he discovered that everyone wanted a piece of what was slowly emerging as "the Warren machine."

It was not something he set out to do. He was by that time fifty-two years of age and, according to one journalist, "a mature man with a paunch

114

and a family."[2] Still, he was suddenly being touted as presidential material even though Warren himself wasn't buying it. As author Robert Coughlan said:

> [His] disquietude is accountable both to Warren's sense of modesty and his sense of political timing. The modesty is based on the fact that the next President must cope with problems to which Warren offhand does not have the answers. As district attorney of California's Alameda County for 13 years, attorney general of California for four years, and governor for only a year and a half, it has not been required of him that he think out a program of global strategy, the conditions of peace, the organization of the new world order, the processes of economic demobilization and similar matters. Accordingly he has not, and as President he would have a good deal of homework to do on these items.[3]

Following Warren's refusal to jump on the Willkie bandwagon in 1944, the Washington pundits were left stewing. Who turns down a shot at a national office to hole up in a governor's mansion? Warren had asked himself that very question several times before he made up his mind to reject Willkie's offer. As he confessed in an article in *Life* magazine in 1944, "It's like putting on a pair of shoes. You get a bad fit in a shoe and it makes you uncomfortable all over. It's the same with this presidential situation: if the shoe doesn't fit, don't wear it. It's a situation that makes me uncomfortable all over. And I wish to God they'd leave me alone."[4]

Tight shoes or not, the national politicos wouldn't leave him alone. Just the contrary, his very aloofness and apparent aversion to running for national office made him that much more mysterious . . . and irresistible. But for Earl Warren, the title of governor fit just fine. As did one other title he wore with equal pride: Dad.

"His political life is a composite, not only of his own qualities but of those of his family," Coughlan wrote. It is very possibly true, as one disgruntled California Democrat claimed, that the people of the state elected the Warrens en masse as much for the warm and human picture they painted in the executive mansion at Sacramento as for the statesmanlike qualities exhibited by the head of the household. "You can beat Earl Warren," Robert Kenny once mused, "but how can you beat that family?"[5]

With the entire Warren clan effectively running for office whenever Papa Warren decided to take the political plunge, the press decided it was time to explore the Warrens' home mystique. *Life*, in its April 24, 1944, issue, ran an in-depth story attempting to peel away the many layers of Earl Warren, governor, that lay just below the surface. And there were lots of them.

Besides Earl and Nina Warren, the family consisted of son James, 20, by then out of school and in the Marine Corps; Virginia, 15; Earl Jr., 14; Dorothy, 12; Nina, 10; and Robert, 9. The family also included Brownie, a middle-aged spaniel; Sonnyboy, a spaniel puppy; and Peanuts, the family's pinto pony. But no one except for the animals ever answered to those names.

Instead, James was called, naturally enough, Jimmy. Dorothy was Dotty. Robert was Bobby. Virginia was often called "La" because that was as close as the children could come to the proper pronunciation of her name when they were learning to speak. Junior was Ju-Ju, and Nina was "Honey Bear," based upon Papa Warren's contention that, as a child, she was a dead ringer for an Australian koala they had often visited at the zoo.

But that's not quite the way the name came about, according to a letter from Honey Bear's younger brother, Bobby, and corroborated by Bobby's nephew, Jimmy Lee:

> When Honey Bear was little, she just *loved* to have stories read to her. From two or three years old, she just loved them. And her favorite book in the whole world was a book called *The Honey Bear*. And she always wanted, you know . . . "What should I read you? How about *Fire Engine*?" And she'd say, "No, *The Honey Bear!*" Always *The Honey Bear*.
>
> Of course, when she was born, she was named Nina after her mother. But unlike Earl Jr., who was named after his dad, you couldn't exactly call her Nina Jr., so that's when they decided to call her Honey Bear, and the name stuck forever.[6]

Jimmy Lee said that he'd been trying for years to find that book, but he couldn't, leading to some speculation about the book's actual origins: "I often wonder if it was perhaps a Winnie the Pooh book or something else that was kind of popular at that time. . . . But Honey Bear just adored that book. Just adored it. And she was just thrilled to be named that."[7]

Up until a few months before the *Life* interview, the family had also owned a Dalmatian named Jerry. A pleasant enough companion at first, he soon learned from Brownie how to bark at strangers and eventually expanded his repertoire to include nipping at their coat sleeves. The Warrens bore the numerous episodes involving delivery boys, legislators, and visiting dignitaries with stoic goodwill but gave up when Jerry took off the entire left sleeve of the tuxedo of the boy who was escorting Virginia to her first high-school dance. Nina sat up until after midnight sewing it back on, and Jerry was given his walking papers.

Like all families, the Warrens had a diverse range of activities and pastimes. That was understandable enough, since the parents encouraged their children to explore life's vagaries at their own pace. Each person was an individual. While La, the oldest daughter, played the piano, liked to dance, and was interested in the usual pastimes of a typical high-school girl (namely, boys), Ju-Ju enjoyed shooting, fishing, and taxidermy and was an avid gardener, winning several prizes for his crops in 1943. Dotty was a devoted Girl Scout, while Honey Bear and Bobby shared their love for horses, spending most of their time after school and on Saturdays at the riding club near the edge of town. Their pinto horse, Peanuts, was an issue between them since he belonged to them both. Still, whenever an argument arose, Honey Bear usually won, and that was understandable, according to Coughlan, because, as he alleged, "[a] conscienceless minx, [Honey Bear] runs the Warren household, including her father. Her power is indicated by the fact that at the Executive Mansion the elder Warrens sleep in what used to be a guest room. Honey Bear got the regular governor's chamber because its bathroom has a shower, and she likes showers."[8]

In reality, Honey Bear *did* occupy the governor's chamber, but not because it had the only shower. In fact, according to Jimmy Lee, *all* the bedrooms had large claw-foot tubs with gooseneck showers. But Honey Bear was "sixteen or seventeen, something about like that, when she contracted polio. It had spread to her school where a bunch of girls were cheerleaders, and a couple of them came down with [it]. She was one of them. It happened quite literally overnight. She was at a football game on Saturday, and on Sunday, her back kind of hurt and her legs were sore."

The diagnosis was a shock. She almost immediately lost total use of her legs, and the family decided she needed additional room to maneuver, to accommodate a wheelchair and crutches and other special-need items. Jimmy Lee recalled how Mama Warren told Earl that they were moving out of the master bedroom, the largest of the five upstairs rooms. "'You're moving across the hall,'" he relayed Nina telling Papa Warren. "'There's a bedroom over there for you,' and she told him that Dotty and Honey Bear would stay in their respective rooms, and Mama Warren moved into the maid's room right next to the master bedroom."[9]

In time, everything worked out well. After months of treatments that included exercise and warm water—plus an intensive trip Nina took with her daughter to Hawaii so the girl could soak in the salt water there—the polio went into complete remission, and she lived the rest of her life symptom-free. "A lot of it was simply the exercise, moving back and forth, keeping the legs going in a warm liquid environment," Jimmy Lee said.[10] Meanwhile, the Warrens kept their same rooms, with Honey Bear occupying the master bedroom while Nina continued to snuggle comfortably into the adjacent maid's quarters.

The conundrum that the governor's private family life might one day contribute to his political ambitions wasn't lost on Warren. Nina, by remaining aloof from politics, had developed into one of her husband's staunchest political weapons. Nearly all women voted not only a president but also a first lady into office, so Warren was ideally situated to get the most from both worlds. He boasted a loving, adoring, devoted family and a campaign tool who, particularly in a year when the proportion of female voters was unusually high, could entice that final push across the finish line.

Toward that end, Nina Warren was perfect. As Coughlan pointed out,

> Until recently, when she became an honorary officer of the Girl Scouts because of Dotty's interest in them, she belonged to no clubs, committees or organizations whatsoever. Beyond being a Baptist (Warren is a sometime Methodist) and a Republican, she has no pressing convictions. She would be astonished if anyone asked her about her ideology. It is not that she lacks the mentality. "When you have six children, five of them in six years," she points out, "you just don't have time for much else."[11]

A significant part of her day played precisely into the role carved out for all women of the day—or felt it did. She spent her hours matching bobby socks and repairing model airplanes, sewing a rip in Bobby's jeans and overseeing the painful new braces on Virginia's teeth—and cooking, baking, and housekeeping, of course. She juggled all those activities against the memories of the time Dotty ate an entire angel food cake and another occasion when Honey Bear was so sick that Nina moved her ironing into her daughter's bedroom to keep her company. She was, in effect, every middle-class mother.

Yet, as the wife of the governor, she also flirted with the public eye during brief interludes of christening ships, overseeing parties at the mansion, meeting with foreign dignitaries, and entertaining a never-ending stream of her husband's honored guests at dinner. She did all that while serving the dual role of providing comfort and support to her husband and ducking into the kitchen to whip up a spontaneous batch of Swedish meatballs or a chocolate cake—not to mention fixing up the old mansion and turning it into a home.

While hardly unique during the war years, when millions of other women bore and raised children, decorated their families' homes, and oversaw their finances, such a first lady in the governor's mansion might have seemed an abstraction to other women everywhere. Instead, Nina appeared to be a supercharged extension of themselves, a tireless worker who was at once both admirable and identifiable. And, every bit as important, it made her husband electable.

It was true that she'd had six children, but it was also true that she brandished a trim figure that made her an American heroine. For Earl Warren, who epitomized the most attractive qualities of the middle-aged American male, his wife was the perfect spouse.

This relationship, gilded with the inevitable consequences of Warren's sociability and vitality, produced positive results. His life was a tribute to planning, right down to the number of children he wanted in his family. But not everything had gone without a hitch. He had always envisioned himself as a husband and father, but he'd also foreseen himself a successful and wealthy trial lawyer. Instead, he had settled for the life of a public servant, culminating with his election to the office of governor. He was happy holding that office, but he was beginning to feel that others around him were conspiring to intervene in his future—for his good or, more likely, for theirs.

But in the middle of the second year of his first term in office, Warren's record both at home and at work remained solid. His sponsorship or approval of various issues resulted in reduced taxes, increased old-age pensions, a reorganized State Guard, an overhauled prison system, a liberal soldier-vote bill, additional funds for childcare centers, and a postwar planning commission. As an administrator and executive, he amazed his electorate with his cordial relations among the traditionally irascible state legislature, overseeing a body somehow serenely at peace within itself.

Of course, some argued that he'd inherited a deck stacked in his favor. His party controlled the legislature, whereas Olson's had not. He came into office with an $80 million surplus, whereas Olson had arrived with a $30 million deficit. He had inherited a wartime truce with labor and hadn't had to face the wracking consequences of the state's labor-employer war, whereas Olson had taken office only a year and a half after a bitter general strike. It is unfair to say, as some anti-Warren voters did, that even Shirley Temple could have made a good accounting as governor. Still, Warren hadn't yet been thoroughly tested.

Of course, he inherited uniquely grave problems of his own based on the war and California's efforts in managing it. Before that, five out of six of the state's workers were employed in agriculture. After his election, more than one-third worked in manufacturing, mostly in durable-goods industries. One out of five California workers was engaged in aircraft construction or shipbuilding. The total labor force increased by nearly one million workers since 1940. After the war, what was to become of the new workers and their fledgling industries as the boys came marching back to their homes and families?

Other states and regions faced similar problems, of course, but the difficulties in California and the West overall were reflected in both degree and potential consequences. Once the European armistice was signed, the industries in the East and the Midwest could begin their conversion from a wartime economy to one of peacetime prosperity. The West, however, was still thoroughly immersed in the continuing war against Japan and, as a result, would trail the rest of the nation in recasting its industries and realigning its priorities to meet a burgeoning postwar economy.

What the West really needed, of course, was someone high up in the ranks of Washington politics to fight for and protect the region's values and economic growth. Some people believed that person was Earl Warren; others felt he was too green, too untested, to slip from the governor's chair in California into the Oval Office in DC. Others pointed to yet another untested politician in earlier days, someone untried and unknown and from an obscure place of origin. Abraham Lincoln not only pulled America out of the quagmire of a grueling half decade of war but also lifted it back up onto its economic feet.

Could Warren possibly turn out to be a better-than-average president, as Alexander Kidd, the old and wizened dean of the law school that Warren had once attended, believed? With all those questions rattling around his head, Warren once again displayed his single-minded approach to dealing with life one step at a time when he said in response to an interviewer asking what he hoped to accomplish in the future, "I hope to be governor of California for a second four years."[12]

6

ON THE ROAD

As 1950 rolled around, Warren, with two terms as governor behind him, contemplated running again. But the conservatives in his party had other ideas. They urged him to enter the race for a vacant seat in the US Senate instead. There he would be pitted against liberal congresswoman Helen Gahagan Douglas, the comely Scotch-Irish American actress and politician. Her entertainment career included success on Broadway, in the opera, and as the star of the 1935 movie *She*, in which she portrayed a villainess who became the inspiration for the evil queen in Walt Disney's 1937 animated film *Snow White and the Seven Dwarfs*. Married for life to popular actor Melvyn Douglas, she was a formidable force in politics. She was also an ultraliberal whom Republicans were desperate to usher out of the state house and out of politics.

Warren might well have been tempted to accept the gauntlet in challenging her for a seat in the Senate and may well have won, but at the last minute, he respectfully declined, noting that he wielded more power as a veteran governor than he could ever exert as a freshman senator.

So, against party urgings, Warren stayed out of the fray, and Helen Douglas's opponent turned out to be none other than Richard Milhous Nixon. In a grueling, hard-fought battle, Nixon ran a typically vicious smear campaign against his opponent, referring to a secret Douglas "slush fund." Nixon also smeared Douglas's patriotism, calling her the "Pink Lady" all the way down to her undergarments. He walked away with the election handily.

Meanwhile, Warren, locked in his own race for a third term as governor, found himself pitted against Democrat James Roosevelt, FDR's son, a development that did anything but delight the seated governor. During the campaign, Eleanor Roosevelt, widow of the recently deceased four-term president, came to California to crusade for James, giving speeches and stumping as hard as she ever had for her husband's reelections. She was furious that President Truman had failed to support her son's bid because of the Democratic president's friendship with Governor Warren—of all things, a Republican!

While Warren viewed the interjection of Mrs. Roosevelt into the race as inevitable, William S. Mailliard, Warren's travel secretary, recalled how much that upset members of the governor's staff. They were concerned about how to deal with "this kind of thing, a legend . . . out there campaigning for her son."

"The only way you can deal with her," Mailliard concluded, "is to absolutely brush it off. If you react, well, by God, she's going to become a significant factor in this campaign."

But the governor only smiled, saying, "Well, I'll tell you what I'll do. I'm just going to issue a statement when we get [back to California]: 'You wouldn't expect [his] mother to be against him, would you?'"[1]

Despite all of Mrs. Roosevelt's concerted efforts, the election on November 7, 1950, ended with Warren trouncing his opponent, winning all fifty-eight counties in the state, the most significant electoral victory in California's history. In an ironic twist of fate, James Roosevelt was later elected to Congress and became one of the Warren Court's most vocal supporters.

Throughout his years as governor, Warren's concern for children spilled over into his political legacy. He created three hundred childcare centers operated by the state's Department of Education for the benefit of the children of working mothers. Most of the centers were housed in public schools and were administered by local boards of education in fifty-one school districts across the state. The cost was borne both by the state and by parents who paid fees ranging from two to six dollars a week per child. The governor also founded the California Youth Authority as an alternative to juvenile prisons, all of which only helped prop up his straight-shooting, family-oriented image.

Throughout it all, Warren's reputation as an honest, progressive, hard-working reformer continued to grow. In July 1951 a Gallup Poll taken randomly reported that if the presidential election had been held that day, Warren would have defeated President Truman by a 52 to 39 margin, an incredible feat considering how popular Truman was during his campaign and his first three years in office. With such glowing support ringing in Warren's head, the governor spent the next four months with friends, family, and colleagues agonizing over his political future. Finally, he made up his mind. Governor Earl Warren of California announced that he would run for the 1952 Republican presidential nomination against Senator Robert

Taft, a conservative Republican from Ohio. In a surprising move, Nixon volunteered to support Warren, pledging to campaign for the governor in the months that lay ahead.

But fate soon intervened, and Warren's attendance at a 1951 pre-Christmas Republican State Committee dinner in San Diego nearly ended in tragedy. The governor took violently ill with severe intestinal cramping and fever. He was rushed to the hospital where tests revealed a malignancy, and surgeons were forced to remove much of his intestine. He remained in serious condition for weeks.

In the meantime, Taft's supporters began spreading the word that Warren was dying of cancer. Others said that, while golfing, they had seen Warren receive a bag full of bribe money totaling $92,000—even though he had been in the hospital on the day of the alleged exchange.

Finally, on January 7, 1952, Governor Warren—with no viable alternative in sight—dropped out of the race for health reasons, and a newcomer to the political arena, a World War II hero and retired US Army general, saw an opening and announced that he was going to run for office on the Republican ticket.

Dwight D. Eisenhower had an impeccable war record and was already extremely popular with the American electorate. The Republican Party, anxious to find a solid candidate whom they could pit against a decidedly beatable Democratic contender in Adlai Stevenson, had encouraged Eisenhower to enter the primary and convinced him that he had a good chance of winning.

As California's primary unfolded, Warren's name continued to be bandied about. He could still win the presidential nomination, his delegation reasoned, as a write-in candidate. Meanwhile, Nixon continued his support for Warren—in public. Behind the scenes, though, he was secretly campaigning for Ike. Despite Nixon's best efforts, Warren carried the primary vote as a write-in candidate in his home state.

When dark-horse western maverick Earl Warren began making newspaper headlines once again, television responded. Warren couldn't have been surprised. He had built a strong organization from the ground up and laid a robust framework for his run for the nomination before his hospitalization. In an April 11, 1952, television interview for *Longines Chronoscope* with David Ross and guest "editors" William Bradford Huie of *American Mercury* magazine and Donald I. Rogers of the *New York Herald Tribune*, Warren was asked what he felt was the one thing that would help pull the Republican Party together to win the presidency for the first time in two decades. He replied, "I believe it's the realization of the need for re-organizing our government, for streamlining it, for cutting out all of the dead wood, for reestablishing integrity throughout the government."

Huie interjected, "I do just want to make this point. Is it fair to say that your criticism of the federal government is a criticism just of management and not a criticism of any theory of government?"

Warren said, "Oh, on the contrary. I want to say to you that I am thoroughly out of sympathy and always have been with the efforts of this administration, and I refer to it as the 20-year administration of centralizing all administrative power in Washington. I believe that they [the Democratic Party] have weakened our institutions. I believe that they have detracted from the efficiency and the importance of both state and local government."

When asked what he meant specifically, Warren replied, "I mean simply this. [With] every program that the federal government initiates that is ... a federal, state and local participation program, the intent on their part is always to centralize the administration of the entire program in Washington, DC. When we do that, we're taking away from state and local governments the responsibility of functioning, and we are weakening our Democratic processes. Now on the contrary, I'm of the opinion that in such programs we ought to put as much of the administrative power as we possibly can in the states and in the local communities and only do so much in Washington as is necessary to see that the purpose of the program is carried out and that the finances of the federal government are protected."

As the day of the 1952 Republican National Convention neared, the California delegates who had signed a pledge to support Governor Warren boarded the train as it departed Sacramento for Chicago. All the representatives were on board.

Except one.

Richard Nixon joined the Warren campaign train at a stopover in Denver on July 4, one night before the train was due to arrive in Chicago. The delegates were in a festive mood, celebrating in orange baseball caps with the letter *W* on the front. Meanwhile, Nixon and his cadre of loyal supporters went through the cars, shaking hands, slapping backs, and whispering that Warren did not have a chance to win the nomination. He told the delegates they should jump on the Eisenhower bandwagon. One stop shy of the Windy City's Union Station, Nixon slipped off the train and into a waiting car that whisked him to Chicago just steps ahead of Warren and his supporters.

When Warren found out about Nixon's dirty tricks, he was furious. "A delegate cannot break his pledge and still be a man of honor," he was quoted in the press the next day. "People of honor keep their word; people of dishonor don't."[2] Nixon, he believed, had dishonored his written pledge. Warren held a visceral repugnance toward his fellow Californian from that moment on.

Former Democratic California governor Pat Brown later recalled the moment: "It all started with the '52 campaign," he said, "when . . . Nixon was on the Warren delegation. He went back and made a deal to support Eisenhower. And he got the vice-presidency as a result of that. But Warren never forgave him; he thought [Nixon] double-crossed him."[3]

Earl Warren Jr. said years later that his father "just detested Richard Nixon with an abiding passion."[4] Brown recalled Warren's calling Nixon "a crook and a thief. He told me that; he's told me that Tricky Dick—that's what he used to call him—he didn't like him at all."[5] Nixon was one of only two persons in his life whom Warren termed an "evil man." The other was the unprincipled president of California's Superior Oil Company, whom Warren had called a "vitriolic multimillionaire."[6]

After finally arriving at Union Station, Warren registered at his hotel before paying a courtesy call on Eisenhower. When the door to Eisenhower's suite opened, Warren was shocked to find the doorkeeper was none other than Nixon's personal assistant, Murray Chotiner. The meeting was anything but civil.

On the floor of the convention the next day, Warren found himself once again bucking the odds, this time against presidential front-runners Dwight D. Eisenhower and Senator Robert A. Taft. Warren's only hope to gain a run at the nation's highest office was to force a deadlock between the two leading candidates . . . but how?

As things turned out, Warren had the perfect opportunity to do just that. But to do so, he would have needed to overcome a nasty streak of morality that plagued his bid to trade his home in Sacramento for a considerably larger residence in DC. He had a three-way deadlock all wrapped up until the California governor himself ensured that wouldn't happen by announcing his support of Eisenhower's position refusing to seat a group of challenged Taft delegates.

Herbert Brownell, Eisenhower's campaign manager, believed that if the contested delegates were allowed to vote on their seating, they would win the vote and give Taft a majority. Because of this, Brownell said, "I . . . drafted the so-called 'fair play amendment' to the rules of the Republican convention which had the effect of disallowing the right of any contested delegate to vote on the confirmation of his seating."[7]

Warren would have gained an advantage by opposing the amendment and supporting the Taft delegates' right to be seated. Doing so could have split the California delegation's votes between the Eisenhower and Taft forces, thus negating them and opening up a very real opportunity for Warren to sneak through to a primary win. But Warren's mind was made up. He believed that allowing delegates to vote on their own contested seats was unfair. So, against his immediate best interest, he urged the California delegates to approve the Eisenhower proposal restricting Taft's supporters.

"You people [will] have to go back to California," he reminded his caucus. "You have an obligation, and it seems to me that you have to discharge that obligation in a way that satisfies your conscience."[8] One of the delegates there at the time later relayed that Warren "made it very plain that this was the way he felt . . . [even though] the Taft delegation's seating . . . might have brought about a deadlock, which would have meant that he would have walked right down the center" to victory.[9]

At the governor's urging, the California delegation ended up casting its seventy votes for the fair play amendment, ensuring the measure's passage and, along with it, Eisenhower's Republican Party nomination. In his memoirs, Ike denied that his appointment of Warren as chief justice was "the payment of a personal political debt, supposedly incurred at the time of my nomination," as several political observers claimed. "The truth was that I owed Governor Warren nothing."[10]

The Republican primary winner insisted that Warren had refused to throw his seventy California votes to him and that it was the Minnesota delegation's switch from Harold Stassen (whose convention floor manager was future chief justice Warren E. Burger) that supplied the votes required for Eisenhower's nomination. But that fails to take into account the governor's support of the fair play amendment that gave Eisenhower the disputed delegates, ending Taft's opportunity for the nomination right along with Warren's.[11]

On the convention floor the next day, Warren, Eisenhower, and the other Republican nominees were offered to the delegates, and the first vote was surprisingly close: Ike received 595 to Taft's 500, Warren's 81, Stassen's 20, and MacArthur's 10. Once Stassen announced that he was throwing his votes to Eisenhower, it was all over. Not long after, Warren learned that Ike had chosen as a running mate none other than Richard M. Nixon. Nixon appeared on the stage, grinning from ear to ear. He had leapfrogged to national prominence after only six short years in public office, almost as quickly as he had hopscotched to a meeting with Ike and his campaign advisers in Chicago before Warren had arrived.

Showing no ill feelings, Warren campaigned doggedly for the Eisenhower-Nixon ticket over the next six months, despite his disappointment in the primary's outcome. He was merely making good on a pledge he had made to the nation in his April *Longines Chronoscope* interview. But Warren's support of Eisenhower was more a reflection of his unshakable belief in and dedication to the Republican Party than his personal love for Ike. The party had backed Warren throughout much of the politico's fledgling public career. So, true to his word, he campaigned hard for the party's choice of Eisenhower, even though he found Ike's habit of mangling syntax grating. He also felt disappointed with Ike's failure to defend Warren's old colleague and benefactor General George C. Marshall against Senator Joseph Mc-Carthy's muckraking charges of treason. Nonetheless, party loyalty spurred Warren to support the Republican presidential nominee, both publicly and privately, over perennial Democratic Party candidate Adlai Stevenson.

Interestingly, Ike's own vice presidential candidate nearly sank the general's campaign and destroyed his political career even before it got started. Two years after Nixon charged his former gubernatorial opponent of harboring a secret slush fund to reimburse her for her expenses, he learned of a leaked 1952 press memo that revealed a similar secret fund used to reimburse *Nixon* for campaign expenses. The California senator, who was stumping with Eisenhower at the time, broke off his campaign tour and flew back to California, where he became one of the first politicians to use the medium of television to deny allegations pressed against him.

In a thirty-minute speech, Nixon coolly refuted the charges, at one point comparing the allegedly illegal campaign gift to the gift of a cocker spaniel dog named Checkers that his family had received. Nixon concluded, "And you know, the kids, like all kids, love [that] dog and I just want to say this right now, that regardless of what they say about it, we're gonna keep it."[12]

The address, which came to be known as the "Checkers" speech, worked. Nixon painted himself as a warm, caring, loving, doting father and family man, and he was exonerated by the very public he had hoped to dupe, much to the relief of future president Eisenhower.

While politics was playing out on the national stage, back in California the political pot continued to boil. Warren had a year left to serve as a lame-duck governor, during which time he was unlikely to get any meaningful legislation passed along to his desk. Worse, a new brand of politician was creating havoc on the stage. Outgoing president Harry S Truman had accused the Republican Party there of turning away from the time-tested policies of their great progressive governor, Earl Warren, choosing instead to follow in the footsteps of another Californian "who is not worthy to lace his shoes." When reporters asked Truman to whom he was referring, the morbidly candid president retorted, "Nixon! [He's] a no-good, lying bastard!"[13]

The words were music to Earl Warren's ears.

7

SCOTUS MEETS *BROWN*

With his unsuccessful bid for president securely behind him and a nebulous future before him, Warren's head danced with a million options while he pondered his next step. He knew he had to do something for a living. He was too young to retire and too energetic not to take a position that befit his experiences.

When Herbert Brownell telephoned Warren to ask if he knew of anyone who could fill the subcabinet position of Chief of the Criminal Division in the Department of Justice for the new Eisenhower administration, Warren recommended Warren Olney III, who eventually was named to the position. Several other people who asked Warren for recommendations went unappointed for one reason or another, and Warren heard nothing more from the new administration until one morning in early December around 7:00 a.m. Warren was still in bed, reading, when the Capitol switchboard operator called and said that General Eisenhower was on the line and wanted to talk to him.

"Governor," the president-elect said, "I am back here selecting my Cabinet, and I wanted to tell you I won't have a place for you in it."

Warren replied, "General, I do not want a place on the Cabinet. I am perfectly satisfied with my job as governor, and I could not afford to move my family back to Washington for such a position."

"Well," he said, "I have been giving you serious consideration for Attorney General, but Herb Brownell has been close to me politically in the campaign, and I feel I need his political advice as well as his legal counsel."

"He will make you a splendid Attorney General," Warren said, to which Eisenhower replied, "But I want you to know that I intend to offer you the first vacancy on the Supreme Court."

Warren, somewhat taken aback, thanked him; Eisenhower said to consider that his personal commitment to Warren.[1]

When Warren told his wife about Eisenhower's promise, she casually inquired as to what the salary of a justice was.

"Twenty-five thousand a year," he replied.

"How could we take the family back to Washington on that?"[2]

Warren told her he didn't know. In reality, it would have been a substantial cut in pay. As governor, he made $25,000 a year. He also received state-furnished housing in the mansion along with an array of guards, automobiles, drivers, janitorial services, $1,000 a month for maintenance, a private plane and pilots, travel expenses, and an office staff that was available for anything Warren needed. Warren told his wife not to concern herself with Ike's offer because he'd heard too many stories about newly elected officials making elaborate promises to their supporters only to forget about them after they'd taken office.

Although Eisenhower and Warren had never been close friends, the Warrens were invited to the presidential inauguration, which they attended with their three daughters. They rode in the parade to the grandstand in front of the White House. Afterward, they attended the Presidential Ball at the Armory, which, according to Warren, "was more or less a shambles. Little attention was paid to seating assignments, and everyone took potluck. But the new president was enthusiastically received. There could be no doubt of his great popularity. 'I like Ike' was the watchword of the hour."[3]

Two days later, the Warrens were back in Sacramento, where the governor wrestled with the problems of a state to which fifteen hundred people a day were moving.

In the meantime, Warren read that King George VI of England had died, and the king's older daughter had been crowned queen. The coronation of Elizabeth II was scheduled for June 2, 1953. President Eisenhower appointed Warren as one of the US delegates to attend. In his *Memoirs*, Warren wrote,

> It was a very gracious thing for him to do, and I have often wondered what prompted his action. I was not one of the international set and had no particular association with the British Empire. I finally concluded that, knowing as he did how young girls would enjoy such an opportunity, it was a generous act on his part to allow my three daughters to view the spectacle.
>
> And it was a great spectacle. I have never seen anything to compare with the coronation ceremonies. It was a difficult time for me . . . because

we were in the closing days of a regular session of our Legislature. As usual, much important legislation was floundering around in committees or conferences awaiting the rush in the closing days when vital changes can be made without drawing immediate public attention because of the confusion that attends adjournment. I also had some concern about what the lieutenant governor might do in my absence with some of the more controversial bills.[4]

Nevertheless, Warren, his wife, and three daughters decided to leapfrog the pond and attend.

Heading the US delegation to Great Britain were General George Marshall and General Omar Bradley representing the armed services and Mrs. Fleur Cowles—at the time wife of Gardner Cowles Jr., publisher of *Look* magazine. The early June weather was anything but cooperative. It was bone-chilling cold; the wind blew to near-gale proportions, and it rained intermittently throughout the two days and nights leading up to the event. Crowds of people lining the parade route remained undaunted. The Warrens had an opportunity to meet the Queen Mother, the Duke of Edinburgh, young Prince Charles, and his younger sister, Princess Anne. Westminster Abbey, where the coronation took place, couldn't accommodate all the guests who had traveled from the four corners of the globe. As Warren recalled:

> I was extremely fortunate in my seating arrangement. I was directly above General Marshall, who had the place of honor in a forward choir seat. Other chiefs of delegations were in the other choir seats. I remember that directly across from the general were the representative of the Soviet Union, Prime Minister Nehru of India, and leaders of the British Commonwealth. When the Queen Mother came to Washington a few years later, I had the honor of sitting with her at a White House or Embassy dinner. We were discussing the coronation, and I was telling her that I recalled her using various motherly devices to keep the little prince interested in the long proceeding. She asked where I was seated, and, when I told her, she laughed. "You had a better seat than I had!"[5]

Warren remained in London for only a day or two following the coronation before he was forced to leave his wife and family and return to Sacramento to deal with some legislative issues. On his way back to rejoin them in Europe, he stopped off in Washington and met Brownell, at the attorney general's request, for lunch at the Statler Hotel. Brownell told the governor that the president wanted to appoint him solicitor general. He said that the president felt that service as solicitor general would be valuable experience before joining the Supreme Court. The governor told him about his financial situation, adding that it was a question of whether he could afford to accept the position and move to DC if the president offered him the position. Brownell asked Warren to think about it while in Europe. They devised a "code" that Warren could send while he was abroad to indicate his decision.

After their meeting, Brownell escorted Warren to the White House for a short social gathering with the president and Mrs. Eisenhower. It was "strictly a social call," Warren recalled. No business or politics were discussed. The next day, Warren returned to London to join his family. All the while, he thought about whether he should accept the position of solicitor general.

It was, he felt, "the most prestigious one in America. To be the principal lawyer for the United States Government in its most important litigation presents a challenge of enormous proportions."[6]

With the offer tucked away in the back of his mind, he joined his family as they prepared to depart for a tour of Scandinavia to explore the lands of their ancestors. Several days later, Warren wired the attorney general of his acceptance. Brownell said, "I was enthusiastic about the idea of [Warren] becoming Solicitor General," and he sent a return cable to show how both he and the president felt about the acceptance.[7]

The attorney general's delight was a given. The governor's was less so. The position of solicitor general is only the third highest in the Department of Justice. Besides that, the shift from governor of California to government counsel arguing before the Supreme Court would have been a step down in most people's eyes. That Warren was willing to do so showed his conviction in the sincerity of Eisenhower's pledge to place Warren on the court as soon as an opening arose. By agreeing to serve as solicitor general, Warren realized the quid pro quo was for the president to appoint him to the first court vacancy.

When the Warren family tour of Scandinavia was complete, the family boarded the liner *Stockholm* at Goteborg and returned home. It was the same ship that would suffer a tragic collision with the Italian liner *Andrea Doria* between New York and Narragansett three years later, resulting in dozens of lost lives.

On September 3, soon after Warren returned to Sacramento, he held a news conference where he announced he would not seek a fourth term as governor, but he declined to answer questions about his future. The following day, a front-page *New York Times* story quoted a "White House source" as saying that, if he wanted it, Warren could have the first vacancy on the

Supreme Court.[8] Meanwhile, the governor was beginning to prepare for the move to Washington to take over as solicitor general. One week later, without any warning, Chief Justice Fred M. Vinson died in bed in the middle of the night.

Vinson's death posed a severe problem for the president. Eisenhower had made a commitment to appoint Warren to the "first Supreme Court opening." But neither the president nor anyone else living in the real world had reason to expect that the vacancy would occur in the court's preeminent position. Vinson was only sixty-three and in apparent good health. He had come from a family renowned for its longevity. Did the Eisenhower commitment really apply to the chief justiceship? The president himself doubted it. In his memoirs, Eisenhower wrote that "neither [Warren] nor I was thinking of the special post of chief justice, nor was I definitely committed to any appointment."[9] Yet Eisenhower had made the offer as a "personal commitment" to the governor, who considered it such. His acceptance of the proposal that he become solicitor general could be justified on no other basis than that!

According to Eisenhower, "I gave serious thought to the possibility of appointing John Foster Dulles."[10] The president spoke to the secretary of state, but Dulles said he had no interest in any position other than the one he occupied. The attorney general met with Eisenhower to see if he thought any of the associate justices on the court could fill the vacancy. Brownell recalls thinking about recommending Justice Robert H. Jackson but decided against it because of Jackson's active role in favor of President Roosevelt's court-packing plan in 1937. Jackson also maintained a long-standing bitter public dispute with Justice Hugo L. Black.[11]

So, with Jackson's appointment to the position of chief justice out of the question, Ike next turned his attention to the possibility of appointing a Democrat to the post. Was that feasible? After scant consideration, the president and his aides agreed that the first Republican administration in twenty years could hardly appoint a Democrat to head the Supreme Court. The solitary Republican on the court at the time was Justice Harold H. Burton. But Brownell recalls that Burton's health wasn't the best, and that was one point against him. Even in perfect health, Burton scarcely had the leadership ability to warrant serious consideration.

That meant the appointment would have to go to someone outside the court. But did that someone have to be Warren? Public speculation focused on the California governor. The day after Vinson's death, the *New York Times* reported that it was commonly accepted on the West Coast that Warren would succeed the chief justice. His political enemies, the report said, would be just as happy to get him out of the state as his friends would be to see him ascend to the highest seat of justice. In his memoirs, Justice William O. Douglas confirmed a popular rumor going around at the time: Vice President Richard M. Nixon was urging Eisenhower to name Warren. According to Douglas, Nixon went to Ike saying something like, "You must get Warren out of California. He has control of the Republican Party machinery there, and we can't do business with him."[12]

Warren's own feelings on the matter were conveyed to the president when, at a White House breakfast, Eisenhower found himself seated next to Representative William S. Mailliard, who had been Governor Warren's travel secretary until Mailliard was elected to Congress. The president asked him, "Do you think that [Warren] would really want to be [on the court] after his years as Attorney General, Governor and all of [that]? Wouldn't it be pretty rarefied for him?"

Mailliard answered, "Yes, I frankly think he'd be very likely to be bored to death" as an associate justice. But Mailliard added, "My answer would be emphatically different if we were talking about the chief justiceship. He could run the place. . . . The Court would have decorum and dignity and it would be well managed."[13]

But Eisenhower was still reluctant to appoint the California governor to head the court. Brownell said, "It was clear to me from [Warren's] discussions with the president on filling Vinson's seat that President Eisenhower did not feel that his prior discussions with Governor Warren had related to a vacancy in the post of chief justice, but that he had had in mind an Associate Justiceship in his original call to Governor Warren about a first vacancy."[14]

At that point, Eisenhower asked the attorney general to fly to California to put the president's view in front of Warren to see if he agreed. Unaware of the president's directive, Warren had taken his sons deer hunting on Santa Rosa Island off Santa Barbara with Oxnard supervisor Edwin Carty. But his trip was cut short on September 25, 1953, when a navy PT boat radioed the island that Warren was "needed back in Ventura."

Warren and Carty sailed to Carty's beach home on the Rincon where Warren placed a call to Brownell, who asked that the governor meet him in Sacramento. Warren flew back the next day, and Brownell flew in on the president's plane from Washington to meet with the governor at McClellan Air Force Base, ten miles from Sacramento. Brownell arrived at 8:00 a.m. to find Warren waiting in a room set aside for the purpose of privacy. The press reported a week later that the conference had lasted three hours; Warren wrote that the meeting took an hour, while Brownell says that they conferred about an hour and a half.

Regardless of the meeting's length, the attorney general told the governor of the president's interpretation of his commitment, saying he felt it applied only to an "ordinary vacancy" in the Supreme Court. He then asked if they could "defer the commitment [for a Supreme Court nomination]." If so, Warren could have any cabinet position he chose. "Name your own," he told the governor.[15]

According to several reports, Warren firmly rejected the offer. He said that he was not interested in any cabinet post and could not afford to take one, which was probably true. Warren was nothing if not a practical man. He also allegedly insisted that Vinson's death had created the first vacancy, and that was all that mattered. Brownell recalled that Warren held fast to the position that he was ready to accept the first justiceship of the court, and that happened to be the one of the chief justice. Warren, however, wrote in his *Memoirs* that he was actually willing to accept *any* position on the court, since all justiceships were basically equal, and that he'd never held out for the slot of chief.

Whether the governor went so far as to expose the president for reneging on his commitment is questionable. In either case, a threat proved superfluous. The attorney general gave in and said that the president would want his nominee for chief justice to accept an interim appointment so that he could be seated at the beginning of its next term. According to an article in the *San Francisco Examiner* recalling the meeting,

> the job would be Warren's, but he had to agree to be in Washington within the week so he could be sworn in on the first Monday in October when the court opened its term.
>
> Eisenhower formally announced the appointment on Sept. 30, and on Oct. 5, just ten days after being interrupted while on his hunting trip, Warren resigned as governor and was sworn in as chief justice of the United States.[16]

Brownell's insistence that the next opening on the court had not applied to the position of chief justice tickled the memory of Warren's son Earl Jr. as to what Warren had told him, claiming that Warren had relayed the information to a member of the Supreme Court. The story was corroborated by Merrill H. Small, Warren's executive secretary from 1945 to 1953. Small confirmed that his distinct impression from the governor was that Warren had "insisted" to Brownell that he be named chief justice. Small went on to say in 1972, "I wrote in the Sacramento Bee of June 7, 1970, that [Warren] held out for the highest job . . . and nothing was said by him about it then or since."[17]

The accounts relayed by Earl Jr., Small, and others were subsequently denied by both Brownell and Warren who, in his *Memoirs*, stated just the contrary:

> I would like to correct something I have seen in print to the effect that I was first offered a place on the Court other than that of chief justice, but that I refused and said I would accept nothing but the chief justiceship. That is positively not the fact. The Attorney General, as I have just related, said the President was thinking of appointing me to the Court and would like to know if I would accept. Nothing was said about my becoming chief justice, and I said unequivocally that I would accept. If the President had chosen to appoint some existing member of the Court to be chief justice and had offered me the vacancy created thereby, I would have accepted as readily. On the Supreme Court, one position is as important as another. They are all equal. Nothing, as far as I can recall, was said by the Attorney General about keeping our meeting a secret. I suppose that was implicit in the nature of his visit. However, the meeting was not made public, and I heard nothing more until Wednesday morning when I received a call from Washington saying that my appointment as chief justice was being announced. I have tried very hard to remember whether it was Attorney General Brownell or President Eisenhower who made the call, but cannot recollect which of the two it was. That might seem strange, but the excitement of the moment, the short notice given for my arrival in Washington, and the fact that at sixty-two years of age I was about to begin an entirely new way of life, three thousand miles from where I had lived and worked during my entire career and in an environment almost totally unfamiliar to me, might possibly account for my cloudy memory of that, to me, pivotal event.[18]

Regardless, Warren realized how little time he had to make the move. He turned the office of the governor over to Lieutenant Governor Knight, his legally prescribed successor. After hopping a plane for Washington, he and Nina arrived in DC on Sunday, October 4, 1953, to be present for the opening of the new Supreme Court term. They were met at the airport by Vice President Nixon, Attorney General Brownell, and other dignitaries, as well as Clerk of the Court Harold P. Willey and Court Marshall T. Perry Lippitt, who drove them to the Statler Hotel and informed Warren that his induction was slated for noon the following day.

"That," Warren later recalled, "was the limit of my immediate instruction as to my duties on the Court."[19]

The day of Warren's initiation as chief justice of the United States was for him the most remarkable and lonely day of his career. The consummation of his entire life's work in public service left him feeling unprepared for the obligations he knew lay ahead. Even as he approached his new position with a reverence he'd never before experienced, so, too, did he realize how unprepared he'd been to undertake such a solemn position on such short notice.

The entire affair was wholly different from the other offices he had held. Before becoming district attorney, he had endured four years of grooming and had distinct ideas as to how it could be improved. On becoming state attorney general, he had many years' background of law enforcement locally, statewide, and nationally. He also knew county government and its relation to the state and felt prepared to plunge into both the civil and the criminal aspects of the job. As governor, his experience in his previous positions acquainted him with many of the problems a leader must face, not to mention how he could successfully tackle them. He also knew the personalities involved and the atmosphere in which he had to work. While he never felt he had answers to all the issues of social growth and America's immersion into World War II, he at least had a reasonable understanding of the best way to approach them.

With the chief justiceship, things were different. Warren wasn't acquainted with Washington or even with the other members of the Supreme Court. He had known Justice Tom C. Clark for several years, both as attorney general of the United States and, before that, as an assistant in the Department of Justice when they had transacted important business together, Warren advocating for the state of California and Clark, for the federal government. He also knew Justice Robert H. Jackson, although not well and not at all officially. He was slightly acquainted with Justice William O. Douglas, but, again, only through legal gatherings that they both attended at various times. The other justices were all strangers to him.

In addition to that disadvantage, he also had to deal with his long absence from the courtroom. Since becoming governor, he hadn't engaged in any legal matters short of dealing with state contracts to assure their legality and studying the bills passed by the legislature to determine if they conformed to state and federal constitutions.

That last responsibility, he realized, could be of *some* help in judging the constitutionality of measures in question before the court, for which he was thankful. During his years as governor, he had signed more than ten thousand bills and vetoed another sizable number, many of them because, in his opinion, they were unconstitutional. Especially in wartime, the legislation had passed a large number of emotionally charged bills targeting anyone who disagreed with the war or with US participation in it.

As district attorney, he had engaged in quite a bit more litigation, both civil and criminal, and had even argued a case in the United States Supreme Court. But as attorney general, his work was confined mostly to administrative matters with a rare court appearance, although he did supervise and collaborate on writing several briefs targeted to be presented to the Supreme Court. He also wrote opinions to state officers on interpreting constitutional questions. But even there, most of his practice had revolved around state courts. His experience with the federal legal system was much more limited. When it came to matters involving regulatory agencies such as the Interstate Commerce Commission, the Federal Trade Commission, and the Federal Communications Commission, most of his courtroom appearances bordered on "negligible."

All these doubts about his lack of practical experience weighed on Earl Warren's mind as he contemplated how, in a few fleeting hours, he'd be presiding over the highest court in the land.

According to Warren's son Earl Jr., "To say my father was a bit nervous would have been a gross understatement."[20]

The court traditionally convened each day at noon, so on the fourth day of October 1953, Warren showed up at the court building around 10:00 a.m. He went to the marshal's office and asked to be taken to the chief justice's chambers. There, he met Margaret McHugh, who had been the executive secretary to Chief Justice Vinson and who, to Warren's great fortune, remained in that position throughout the new chief's tenure in office. He also met three law clerks—William Oliver, who had served with Chief Justice Vinson and would later become a law professor at the University of Indiana, and Earl Pollock and Richard Flynn, both of whom had recently graduated from the law school of Northwestern University. They had reported for work only a short time before Vinson's death. Both later became prominent lawyers in Chicago and Washington, DC, respectively. Finally, Warren met two elderly messengers, one of whom died during the chief justice's first term and the other who was retired under the new compulsory retirement act one year later.

And that was Mr. Chief Justice Warren's entire personal staff.

The transition from governor to chief justice went as smoothly as could be expected, which is a kinder way of saying that it was blatantly painful. Warren's duties included managing the Supreme Court building and the administration of the court itself. It was difficult to find out anything from official records regarding the offices of the clerk, the marshal, the librarian,

or the reporter of decisions. When he asked about their practices or procedures, he was informed there was nothing in writing. All the court officers
told him was that their predecessors had always done things in a certain way,
and that's how they were expected to continue to do things.

Luckily, McHugh had been with Chief Justice Vinson long enough to
have grasped every aspect of staff relationships, so she worked with her new
boss to handle all the issues that came their way without having to rely on
outside help.

After introducing Warren to staff members, McHugh escorted the new
chief to the chambers of Justice Hugo L. Black, the senior associate justice.
"He welcomed me to the Court and offered his assistance in every possible
way. He then took me to the chambers of the other members of the Court
who were also most cordial in their welcome."[21]

Black took several minutes in the conference room to explain the
court's operating procedure. He advised Warren on some of the several
dozen new cases awaiting the court's attention, some of them urgent. Warren asked Black if he would manage a few of the conferences until he could
familiarize himself with procedures, and Black agreed.

Since Warren's appointment to the court had come about so quickly,
he was forced to wear someone else's robe, which turned out to be several
sizes too large for him but was certainly better than nothing. Then, all too
quickly, the time had come for the justices to gather in the conference room
so that Warren could take the Constitutional Oath—the same one that all
federal officers take—in front of the other eight justices:

> I, Earl Warren, swear that I will support and defend the Constitution of
> the United States against all enemies, foreign and domestic; that I will
> bear true faith and allegiance to the same; that I take this obligation
> freely, without any mental reservation or purpose of evasion; that I will
> well and faithfully discharge the duties of the Office on which I am
> about to enter.

Although that oath was all the Constitution required, tradition dictated
he take a second Judicial Oath in open court, so the new chief justice stood
up to be led into the courtroom. Tall, broad, and impressive, Warren cut an
imposing figure, standing six-foot-one but seeming larger than his height.
He was square-shouldered, brawny, and chiseled. He held his two hundred
pounds erect, feet spread slightly to shoulder width. His sky-blue eyes shone
like the crystalline waters of Norway's Hardanger Fjord, where Warren had
recently spent time with his family. His fair, clear complexion confirmed

his Scandinavian ancestry. As one former official visiting him in his spacious office in Sacramento described him, "He himself was a man as big as the room, in a sense. He had a large body—he fitted into that spaciousness and, you know, the sense of California: Large!"[22]

Precisely at noon, the marshal of the court pounded his gavel, and the justices walked single-file into the courtroom—Mr. Justice Black in the lead followed by the other associate justices according to seniority: Stanley Reed, Felix Frankfurter, William O. Douglas, Robert Jackson, Harold Burton, Sherman Minton, and Tom Clark. The ornate marble courtroom was packed with dignitaries, including President and Mrs. Eisenhower and Vice President and Mrs. Nixon. Nina Warren, wearing a red hat and orchid, sat in the box in front of and to the left of the bench, between the vice president and Mrs. Nixon. It was the first time that the Eisenhowers and Mrs. Warren had ever been in the court building.

The chief justice, according to ceremonial custom, filed into the courtroom last. Each of the associate justices took his proper seat: Mr. Justice Black on the right of the empty chair of the chief justice, Mr. Justice Reed to the left, with the others alternating right and left according to their seniority. The seat of the chief justice remained vacant while Warren was shown to a chair behind the clerk at the right of the court.

The marshal intoned the opening of the 1953 term of the Supreme Court in this solemn language, as he does every session of the court:

> Oyez! Oyez! Oyez! All persons having business before the Honorable, the Supreme Court of the United States, are admonished to draw near and give their attention, for the Court is now sitting. God save the United States and this Honorable Court![23]

For the first order of business, Justice Black read a statement regarding the death of Chief Justice Vinson. Then, while the magistrates and the audience stood, the clerk read the commission appointing Earl Warren to an interim term, pending the return and confirmation of Congress following their recess.

> Dwight D. Eisenhower
> President of the United States of America
> TO ALL WHO SHALL SEE THESE PRESENTS, GREETING:
>
> Know Ye: That reposing special trust and confidence in the Wisdom, Uprightness, and Learning of Earl Warren, of California, I do appoint him chief justice of the United States, and do authorize and empower him to

execute and fulfill the duties of that office according to the Constitution and laws of the said United States, and to Have and to Hold the said Office, with all the powers, privileges, and emoluments to the same of right appertaining, unto Him, the said Earl Warren, until the end of the next session of the Senate of the United States and no longer; subject to the provisions of law.

The confirmation continued, followed by the judicial oath, as required of all federal judicial officers in addition to the constitutional oath already taken in the conference room. It was administered to Warren by the clerk of the court:

I, Earl Warren, do solemnly swear that I will administer justice without respect to persons, and do equal right to the poor and to the rich, and that I will faithfully and impartially discharge and perform all the duties incumbent upon me as chief justice of the United States according to the best of my abilities and understanding, agreeably to the Constitution and Laws of the United States. So help me God.

Finally, Warren was conducted to the seat of the chief justice, a high-backed chair in the center of the raised bench. On his way, he tripped over the hem of his oversized robe and nearly fell as the courtroom spontaneously gasped. Warren commented later that he had literally "stumbled onto the bench."[24]

His discomfort was eased somewhat when, a few moments later, during the order of business called "Admission to Practice," Vice President Nixon approached the podium flanked by two old friends to move their admission to practice before the Supreme Court. The friends were Warren Olney III and Stanley M. Barnes, both Californians and both assistant United States attorneys general. Instead of moving their admission in the usual form, the vice president unwittingly said, "Mr. Chief Justice, I have the honor to move the nomination of . . ." It was a solemn moment, and the slip of the tongue passed unnoticed by everyone except Warren, who said later that it helped relieve some of the tension he'd had going in.

The first order of business after the chief justice took his seat was the presentation to the court of Attorney General Herbert Brownell by Acting Solicitor General Robert L. Stern. According to ritual, Warren welcomed Brownell to the court. Warren wasn't sure why that formality had taken so long in coming, since Brownell had been attorney general for nearly nine months, but he was nonetheless happy to welcome the man because they had been friends in politics for years. As close as Brownell was to the president both politically and personally, Warren surmised that the attorney general must have played a significant role in his appointment to the bench.

Contrary to custom, President and Mrs. Eisenhower graciously attended the induction ceremony, which Warren said later he appreciated. The first couple sat with Nina and the families of the other justices in the box in front of and to the left of the bench.

The session took around twenty minutes, after which the court rose and retired as the marshal announced a recess for one week.

The president and Mrs. Eisenhower left immediately, before Warren had a chance to speak to them, but later that afternoon, the new chief justice received an invitation to the White House, where Mrs. Eisenhower and Nina chatted while the president, Brownell, and Warren retired to another room. After a cordial visit, Nina and Earl returned to their hotel, and the next morning Nina flew back to California to continue closing out the governor's mansion, a Herculean task she had to complete by herself within a month.

During the week following Warren's induction, the court met daily in conference to discuss the appeals and petitions for certiorari that had been filed since the court had adjourned the preceding June. The conference was to determine which merited oral argument and which could be disposed of summarily. With no prior knowledge of the cases or opportunity to review them, Warren played no part in their disposition. However, in his first written opinion, he took a case of little notoriety that was argued on the third day of the term—one that should, in his opinion, have received a unanimous opinion all along its route through the courts. But it had not, and, unless reversed by the Supreme Court, it could have resulted in a weakening of the Federal Longshoremen's and Harbor Workers' Compensation Act by threatening to deprive injured workers of payments due them. The rationale was nebulous at best. The employers said the workers had the responsibility to notify them of any accidents or injuries. Failure to do so, the employers claimed, negated their rights to compensation.

The Department of Labor's deputy commissioner of the Bureau of Employees' Compensation found in favor of the employee; the district court reversed that decision and enjoined further payments under the act. The court of appeals, by a divided vote, sustained the district court, and the Supreme Court had granted certiorari to review that decision. Warren's opinion was reported on November 9, 1953, the first he signed during his tenure as chief justice. It unanimously reversed the court of appeals ruling and established the claim of the workers in *Voris v. Eikel*.

In a matter of hours after first being seated on the court, Warren had learned a few things about the thorniest of cases facing the Brethren in the weeks to come. One of those cases was a series of five suits lumped together under the banner of the "school desegregation cases."

The five suits were from Kansas, Virginia, South Carolina, Delaware, and the District of Columbia. While the latter was in a somewhat different setting because it did not involve state law, they all concerned the so-called separate but equal doctrine that had been established by the Supreme Court in the case of *Plessy v. Ferguson* all the way back in 1896. That decision declined to prohibit separate railroad accommodations for blacks and whites. It sought to justify racial segregation for almost every movement or gathering as long as "separate but equal" facilities were provided. The court's finding in *Plessy* was known as the Jim Crow doctrine.

The case was not new to the Supreme Court—at least not to the Vinson Court, which had begun hearing oral arguments in spring 1953, several months before Vinson's death and Warren's October 1953 interim appointment. Since Vinson had died before the court could vote on the case, the court held it over for reargument pending the installation of a ninth justice—Earl Warren.

So, for the issue that had initially come before the Vinson Court, the matter taken up by the new court was this: Does segregation of children in public schools solely on the basis of race, even though the physical facilities and other "tangible" factors may be equal, deprive the children of the minority group of equal educational opportunities?[25]

But in reality, the question dug much deeper.

Just before the turn of the century, most of the southern United States was still segregated, providing separate and different educational facilities for blacks and whites. In *Plessy*, the court had ruled that segregation was permissible as long as "separate but equal" facilities were provided to blacks. Nearly sixty years later, the Brown family and their attorneys from the National Association for the Advancement of Colored People (NAACP) were arguing that, in education, there was no place for separate facilities.

Linda Brown was the seven-year-old daughter of Reverend Oliver Brown. In the fall of 1950, her father took her by the hand and walked her to the Sumner Elementary School in Topeka, Kansas. There, Brown was met by school officials who told him what he already knew. The school board had decided that although the Browns lived in an integrated neighborhood, Linda could not attend the all-white public school only four blocks from her home. Instead, the girl had to leave her white and Mexican American playmates and be bused nearly two miles to a "Negro" school.

Oliver Brown went to see Charles Scott, a personal friend and former classmate at Topeka High School and a local attorney for the NAACP.

Scott agreed to file suit against the Topeka school board. Black attorney and civil rights advocate Thurgood Marshall saw the moment he had been waiting for. The NAACP and Marshall joined the Brown case with four other school segregation cases. All of the cases had initially been presented together under the title *Brown v. Board of Education of Topeka, Kansas* a full year before Earl Warren had been named the chief of the court.

Preparing to argue the original case before the Vinson Court, Marshall crafted the organization's brief. Working alongside him were his deputy, Jack Greenberg; some of the best black lawyers in America; and a large group of the most noted white lawyers working for the ACLU and on law school faculties throughout the nation. Marshall also enlisted the aid of nineteen amicus curiae, or friends of the court. They, too, filed briefs criticizing the treatment of Linda Brown and the concept of "separate but equal" education. Organized associations such as the Congress of Industrial Organizations, the American Jewish Congress, the American Civil Liberties Union, the Japanese American Citizens League, the Catholic Interracial Council, the American Federation of Teachers, and the American Veterans Committee were all firmly against segregation.

Finally, on December 9, 1952, the big day arrived. Marshall and his legal staff prepared to present their oral arguments. It wasn't going to be an easy case for them. Sitting across the courtroom from Marshall and his team were nine exceptionally earnest, austere, white male justices:

- Chief Justice Fred M. Vinson, sixty-two years old, a conservative Kentuckian who had been appointed to the court by Harry S Truman.
- Stanley F. Reed, sixty-eight years old, another Kentuckian who had delivered the crushing decision in the Lyons murder case that Marshall had handled years earlier.
- Felix Frankfurter, seventy years old, a former Harvard Law School professor and a noted conservative who hated to see any ruling change unnecessarily.
- Robert H. Jackson, sixty years old, the former chief counsel for the United States at the Nuremberg trials following World War II.
- Harold H. Burton, sixty-four years old, the former mayor of Cleveland, Ohio.
- Tom C. Clark, fifty-three years old, the former United States attorney general from Texas.
- Sherman Minton, sixty-two years old, a former conservative senator from Indiana.

- Hugo Black, sixty-six years old, an Alabaman and former member of the Ku Klux Klan who had somehow managed to put his past behind him and was now considered an outspoken defender of civil liberties.
- William O. Douglas, fifty-four years old, a vocal supporter of racial equality.

Of the nine Justices, Marshall was confident of winning over at least two—Black and Douglas. A third, Robert Jackson, was a possibility but by no means a certainty. Marshall needed two more justices to come to his support if he were to win the case. No one, least of all Marshall himself, could predict which of the remaining justices might come around to his way of thinking.

So, as he prepared to present his opening argument, he focused mainly on the Fourteenth Amendment, which he read aloud:

> All persons born or naturalized in the United States and subject to the jurisdiction thereof are citizens of the United States and of the state in which they reside. No state shall make or enforce any law which shall abridge the privileges or immunities of citizens of the United States; nor shall any state deprive any person of life, liberty, or property, without due process of law; nor deny to any person within its jurisdiction the equal protection of the laws.[26]

Opposite Marshall in the courtroom sat several states' attorneys. They were led by noted constitutional lawyer John W. Davis. Marshall, together with the NAACP, was operating on a shoestring budget consisting mostly of small donations from individual supporters. Davis, a one-time presidential candidate, brought with him all of the money and the unlimited social power of the segregated South. In response to Marshall's reading of the Fourteenth Amendment, Davis said: "The Fourteenth Amendment never was intended to do away with segregation in schools. It is a proper use of the police powers of a state to separate the races if the state believes segregation to be in the interest of common welfare. Segregation in schools is not in conflict with the Constitution as long as equal facilities are provided for the two races. A state has as much right to classify pupils by race as it does to classify them by sex or age."

Marshall rose to the challenge. In an emotive statement, he outlined the reasons the doctrine of "separate but equal" did not work:

Three generations of the Warren family face the camera for the first time at the Warren home at 88 Vernon St, Oakland. James Lee Warren, three weeks old, is held in the arms of his beaming father, Marine Lt. James Warren, while Gov. Earl Warren, a proud grandfather, looks on. It was the first time either father or grandfather saw the child with Warren on his first visit home before being restationed at San Francisco.—Warren Family Album (Used with Permission)

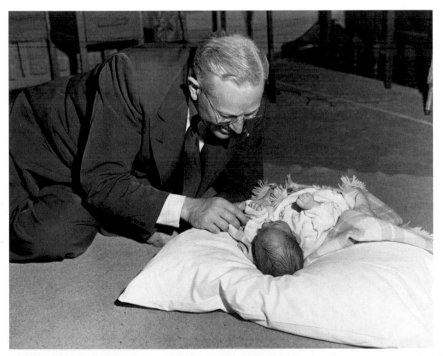

Papa Warren and grandson James Jr. (Jimmy Lee), at about one week.—Warren Family Album (Used with Permission)

On the steps of Santa Barbara Mission after attending Solemn Fiesta Mass and visiting the Sacred Garden, Thursday, August 24, 1950. Shown are from left, Dorothy (19), Virginia (21), Warren, Honey Bear, and Nina.—Warren Family Album (Used with Permission)

Papa Warren with sons Bobby, left, and James Sr.—Warren Family Album (Used with Permission)

*Christmas circa 1963, with Earl and Nina Warren (seated, center) surrounded by family. —
Warren Family Album (Used with Permission)*

*Earl's wife, Nina Elisabeth Palmquist Meyers. —
Warren Family Album (Used with Permission)*

Christmas at the Warren family ranch, St. Helena, California, circa 1962. First row: Honey Bear Brien, Earl Brien, Jaime Daly, Warren Daly, Heather Brien, Margaret Warren. Second row: Willie Brien, Papa and Mama Warren. Third row: John Daly, Florence Jessee (Jimmy Lee Warren's maternal grandmother), Dottie (Dorothy) Warren, Jocko Warren, Jeff Warren, Virginia Daly, Jimmy Lee Warren, Jim Warren. —Warren Family Album (Used with Permission)

Mama and Papa Warren in St. Helena, California (Christmas, circa 1959), with Jocko, Jeff, and Jimmy Lee holding Peter Pan the lamb. —Warren Family Album (Used with Permission)

Mama and Papa Warren (about 1946–47) on the grounds of the Sacramento capitol with grandson, Jimmy Lee, in the middle, Margaret and Jim Warren in the rear.—Warren Family Album (Used with Permission)

Left to right: Attorneys for the plaintiffs, Brown vs. Board of Education, Harold P. Boulware (Briggs case), Thurgood Marshall (Briggs case), and Spottswood W. Robinson III (Davis case).—Library of Congress (Public Domain)

Earl Warren and Nina Elisabeth Meyers, Marriage Certificate.—Warren Family Album (Used with Permission)

May 7, 1954

TO THE MEMBERS OF THE COURT:

As suggested by the Conference, I submit the attached memoranda as a basis for discussion of the segregation cases.

It seemed to me there should be two opinions - one for the state cases, and another for the District of Columbia case. Also, because of the divergent conditions calling for relief and because this subject was subordinated to a discussion of the substantive question in both the briefs and oral argument, the cases should be restored to the calendar for further argument on Questions IV and V previously submitted by the Court for the reargument this year. It also occurred to me that we might appropriately invite the Attorney General of the United States and the Attorneys General of the States requiring or permitting segregation to present their written and oral views should they desire to do so.

The memos were prepared on the theory that the opinions should be short, readable by the lay public, non-rhetorical, unemotional and, above all, non-accusatory.

Ew.

Warren memo to the Court regarding the Brown opinions: some thoughts by Chief Justice Earl Warren.—Library of Congress (Public Domain)

Warren seated in suit.—Library of Congress (Public Domain)

Earl Warren, seated in robes.— Library of Congress (Public Domain)

Warren swearing in President John Fitzgerald Kennedy, with Jacqueline Kennedy, left; Lyndon Johnson, second from right;and Richard M. Nixon, right, observing.—Library of Congress (Public Domain)

January 20, 1965. Warren swearing in President Lyndon Baines Johnson as the 36th president of the United States in the Capitol Plaza, with Lady Bird Johnson and Vice President Hubert H. Humphrey observing.—Library of Congress (Public Domain)

Warren swearing in President Richard M. Nixon, with Pat Nixon, center; and Hubert Humphrey, far right, observing.—Library of Congress (Public Domain)

I got the feeling on hearing the discussion yesterday that when you put a white child in a school with a whole lot of colored children, the child would fall apart or something. Everybody knows that is not true. Those same kids in Virginia and South Carolina—and I have seen them do it—they play in the streets together, they play on the farms together, they separate to go to school, they come out of school and play ball together. They have to be separated in school. . . . Why, of all the multitudinous groups of people in the country, [do] you have to single out the Negroes and give them this separate treatment?

It can't be because of slavery in the past, because there are very few groups in this country that haven't had slavery some place back in the history of their groups. It can't be color, because there are Negroes as white as the drifted snow, with blue eyes, and they are just as segregated as the colored men.

The only thing it can be is an inherent determination that the people who were formerly in slavery, regardless of anything else, shall be kept as near that stage as possible. And now is the time, we submit, that this Court should make clear that that is not what our Constitution stands for.[27]

One of the most vexing problems facing the court was that the justices were being asked to make law rather than to interpret it. Passing legislation was something only Congress is supposed to do. But in the case of *Brown* and desegregation, Congress didn't dare do it. If the Supreme Court ruled that racial segregation was wrong, their ruling would affect twenty-one states (those that supported segregation) plus the District of Columbia. Paul Wilson, the assistant attorney general of Kansas, pointed that out. He asked the court if all those states had been wrong for seventy-five years in believing that separate facilities, although equal, were legal within the meaning of the Fourteenth Amendment.

In response, Justice Burton asked if Wilson didn't think it possible that, during those seventy-five years, the social and economic conditions of the nation might have changed, intimating that what might have been a valid interpretation of them seventy-five years ago might not be valid today.

"We recognize that as a possibility," Wilson conceded. "We do not believe that the record discloses any such change."

"But that might be a difference between saying that these Courts of Appeal and state supreme courts have been wrong for seventy-five years," Burton added.

"Yes, sir," said Wilson. "We concede that this Court can overrule the Plessy doctrine [which established the 'separate but equal' concept], but nevertheless, until it is overruled, it is the best guide we have."

Justice Frankfurter suddenly broke into the conversation: "As I understood by brother Burton's question or as I got the implication of his question, it was not that the Court would have to overrule those [separate but equal] cases; the Court would simply have to recognize that laws are kinetic, and some new things have happened, not deeming those decisions wrong, but bringing into play new situations toward a new decision."

"We agree with that proposition," said Wilson, "but, I repeat, we do not think that there is anything in the record here that would justify such a conclusion."

After several more minutes of arguments, the court adjourned for the day to continue the following morning with a line of questioning concerning the other four cases being presented along with *Brown*. When the next day's proceedings began, Davis—the gray-haired former solicitor general, former ambassador to Great Britain, and noted constitutionalist—stood up. He grabbed onto a question previously placed to Marshall. He emphasized that if the states were forbidden to discriminate in their schools by race, they would also be prohibited from segregating its pupils on the grounds of sex, age, or mental ability.

Davis then made an unpardonable mistake. He told the justices how they had to think.

"It is the duty of the Court," he emphasized, "to interpret the Fourteenth Amendment by placing the Court 'as nearly as possible in the condition of those who framed the instrument [the Constitution].'"

Justice Burton, obviously irritated, replied, "But the Constitution is a living document that must be interpreted in relation to the facts of the time in which it is interpreted!"

Davis replied by saying that circumstances may change within the span of a century. However, he claimed that these circumstances did not alter, expand, or change the language that the framers of the Constitution had initially used. Davis then went on to quote a magazine article by Mississippi editor Hodding Carter that justified the continuation of school segregation.

When it was once again Marshall's turn to speak, he referenced Davis's allusion to the article.

"The article quoted was of a newspaperman answering another newspaperman. I know of nothing further removed from scientific work than one newspaperman answering another," he said.

Frankfurter rocked forward in his seat and replied, "I am not going to take issue with you on that!"

Later in the hearing, Justice Reed asked Marshall if he couldn't accept the proposition that segregation in the schools was legislated "to avoid racial friction." Marshall replied:

> I know of no Negro legislator in any of these states, so the people disadvantaged have had no say in this policy. . . . I know that in the South, where I spent most of my time, you will see white and colored kids going down the road together to school. They separate and go to different schools, and they come out and play together. I do not see why there would necessarily be any trouble if they went to school together.[28]

Reed then commented that the question of segregation was more a matter for the legislature than for the Supreme Court. Marshall expressed his disagreement. He insisted that the rights of minorities were protected not by government but by the courts.

With that, the arguments ended and the justices filed out of the courtroom. Marshall admitted later that he did not believe he had swayed the five justices he needed to his side.

While they were awaiting the court's decision, the press presented the case to its readers in details more glaring than any other case before. As *Brown* had unfolded in the courtroom, millions of Americans were suddenly exposed through newspaper and magazine articles and radio and television newscasts to a wide range of bizarre discriminatory laws they had not known existed. Among them:

- Florida and North Carolina required that textbooks used by blacks and whites must be stored separately and must never be mixed together.
- Oklahoma required that separate telephone booths for blacks and whites be provided.
- Louisiana and South Carolina required separate black and white seating at circuses.
- Mississippi prohibited anyone from printing or circulating printed matter in favor of social equality or interracial marriages.
- Alabama, Mississippi, and South Carolina required black nurses for black patients in hospitals and white nurses for white patients.
- Alabama, Arkansas, Florida, Georgia, and North and South Carolina prohibited chaining black and white prisoners together.

As the days went on, the NAACP received thousands of letters and even more telephone calls supporting its handling of the *Brown* case. Win or lose, one thing was sure: The question of segregation was before the American public as it never had been before.

Finally, in June 1953 the court reconvened, presumably to announce its decision. Instead, Marshall learned that the court was requesting additional information on the combined school segregation cases. The cases, it declared, would have to be reargued before the Vinson Court the following fall.

Marshall was crushed. He blamed Vinson for the delay. The chief justice, he was sure, was dead set against integration, against voting down decades of "separate but equal." So long as Chief Justice Vinson had his way, it was unlikely that the remaining justices would buck him. Marshall said later that he thought about Vinson and his pending decision every day. He wondered if the chief justice would vote his personal biases or constitutional law.

But before Vinson had the chance to vote at all, something happened to change the makeup of the court and alter the course of US history. On the evening of September 8, 1953, Vinson told his wife that his stomach was bothering him. Several hours later, he was dead.

After Vinson's death, the justices announced that there would be no reargument of the case until a new chief justice was appointed to the bench. One month later, there was.

Less than three months after Vinson's death, on December 7, 1953, a total of nine justices sat to hear the reargument of the case, scheduled for December 7–9, this time before the Warren Court.

The Supreme Court building was filled with anxious spectators. It was stuffed with attorneys, too. Presenting the state of Kansas's arguments in favor of segregation were some of the best attorneys in America, including John W. Davis, who had presented the state's original argument before the Vinson Court. The state's other two attorneys included T. Justin Moore and Attorney General J. Lindsay Almond, two of the most prestigious lawyers the state of Virginia had ever produced. The attorneys represented the state along with the same four additional cases involving segregation in Virginia, South Carolina, Delaware, and the District of Columbia.

On the opposing side, NAACP lawyer Thurgood Marshall, who would eventually become a Supreme Court justice himself, was once again set to argue the case for Brown.

After two days of passionate rhetoric both for and against segregation, the Warren Court adjourned, and both sides walked out of the building as unsure as ever of the court's pending decision. The fate of discrimination in the schools was now entirely in the hands of the justices. As Burton wrote in his diary just before the court handed down its unanimous decision, "This [decision] would have been impossible a year ago. . . . However the postponement then [by the Vinson Court] was with the hope of a better result later."[29]

Throughout the three days spent in conference, the new chief justice had intervened in the argument only three times, typifying what was to become the Warren approach during oral arguments: to try to bring the discussion down to the core facts and issues, showing his impatience with attempts to avoid decisions by technical requirements.

The same was not the case when the justices met on Saturday, December 12, for their first conference on the segregation case direction before the new chief justice. Until that time, his brethren had found in Warren a convivial colleague who disarmed them with his friendliness and lack of pretension. Now they would learn that their chief was a born leader whose political talents were to prove as useful in the judicial palace as they had been in the governor's mansion.

On March 17, 1954, at 12:52 p.m., Chief Justice Warren entered the chambers. Thurgood Marshall was ailing at the time, as much from the neglect of his health from years of overwork as anything. He had failed to pay much attention to his body's warning signs because he was so consumed by his commitment to the NAACP.

But Earl Warren wasn't ailing. He slipped into his chair and picked up a document from the bench. He announced with a somber, resonant voice that the judgment and opinion of the court in the case of "Oliver Brown v. Board of Education of Topeka" had been reached.

As the journalists who had been waiting in the press room scurried back into the courtroom, Warren began reading the decision. The Associated Press wire service dashed off a bulletin to an anxious nation: "Chief Justice Warren today began reading the Supreme Court's decision in the public school desegregation cases. The court's ruling could not be determined immediately."[30]

Indeed, it would be some while before anyone in the courtroom could determine what the court had decided once the silver-haired orator began his long, rambling pronouncement, alluding to the evidence of psychologists, sociologists, and educators on the effects of segregation on black students. He discussed the merits of *Plessy v. Ferguson* and the Fourteenth Amendment. After talking about the history of black education in America, he called education "the most important function of state and local governments."[31]

Finally, more than an hour after he had begun reading the court's decision, Warren arrived at the core of the court's ruling.

In approaching this problem, we cannot turn the clock back to . . .1896 when Plessy v. Ferguson was written. We must consider public education in the light of its full development and its present place in American life throughout the Nation. Only in this way can it be determined if segregation in public schools deprives these plaintiffs of the equal protection of the laws.

Today, education is perhaps the most important function of state and local governments. Compulsory school attendance laws and the great expenditures for education both demonstrate our recognition of the importance of education to our democratic society. It is required in the performance of our most basic public responsibilities, even service in the armed forces. It is the very foundation of good citizenship.

We come then to the question presented: Does segregation of children in public schools solely on the basis of race, even though the physical facilities and other "tangible" factors may be equal, deprive the children of the minority group of equal education opportunities? We believe that it does. . . .

To separate them from others of similar age and qualifications solely because of their race generates a feeling of inferiority as to their status in the community that may affect their hearts and minds in a way unlikely ever to be undone. The effect of this separation on their educational opportunities was well stated by a finding in the Kansas case by a court which nevertheless felt compelled to rule against the Negro plaintiffs:

Segregation of white and colored children in public schools has a detrimental effect upon the colored children. The impact is greater when it has the sanction of the law; for the policy of separating the races is usually interpreted as denoting the inferiority of the Negro group. A sense of inferiority affects the motivation of a child to learn. Segregation with the sanction of law, therefore, has a tendency to [retard] the educational and mental development of Negro children and to deprive them of some of the benefits they would receive in a racial[ly] integrated school system.

Whatever may have been the extent of psychological knowledge at the time of Plessy v. Ferguson, the finding is amply supported by modern authority. Any language in Plessy v. Ferguson contrary to this finding is rejected.

We conclude that in the field of public education the doctrine of "separate but equal" has no place. Separate educational facilities are inherently unequal. Therefore, we hold that the plaintiffs and others similarly situated for whom the actions have been brought are, by reason of the segregation complained of, deprived of the equal protection of the laws guaranteed by the Fourteenth Amendment.[32]

The spectators in the courtroom sat silently for several moments as if a shroud had been lowered over them. An eternity passed before anyone could work up the courage to break the silence, to say something, applaud, cough—or even shift in his seat. When word of the decision finally reached Marshall and attorney Roy Wilkins at the New York offices of the NAACP, Marshall turned to his coworker. They had hit the jackpot. He had just won a unanimous decision from the nation's highest court, a decision destined to change the shape and future of America.

In later years, Marshall, when recalling the *Brown* case in his memoirs, pointed out Warren's reflection upon the strange course the arguments had taken during the hearing:

> One might expect, as I did, that the lawyers representing black school-children would appeal to the emotions of the Court based upon their many years of oppression, and that the states would hold to strictly legal matters. More nearly the opposite developed. Thurgood Marshall made no emotional appeal, and argued the legal issues in a rational manner as cold as steel. On the other hand, states' attorney Davis, a great advocate and orator, former Democratic candidate for the presidency of the United States, displayed a great deal of emotion, and on more than one occasion broke down and took a few moments to compose himself.[33]

The court's unanimous decision was met almost instantly by resistance from the South. With centuries of racist attitudes behind them, southern politicians who believed in the concept of white supremacy groused openly that no nine "honest men" could possibly have reached the conclusion they reached in *Brown.*

"I shall use every legal means at my command to continue segregated schools in Virginia," the governor of that state said.[34]

Similar responses echoed throughout the South. The governor of Georgia claimed the decision turned the Constitution into "a mere scrap of Paper." North Carolina's governor said he was "terribly disappointed." South Carolina's governor said he was "shocked."[35]

Before long, there would be battles in Jackson, Mississippi; riots in Selma, Alabama, and boycotts in Memphis, Tennessee. Some southern school officials vowed that blood would run in the streets of their towns before even one southern white girl would be allowed to attend school with "overgrown Negro males."[36]

Adding to all the chaos following the decision was the fact that the Eisenhower administration, while not openly condemning the court's ruling, did not support it, either. In fact, the administration seemed to be distancing itself from the decision by saying that the White House could not be blamed for striking down segregation since it was the Supreme Court and not the Eisenhower administration that did so.

Warren later relayed an incident that occurred shortly before the court reached its groundbreaking decision, while the justices were still deliberating. Eisenhower had instituted a policy of holding White House dinners for select groups of people where the guests were asked for their opinion on any one of numerous issues of national importance.

Warren was invited to one such dinner. Since the chief justice was the ranking guest, he was seated to the right of the president and very near attorney John Davis, the state of Kansas's pro-segregation counsel in *Brown*.

After dinner, the president took Warren by the arm and, leading him to a room for coffee and after-dinner drinks, leaned close to him. "These are not bad people," he said, referring to the people of the segregationist South. "All they are concerned about is to see that their sweet little girls are not required to sit in school alongside some big, overgrown Negroes."[37]

Not long after the *Brown* decision was read, Warren's cordial relationship with the president soured, with Eisenhower remarking that nominating Earl Warren to the US Supreme Court had been "the biggest damned-fool mistake I ever made."[38]

The loss of Eisenhower's confidence was a sacrifice that Warren made gladly. The court's decision to strike down once and for all the undemocratic and heinous principles surrounding segregation would become the most famous, if not the farthest-reaching, decision of Warren's judicial career.

Despite stubborn opposition from southern administrations and a few district courts, the principles of *Brown* eventually extended into every area of racial relations, becoming the cornerstone for the great civil rights campaigns of Martin Luther King Jr. during the 1960s. They also began to change the attitudes of whites toward blacks in America forever.

Interestingly enough, while deliberations were going on at the Supreme Court, so, too, were they unfolding on the floor of the US Senate, where Congress had reconvened for the 1954 session. First on the agenda was the matter of confirmation of the interim chief justice of the United States, Earl Warren.

Warren's interim appointment by Eisenhower had been temporary pending his confirmation by the Senate. If the Senate voted him down, his tenure would lapse. But tradition dictated that a president's Supreme Court nominee was a shoo-in. Furthermore, everyone knew it—everyone, that is, except the US Senate.

Contrary to tradition, the new chairman of the Senate Judiciary Committee, North Dakota's William Langer, delayed the nomination for weeks—not because he had anything against Warren personally but rather as a protest against the lack of patronage the Eisenhower administration had shown for Langer's home state. Another delay arose when the committee asked the FBI to investigate Warren's background—something that had never been done before for any Supreme Court candidate. The FBI agreed, and when its investigation was concluded, Warren passed with flying colors.

The entire senatorial circus enraged sitting Justice Felix Frankfurter to the point where he grabbed a pen and paper and scribbled a scathing note to a close friend: "I know nothing that has made me more morally outraged . . . than the fact that . . . a man whom the President of the United States has named as the chief justice and who has been discharging that office for four months with true regard to its highest standards . . . should have to have his confirmation held up until some cops report whether or not he is a security risk or otherwise not qualified for the chief justiceship."[39]

As the charade plodded on, Warren personally declined an invitation to appear at a subcommittee confirmation hearing—a wise move considering that he had been seated and functioning as the chief justice for months, but a range of anti-Warren testimony, mainly by right-wing extremists, blew into the Senate chambers. That, predictably, generated a firestorm of protests from supporters of the nominee, from the president on down.

Finally, the Judiciary Committee approved Warren's nomination by a vote of twelve to three, and the Senate voted to confirm him by voice vote without dissent on March 1, 1954.

"One must hope," a *New York Times* editorial commented, "that this kind of circus . . . will not play Washington again."[40]

8

ONE MAN, ONE VOTE

The storm only intensified. It reached its apex when Alabama governor George Wallace took the oath of office on January 14, 1963, standing on the gold star marking the spot where, nearly 102 years earlier, Jefferson Davis was sworn in as provisional president of the Confederate States of America. In his inaugural speech, Wallace said: "In the name of the greatest people that have ever trod this earth, I draw the line in the dust and toss the gauntlet before the feet of tyranny, and I say segregation now, segregation tomorrow, segregation forever."[1]

Wallace was not alone in his defiance of integration throughout the South during the sixties. But the problem had begun years earlier, as Warren himself noted in his *Memoirs*:

> The Court expected some resistance from the South. But I doubt if any of us expected as much as we got. Nor did I believe that there would develop in the Republican Party, which freed the slaves through the Civil War and the Thirteenth Amendment and granted them all the attributes of citizenship through the Fourteenth and Fifteen [*sic*] Amendments, a Southern strategy which had for its purpose a restriction of such rights in order to capture the electors of those states and achieve the presidency. I, for one, thought it would be wonderful if, by the time of the centennial of the Fourteenth Amendment (1968), the principle of desegregation in Brown v. Board of Education could be reality throughout the land. And I still believe that much of our social strife could have been avoided if President Eisenhower had at least observed that our country is dedicated to the principle that . . . "We hold these Truths to be self-evident, that all Men are created equal, that they are endowed by their Creator with certain unalienable Rights, that among those are Life, Liberty and the Pursuit of Happiness . . ." (Declaration of Independence).[2]

But that hadn't been the case, and for years afterward, the aftermath of more than a century of slavery reared its ugly head in one form or another and would continue to do so, some people argue, to this very day and beyond.

The court's role in America has never been to enact social justice but rather to confirm the legality of the mechanisms by which it functions. That's what laws that are passed by Congress and enforced by the Executive Branch are for—to create a climate in which the country can live up to the guarantees of the US Constitution.

Toward that end, the staggering reach of *Brown* and the changes it brought about nationally induced many people to believe that it was the most significant case of Earl Warren's tenure on the court, although he never felt that way. In his *Memoirs*, he wrote, "It seemed to me that accolade should go to the case of Baker v. Carr (1962), which was the progenitor of the 'one man, one vote' rule."[3]

While acknowledging his understanding that *Brown v. Board of Education* was of tremendous importance and left a lasting impact on the nation, the principle that declared equal educational opportunities for all races was grounded solely on the Fourteenth Amendment to the Constitution without any input from Congress. That wasn't the fault of Congress, as Warren realized, since the court in its early decisions had limited the scope of the Fourteenth Amendment, particularly by the "separate but equal" doctrine of *Plessy v. Ferguson*, so that further congressional "tinkering" seemed to be superfluous. The ruling in *Brown* slashed to pieces three centuries of slavery and its remnants based on the white supremacy theory long prevalent in America and throughout much of the world. If Congress had intervened beforehand and passed remedial legislation a generation or more before having to enforce *Brown's* provisions for integration, Warren later wrote, "the blacks and other minorities would have achieved their rights by the middle of the twentieth century, and much of the emotional heat undoubtedly would have been avoided."[4] Warren continued:

> [*Baker v. Carr*] arose in Tennessee, which was one of the most malapportioned states in the Union, although the legislatures of more than forty states were so unbalanced as to give people in certain parts of them vastly greater voting representation than in others. In Tennessee, for example, although there had been a conspicuous shifting of population from country to city, districts retained the same voting strength in the State Legislature that they had had for more than sixty years. Representation was distorted to the point where one district had only a few hundred voters while another embraced tens of thousands, yet both districts were

given equal weight in legislative decisions. The situation approached the "Rotten Borough" era in England, where a few families were given parliamentary power equal to that of thousands of people in other parts of the country, thus bringing government to a very low estate until remedied. Tennessee had more small districts than large ones, and the representatives of those districts would not vote to redistrict the state to bring about fairer distribution of voting power because it would cause some of them to lose their seats and to relinquish control over the larger metropolitan areas. Neither would they vote to change or implement the State Constitution, and it could not be changed unless a measure to do so were submitted to the people by the Legislature. As a result, the cities and suburbs, where most of the people lived, had little to say about the manner in which they were governed. They were deprived of an opportunity to do many of the things that were essential to their orderly development.[5]

The situation was far from unique to Tennessee. Fewer than a handful of states had equitable representation in both houses of their legislatures. Warren recalled that Justice Black, who had been in public life for half a century, told him that as far back as he could recall, every governor of Alabama had run on a platform to equalize representation in the legislature, and every one had been foiled by that same body. In the state of Georgia, under what was called the Unit Rule, the largest city, Atlanta, had little more weight than one of the smallest counties in the election of the governor and other state officers. Another justice from a populous state told Warren that to stop any legislation to which a high-paid lobbyist disapproved, he had only to control the votes of nine senators, and they could be from the least populous counties in the state!

To all of this, the reticence of the Supreme Court had in the past contributed to the growing problem, making change all but hopeless. The court refused to enter or to permit lower federal courts to consider any litigation seeking to remedy unequal apportionment because it was considered a political problem, not a judicial one, to be handled by the political agencies of the states.

From the beginning, Warren ran into trouble with Justice Frankfurter, who resented the court's meddling in what he chose to call the "political thicket," contending that it would involve the courts in matters outside their constitutionally mandated domain. But in *Baker v. Carr*, Justice Brennan wrote for a majority of the court that the question of whether people underrepresented in their government were being deprived of equal protection of the laws was a just one, subject to the jurisdiction of the federal courts.

From the doctrine of that case developed the "one man, one vote" rule, and in the space of a very few years, it covered the entire spectrum of representative government—federal, state, and local. While occasionally some aberrant piece of litigation springing from a flagrant disregard for the will of the electorate violated the "one man, one vote" principle, the doctrine was quickly adopted universally and came to exemplify US political life. Warren elaborated:

> The reason I am of the opinion that Baker v. Carr is so important is because I believe so devoutly that, to paraphrase Abraham Lincoln's famous epigram, ours is a government of all the people, by all the people, and for all the people. It is a representative form of government through which the rights and responsibilities of every one of us are defined and enforced. If these rights and responsibilities are to be fairly realized, it must be done by representatives who are responsible to all the people, not just those with special interests to serve. . . .
>
> The right to vote freely for the candidate of one's choice is of the essence of a democratic society, and any restrictions on that right strike at the heart of representative government. And the right of suffrage can be denied by a debasement or dilution of the weight of a citizen's vote just as effectively as by wholly prohibiting the free exercise of the franchise.[6]

Legislators represent people, Warren stressed, not trees or acres. They are elected by voters, not farms or cities or economic interests: "As long as ours is a representative form of government, and our legislatures are those instruments of government elected directly by and directly representative of the people, the right to elect legislators in a free and unimpaired fashion is a bedrock of our political system (Reynolds v. Sims, 1964)."[7]

When *Baker v. Carr* came to the Supreme Court in 1958 on the constitutional question of whether each voter was being given equal protection of the laws, Warren recalled the effect that disproportionate representation had in Tennessee. The problem was even worse in his home state of California, where Los Angeles's representation had outgrown that of every other local jurisdiction five to one.

In turning to the federal courts, the plaintiffs in *Baker* pointed out that the courts were the only forum that offered any promise of relief and asked for a declaratory judgment that the Tennessee apportionment act was unconstitutional. They also requested an injunction to prevent state officers from conducting any more elections until the matter was adjudicated. The three-judge district court, following established precedent, dismissed the complaint on the grounds that the relief requested and the legal wrongs alleged were not within the scope of judicial power conferred on federal courts by Article III of the Constitution. Additionally, the district court found that, even if the courts had jurisdiction, the questions presented to it were nonjusticiable—that is, political rather than judicial in nature.

On direct appeal to the Supreme Court, several urban-based groups joined Solicitor General Archibald Cox in filing amicus briefs on behalf of the recently elected Kennedy administration. As Justice Tom Clark pointed out in his concurring opinion, *Baker v. Carr* was one of the "most carefully considered" Supreme Court decisions of modern times. The court heard three hours of oral argument on April 19 and 20, 1961, three times longer than the amount of time it normally allocated. The brethren also held the case over for another three hours of argument at the opening of the 1961 term. As Justice Clark said, *Baker* was considered "over and over again by us in Conference and individually."[8]

The court announced its decision on March 26, 1962, in five opinions totaling 163 pages. The opinions were exceptionally biting in tone. Justice Clark characterized Justice Felix Frankfurter's 64-page dissent as "bursting with words that go through so much and conclude with so little."[9]

Justice Brennan, speaking for the court, carefully avoided explicit discussion of the merits of the case, although he made clear that the majority felt that Tennessee had acted unconstitutionally. Brennan distinguished between the two grounds relied upon by the district court, jurisdiction and nonjusticiability, concluding that the matter was within the jurisdiction of federal courts and that the plaintiffs had a sufficient interest in the weight of their votes to have standing. Ultimately, he concluded, pointing out Chief Justice Roger B. Taney's opinion in *Luther v. Borden* (1849), the court was found to have judicial standing:

> Prominent on the surface of any case held to involve a political question is found a textually demonstrable constitutional commitment of the issue to a coordinate political department; or a lack of judicially discoverable and manageable standards for resolving it; or the impossibility of deciding without an initial policy determination of a kind clearly for nonjudicial discretion; or the impossibility of a court's undertaking independent resolution without expressing lack of respect due coordinate branches of government; or an unusual need for unquestioning adherence to a political decision already made; or the potentiality of embarrassment from multifarious pronouncements by various departments on one question.[10]

Although in *Baker* the court limited its holding to jurisdictional matters, it didn't restrict itself to situations such as that in Tennessee, where the legislature had failed to comply with its own constitution, clarifying that any state legislature that failed to reapportion its districts in such fashion as to reflect the equality of its population was in jeopardy of violating the Equal Protection Clause. His opinion thus called into question the constitutionality of legislative apportionment in practically every state in the union. "We conclude," he wrote, "that the complainant's allegations of denial of equal protection present a justiciable constitutional cause of action upon which appellants are entitled to a trial and a decision."[11]

Justices William O. Douglas, Tom Clark, and Potter Stewart, while joining the opinion of the court, wrote separate concurrences. To Justice Douglas, the issues were uncomplicated: It was a voting rights case, and voting rights have long been within the protection of federal courts. Justice Clark took issue with Justice Harlan's dissenting opinion, which contended that the court's decision would mean that the Equal Protection Clause required "mathematical equality among voters," concluding that all the court needed to decide was that Tennessee's apportionment is a "crazy quilt without rational basis."[12] Unless the federal courts provided relief, he claimed, there could be no remedy for what he believed to be a patent violation of the Equal Protection Clause.

Justice Stewart emphasized the court's threefold finding: that federal courts possessed jurisdiction of the subject matter, that the appellants had standing to challenge the Tennessee apportionment statutes, and that reapportionment was a justiciable issue.

Justice Frankfurter, in the last opinion he wrote before his retirement from the court, expressed his belief that the federal courts should not intervene in the "essentially political conflict of forces by which the relation between population and representation" has already been determined.[13] Justice Harlan similarly dissented, contending that even if federal courts had jurisdiction, which he believed they hadn't, there existed no federal constitutional requirement that state legislatures must be structured to reflect equally the voice of every voter.

What followed on the heels of the court's findings in *Baker* constituted a predictable spate of legal attacks against the makeup of several state legislatures. In light of the heat of the situation, Warren decided to tackle any questions of state malapportionment personally, even though he knew doing so would create a good deal of controversy. But, in his mind, he had the stamina to face down any adversary in light of truth and justice—and fairness.

In his June 1964 opinion in *Reynolds v. Sims*, one of a group of decisions that came to be known collectively as the Reapportionment Cases, Warren declared that representation in state legislatures must be based primarily on population. One week later, the court handed down similar rulings (without opinions) involving nine more states, emphasizing that our form of government requires fair representation; that fair representation means equal representation in which one man's vote has the same value as another's, and that legislatures that are not elected on that basis are unconstitutionally founded.

Not surprisingly, the rulings created a maelstrom of controversy, particularly among those threatened with losing their positions through redistricting. The Council of State Governments was so vehemently opposed to the rulings that it threatened to propose a constitutional amendment to negate the decision. Among those states that endorsed the amendment, several agreed to do so only after substituting language of their own. Others eventually withdrew their petitions. Whatever the number of states supporting a constitutional amendment, nearly all of them did so behind the cloak of secrecy. The only notice the press gave of a state's support for the amendment was a small article buried deep within the daily papers announcing a call for a constitutional convention resolution under Section V of the Constitution. Warren recalled the furor:

> The only method ever used before this [time] to amend the Constitution was submission by both houses of the Congress for a specific Amendment. That procedure was well understood by the nation, but the Amendments submitted to annul the decisions of Baker v. Carr and its progeny came under the portion of Article V which authorized Amendments "on the application of the Legislatures of two-thirds of the several States," etc. This procedure had never been attempted in the history of the nation. Congress had not enacted any procedure in the event of its use, and it was not at all certain whether a convention called in this manner would be limited to consideration of the particular Amendment suggested or whether it might be used to amend the Constitution to any extent it happened to choose.[14]

Two even more ominous proposed amendments cropped up around the same time. One would have gutted the US Supreme Court entirely by establishing a Court of the Union made up of the fifty chief justices of the state supreme courts, which would have had the authority to review and overrule any decision of the United States Supreme Court in cases involving federal and state relations. The Court of the Union would be called to convene through the application of a required number of states. "This," Warren felt, "would have changed the character of our national institutions and would have impinged upon the Supremacy Clause of the Constitution (Article VI) to an uncharted extent in the enforcement of federal law as interpreted by the Supreme Court under Article III." The relevant portion of Article VI (Section 2) reads:

> This Constitution, and the Laws of the United States which shall be made in Pursuance thereof; and all Treaties made, or which shall be made, under the Authority of the United States, shall be the supreme Law of the Land; and the Judges in every State shall be bound thereby, any Thing in the Constitution or Laws of any State to the Contrary notwithstanding.[15]

Despite the grave implications of the twin proposals, little national debate arose. The state legislatures proceeded with their activities without undue discussion or examination by the press or anyone else. Not even the American Bar Association spoke up against the dangerous waters on which the state houses were treading, lending its implied support to the proposals. "It can reasonably be said," Warren wrote, "that one man, Arthur Freund, a prominent lawyer of St. Louis, was more responsible than all others combined in finally bringing the danger of the proposals into public view." When it looked as though either or both of these amendments might succeed in obtaining the endorsement of the requisite number of states, Freund made a one-man crusade of the issue. He wrote to legislators, lawyers, scholars, and newspapers until finally a few of the country's main newspapers recognized the importance of the situation, wrote articles about it, and pinpointed its dangers. Only then did the movement die stillborn.

The American Bar Association reacted to the state proposals as it did to the anti-court activities of Senator Joseph McCarthy—that is, not at all. Its weight and influence during those years fell in line with McCarthy's anti-Communist rants and his diatribes against everyone who refused to join in his unsubstantiated attacks.

The Warren Court almost from Day One succumbed to similar unrelenting attacks. The first storm, Warren recalled, came immediately on the heels of *Brown*:

> Most of the Southern legislators joined the Southern Manifesto, a statement condemning the decision, arousing the people to thwart it, and pledging themselves to employ all possible means to that end. There were fulminations on the floors of both houses, and threats to apply the dead hand of nullification. The Court received no support of any kind

from the American Bar Association as we were pilloried and reviled. I
was personally held to be a modern-day Thaddeus Stevens. Such heated
criticism, in spite of the lip service more recently given to the Brown
ruling, has never subsided. To this day, every decision enforcing the equal
protection or due process clauses of the Constitution in civil rights cases
is the occasion for some people in Congress to assail the Court for the
abuse of its function and the exercise of naked power.[16]

Throughout the McCarthy era, the Warren Court was under attack for
being "soft on Communism." It wasn't simply a catchphrase; it was politically chic. During the most despicable days in the modern history of the
House, those Americans who weren't supportive of McCarthy and his rampant abuse of the principle of guilt by association were against him, meaning
they were Communist conspirators or, at best, sympathizers. Warren and the
court did their best to try to rein in such unmitigated hatred and innuendo
by neutralizing the effects of "rabid congressional committees"[17] intent
on exposing innocent people for the sake of exposure, establishing guilt
by association, and compelling witnesses to implicate themselves without
regard to the Fifth Amendment protection against self-incrimination. Even
some of the lower courts were not immune to McCarthy's broad-sweeping,
witch-hunting tactics. In one case, a federal judge sentenced a witness to
one year in prison for refusing to name associates with whom he was in
college fifteen years earlier! The inquiry was to show that he had fraternized
with students who were said to have been Communists at the time.

And that was only the beginning of the attacks on the court's lofty
position. Senators William Jenner of Indiana and John M. Butler of
Maryland sponsored legislation designed to strip the Supreme Court of
jurisdiction in some of the "subversive activities" fields in which the Mc-
Carthy group was deeply embroiled. According to Warren, "Some of this
legislation, evoking as it did the atmosphere of Cold War hysteria, came
dangerously close to passing."[18]

General Eisenhower had campaigned in favor of the powerful oil and
gas interests of the southern states, particularly Texas, and promised that if
elected he would see that the producers were kept free of federal regulation.
The ramifications were far-reaching. Tens of millions of people throughout
the country were dependent upon the oil and gas of the Gulf States as it
came to them through interstate pipelines that reached to the Great Lakes
and to both the North Atlantic and Pacific coasts. A sweeping federal hands-
off policy would need to be accomplished through congressional action
exempting the sales of the gas and oil from regulation by the Federal Power
Commission, which had been established to control the interstate commerce

of the electrical, oil, and gas industries. Such a maneuver had been attempted in the administration of President Truman through a bill introduced by Senator Robert Kerr of Oklahoma, one of the advocates of big oil and gas interests. Because of irregularities in the passage of the act, Truman vetoed it.

After Eisenhower's election, the bill was introduced again, and again it passed. But corruption reared its all-too-familiar head, and the president learned that several legislators had accepted bribes to vote for the bill. Eisenhower, like his predecessor, was forced to veto it. Most of the congressional shenanigans revolved around representatives of the Superior Oil Company, with whom Warren had tangled in the past. Faced with two consecutive presidential vetoes, the oil company chose not to go back to Congress a third time but, instead, shifted its substantial leverage to the courts. Through a series of cases, the company ultimately laid its arguments before the Supreme Court, but the Warren Court was having none of it and promptly denied the relief the company had sought.

Next, the government brought a suit against the El Paso Gas Company for monopolizing the gas industry in the western states. The court decided in favor of the government and against a merger that El Paso had wanted, but after the court's decision, the government capitulated and joined in an endeavor to nullify the court's mandate. Again, the court failed to accommodate El Paso and sent the case back to the lower trial court twice to have its order implemented.

While these assaults against the court were ongoing, the electric power interests decided to enter the fray. Led by the Roosevelt administration's brainchild Tennessee Valley Authority, the bête noire for the private power sector, as Warren termed it, the TVA rattled the nation with claims that El Paso Gas was communistic, socialistic, and the mortal enemy of private enterprise. In 1952, General Eisenhower campaigned on a pledge to contain the TVA to prevent its future land grabs and encroachments on private enterprise. When elected, Eisenhower set up an interdepartmental committee to reign in the governmental agency.

In 1954, the United States Atomic Energy Commission (AEC) entered into the Dixon-Yates contract with two private energy companies, Middle South Utilities and the Southern Company, which agreed to supply 600,000 kilowatts of power to the AEC for its Tennessee plant. This power was to replace that which the TVA was scheduled to provide, freeing up the TVA's ability to sell its energy to the city of Memphis to meet that city's booming demands. The TVA had asked for federal funds to build additional generating capacity for Memphis, but Eisenhower opposed using taxes for tax-free, low-interest financing to benefit one metropolitan area over another.

The Dixon-Yates contract was named after its two signatories: Edgar Dixon, president of Middle South Utilities, and Eugene Yates, chairman of the board of the Southern. AEC chairman Lewis Strauss and President Eisenhower favored the proposal, which was approved by the Joint Committee for Atomic Energy (JCAE) when it was still controlled by Republicans.

But in 1954, Democrats won the congressional elections and gained chairmanship and majority control of the JCAE. The new chairman, Senator Clinton Anderson, reopened the Dixon-Yates hearings to force the AEC to cancel the contract. Most of the issues between the TVA and the AEC were resolved while Kenneth Nichols was general manager, but under a plan developed by Walter von Tresckow, a New York financial consultant, the city of Memphis created an alternative solution to its power needs, and the contract was canceled.

The Dixon-Yates utility claimed damages, and the case came before the Supreme Court, which decided in favor of the government. Warren later recalled, "[T]he thing I most remember about the argument was that after Solicitor General Lee Rankin, with his customary candor and straightforwardness, argued the conflict of interest issue and the cancellation of the contract, counsel for Dixon-Yates read a letter from the President saying it was the greatest contract of its kind which had ever been executed. This decision did not endear us to the electric power industry."[19]

Another attack against the court came with the breakup of the association between giant auto manufacturer General Motors and E. I. du Pont. Even though the court ruled with congressional mandates forbidding violations of the antitrust laws, the ruling created a sensation. Legislators of both parties rushed to pass legislation relieving both of any of the legal consequences of their violations, and Congress amended the tax laws to minimize potential tax losses.

That case was one of many examples of the court interpreting the antitrust laws strictly, all of which served to give Warren's brethren a bad name among big business. Warren voted with the majority most of the time in sustaining the provisions of the antitrust laws. He commented, "I always disliked monopoly and the more I saw of business and government the more committed I became to the theory that the greatest danger to our private enterprise system is a monopoly. I therefore felt that whenever Congress determined that certain conduct was monopolistic and proscribed it, it was our solemn duty to enforce such legislation without equivocation."[20]

Such strict interpretations failed to endear the Warren Court to industrial America, particularly with the railroads when the court ruled that a merger of mega-giant railways Pennsylvania and New York Central was illegal. Nor did the brethren ingratiate themselves to some of the nation's largest banks when they forced those institutions to dissolve their monopolistic mergers.

Beyond the field of business, Warren and his brother justices also made staunch enemies in both the public and the legislative arenas when the court declared compulsory prayers in the public schools to be unconstitutional. The press had a field day with that ruling, as Warren recalled:

> I vividly remember one bold newspaper headline saying, "Court outlaws God." Many religious denominations in this same spirit condemned the Court, although most of them have receded from that position. Scores of Constitutional Amendments and legislative bills were proposed in the Congress to circumvent the decision but were later abandoned when the public came to recognize that the ruling was not an irreligious one. Rather it tried to maintain the separation of church and state guaranteed by the First Amendment.[21]

History, Warren went on to explain, was "replete" with the battle scars of terrible wars between different denominations of the Christian religion. He wrote:

> In Philadelphia in the last century, bloody strife, murder, and arson were rampant because of a controversy over whether the Protestant or Catholic Bible should be used in public school devotions. The majority of us on the Court were religious people, yet we found it unconstitutional that any state agency should impose a religious exercise on persons who were by law free to practice religion or not without state interference. Among other things, this assured that conflict between religious factions could be avoided.
>
> Because the Court, over the years, sought to make our criminal procedures conform to the relevant provisions of the Constitution and be a reality for the poor as well as the rich, it was made the target for widespread abuse. Many of these cases dislodged old law enforcement practices that had become tarnished with brutal intimidation of prisoners and suspects along with other injustices. Because police and indignant citizens were overwhelmed with the wave of violence that flooded the land, they found in the Court a stationary target and made us responsible for the increasing crime rate. We were "soft on criminals," they said.[22]

The public attack on the court about law enforcement centered around the case of *Miranda v. Arizona*. In it, SCOTUS held that, before a prisoner (as opposed to a suspect merely being detained for questioning)

could be interrogated by police, he must first be informed of his constitutional rights regarding the purpose of the arrest along with his right to
have a lawyer present during questioning. The court also stipulated that the
police had to tell a defendant that, if he couldn't afford a lawyer, the state
would assign him one free of charge. Furthermore, he needed to be advised
that he couldn't be forced to answer questions, but, if he did so, everything
he said could be used against him in a court of law. Warren explained:

> There was really nothing new in this except to require police and pros-
> ecutors to advise the poor, the ignorant, and the unwary of a basic con-
> stitutional right in a manner which had been followed by Federal Bureau
> of Investigation procedures for many years. It was of no assistance to
> hardened underworld types because they already know what their rights
> are and demand them. And so it is with all sophisticated criminals and af-
> fluent prisoners who had ready access to their lawyers. However, because
> so many people who are arrested are poor and illiterate, short-cut meth-
> ods and often cruelties are perpetrated to obtain convictions. Hence a
> large percentage of police officers and prosecutors rebelled against such
> an articulation of a defendant's rights by the Supreme Court.[23]

But it wasn't only law enforcement that seized upon the opportunity to
target the court for America's rising crime rate. It was America at large looking for someone to blame. It wasn't enough to fault the nation's destabilizing
ghettos, growing ignorance, increasing poverty, expanding drug trafficking,
skyrocketing unemployment, and rampant organized crime (often made possible through corrupting law enforcement officials). The more obvious rationale was the nation's increasingly arrogant court system—and particularly the
Supreme Court. That attitude, according to Warren, led to the so-called law
and order campaign of 1968, a one-sided affair in which the courts were prohibited from debating the wisdom or propriety of their decisions, opening
the judiciary up to the "wildest and most emotional charges" often leading
to increased legislation aimed squarely at denigrating the courts:

> The House of Representatives became extremely critical when we
> granted certiorari to review a decision of the Court of Appeals of the
> District of Columbia which confirmed the House's action in excluding
> Representative Adam Clayton Powell from its membership. His expul-
> sion occurred in spite of his valid election to a seat from New York and
> his possession of the three constitutional requirements for the position:
> citizenship, qualifying age, and residence. The House employed special
> New York counsel and claimed that our exercise of jurisdiction to re-
> view an act of Congress refusing to seat an elected member of that body

was an unwarranted confrontation of one of the three branches of government by another. They contended that the decision of Congress was not reviewable in any court. We eventually held, in an opinion written by me only one week before my retirement, that the House of Representatives had exceeded its constitutional powers in excluding Powell from membership by the requirement of only a majority vote. Correct procedure called for expulsion from membership for misconduct only after a trial and by a two-thirds vote. Powell had, after all, been seated according to the wishes of the voters of his congressional district.

This action of the Congress, though clearly beyond that body's constitutional powers, was provoked by the flamboyant, abrasive, and insolent actions of the congressman. It also had racial overtones because Powell was black. Although other members of Congress have been charged with corruption in the courts and even convicted and sentenced to imprisonment, the House traditionally has permitted them to go unscathed as congressmen, even to the extent of permitting them to retain committee chairmanships and control vital legislation.

. . . [T]he Supreme Court, if it defies the status quo, is bound to build up a formidable array of dissenters in powerful places. I hope the Court can always be criticized as publicly and as forcibly as desired. Justices must live with their judgments and be judged by them, not only at the time of their rendition, but through the indefinite future.[24]

As bitter a pill as such criticism was for the judiciary to swallow, Warren was astute enough to realize that the alternative would have been far worse for a democratic republic. While a growing number of judges and lawyers felt that the courts should have had the power to respond to unfair criticism, the Warren Court moved in the opposite direction. Even in matters as seemingly mundane as punishing witnesses for contempt, they felt such proceedings should be confined to specific areas with limited punishments after a trial to conform to the principles of due process. "This in my opinion," Warren said, "is essential to the preservation of a humane administration of justice that eschews arrogance."[25]

In his support, he wrote of a classic example of a female witness in the West Coast trial of many rank-and-file members of the Communist Party. The witness was being interrogated about her association with others who were alleged to have been connected with the party's activities. Warren recalled that she told the court she would testify as to her own actions but that she would not be an informer against others:

After testifying, she was asked eleven questions such as, "Did you know A or B, etc.?" all of which she refused to answer. At the conclusion of the trial, the judge summoned her before him for contempt of court for failure to answer the questions, and angrily sentenced her to serve one year in prison for each separate refusal. The sentences were to be served consecutively, thus resulting in an aggregate of eleven years of imprisonment for contempt of court, all this without a trial by a jury or even by a judge who was detached from the incident and presumably free from bias.

This was at the height of the Cold War era when the hysteria created by Senator McCarthy was abroad and many people—in fact, a large segment of our citizenry—were inflamed against anyone who espoused the political philosophy of Communism or was suspected of associating with anyone who did. As a result, the Supreme Court was soundly traduced for setting aside this outrageous conviction and for reversing the convictions of the defendants in the case on the ground that the government had failed to show any illegal acts on their part; it had merely discovered that they advocated Communism as a political philosophy. Many politicians made anti-Supreme Court sentiment a basis of their campaigns for election, and some with long careers in high office maintained their tenure by such an appeal.[26]

In a free country, the chief stressed, people who feel they have been wronged by the government have a right to complain. That right is protected by the First Amendment's guarantee of freedom of speech, press, and the ability to "petition the Government for a redress of grievances." If citizens are forced to surrender that right, the government is no longer responsible to the will of the voters who elected them. "Although federal judges are not elected," Warren wrote, "the principle applies equally to them as well as to the officers of the legislative and executive branches."[27]

The judging process is particularly vulnerable to such faultfinding because in every case the judge decides for someone and against someone else after a courtroom confrontation that involves self-interest, reason, and emotions by both parties. Judges must understand that protest is one of the constituents of the process, and if they can't tolerate that, they shouldn't be on the bench. To use the admonition of President Truman, "If you can't stand the heat, stay out of the kitchen." Criticism of judges is both normal and healthy, Warren wrote, whether the judging is in a courtroom or on an athletic field. That criticism is not an expression of ill will but rather a demonstration of the public's right to place blame.

The Supreme Court is particularly subject to criticism because most of its decisions are, as they say in athletic events, "close decisions" or "judgment calls." As a case wends its way to the Supreme Court, it becomes charged with emotion from the publicity it generates and the discussion that inevitably follows. The questions presented to the court are public questions that often affect large groups of people. Add to them the understanding that the court's decisions are final, and we can easily see why SCOTUS would attract more criticism than other courts. And that criticism becomes effective precisely because it is a one-sided affair.

"Justices must take it in silence," according to Warren, "leaving it to the people to form their own opinions concerning the Court's actions. This limitation and others make the life of a Justice of the Supreme Court an austere one, yet I could generally accept denunciation as a part of the job without resentment, except for one phase of it."[28]

That phase, Warren went on to write, came from the least anticipated segment of American society. It came from the American Bar Association itself.

9

UNDER EVERY BED

Eighteen months after the first *Brown v. Board of Education* decision, a weary black woman returning from work as a seamstress at the Montgomery Fair department store in Montgomery, Alabama, refused to surrender her seat on a city bus to a white man. It was an unpardonable affront. Arrested on a charge of violating the state's bus segregation law, Rosa Parks was summarily convicted on December 5, 1955, and fined fourteen dollars.

That day, Montgomery's long-suffering black population invoked a boycott of the city bus line. It was spearheaded by a reluctant young minister named Martin Luther King Jr. The guerrilla war of civil rights demonstrations in the streets of the Deep South had begun.

On February 1, 1956, two days after a bomb shattered the King home, the local NAACP challenged Alabama's bus-segregation law. Expanding upon the findings in *Brown*, the NAACP's federal suit sought to expand the application of the rule that separate was not equal—whether in public schools or on publicly regulated buses.

Fearing the end of an all-too-comfortable lifestyle, nineteen senators and eighty-two representatives—virtually the entire congressional delegation from states that had once made up the Confederacy—issued a Southern Manifesto condemning the Supreme Court and its decision in *Brown*.

The mid-March statement asserted the justices had ignored a century of precedent, and, "with no legal basis for such action, undertook to exercise their naked judicial power and substituted their personal, political and social ideas for the established law of the land."[1]

No longer restrained, South Carolina governor James Byrnes insisted, "The Supreme Court must be curbed."[2] As a former secretary of state and associate justice himself, Byrnes lent an air of respectability over the patina of racism.

But, true to segregationists' worst fears, *Brown* was only the begin-ning. On June 4, 1956, the federal circuit court voted two to one to hold Alabama's bus-segregation practices unconstitutional. When city and state attorneys appealed, the Supreme Court summarily disposed of the case on the initial pleadings filed with the clerk. The succinct, unsigned opinion on November 13, 1956, granted the NAACP's motion to affirm the lower court decision. The very fact that there had been no oral argument and no written opinion suggested just how firmly the court stood behind *Brown*.

Tainted as bigots, southern critics of the court might have remained on the political fringe had the brethren in April 1956 not taken up the case of Steve Mesarosh, secretary of the Communist Party in Pennsylvania.

Under his party name of Steve Nelson, Mesarosh had been convicted in a Pennsylvania state court for advocating the overthrow of the US gov-ernment. On appeal, the Pennsylvania Supreme Court reversed the convic-tion. The court reasoned that the federal government had passed the similar Smith Act in 1940 and thereby preempted enforcement of state sedition laws. State prosecutors appealed to the United States Supreme Court.

The issue was simple: Given the federal law, did the forty-two states as well as the territories of Alaska and Hawaii that had similar sedition statutes require the additional protection?

Warren, the former governor who had once signed a bill imposing a loyalty oath on state employees, argued in conference there would be "no loss to the US if these acts are stricken."[3]

The former California deputy DA, who decades earlier had helped convict the Wobblies under a similar state criminal syndicalism law, now moved to end such local prosecutions. "My general impression is that for him, the witch-hunt was worse than whatever danger there was [from Communists]," court clerk Samuel Stern explained.[4]

Although seasoned practical reasoning agreed with Warren, much of the nation, still caught up in the Red Scare of Joseph McCarthy, did not. To them, the Supreme Court seemed to be freeing an acknowledged Commu-nist. Worse, the court was preventing the states from defending themselves from the scourge of Communism.

Aware of the political sensitivity of the case, Warren assigned the opin-ion to himself. As chief justice, he felt only he should bear the unpopular brunt of the work of his court.

In drafting the 6–3 opinion for *Nelson*, Warren relied heavily on the Pennsylvania Supreme Court's earlier decision. "Sedition against the United States is not a local offense," he wrote. "It is a crime against the Nation. As such it should be prosecuted and punished in the Federal courts where this defendant has in fact been prosecuted and convicted and is now under sentence."[5]

Not yet finished shooting itself in the foot, the court compounded its problems a week later when a majority held that the New York City Board of Regents could not dismiss a Brooklyn College faculty member merely because he invoked his Fifth Amendment right against self-incrimination while testifying before the House Un-American Activities Committee (HUAC). Justice Tom Clark wrote for a 7–2 majority that due process required Professor Harry Slochower be granted a hearing before he could be fired.

With Nelson and Slochower, the infuriated South took up its anti-Communist cudgels to batter the court. "Something has got to be done to stop the Supreme Court," thundered Congressman Mendel Rivers of South Carolina. "They are a greater threat to this Union than the entire confines of Soviet Russia."[6]

The Supreme Court was made up of "politicians instead of lawyers," according to Senate Judiciary Committee Chairman James Eastland of Mississippi. "Surfacing momentarily from his alcoholic fog," as author Ed Cray wrote, "Joe McCarthy agreed. 'We made a mistake in confirming as Chief Justice a man who had no judicial experience, who had practically no legal experience except as a district attorney for a short time and whose entire experience was as a politician."[7]

In Senate Judiciary hearings a month later, Eastland and McCarthy reaffirmed the expedient pact between southerners and conservative anti-Communists.

"You have heard one communist after another come before this committee and take the position that the Communist Party was just another political party; in fact, that is the Communist line, is it not?" Eastland asked rhetorically.

"That is strictly the Communist line," McCarthy replied.

"Is not that the line that the Chief Justice of the United States takes?"

"Unfortunately, yes, Mr. Chairman," McCarthy agreed. "And I may say that I follow what is said in communist publications, to follow their line, rather closely. And the communist *Daily Worker* applauded this decision, the *Nelson* decision, and other decisions of the Supreme Court. In their book Earl Warren is a hero."[8]

Warren could say nothing. As he wrote a sympathetic California acquaintance, "Members of the Court can neither resent nor refute criticisms no matter how far-fetched they may be."[9] Within the privacy of his chambers, however, he dismissed the Wisconsin senator as a "querulous, disreputable liar."[10]

Concern about an increasingly liberal Supreme Court spread well beyond segregationists and red-baiters. Conservative business organizations such as the National Association of Manufacturers and the National Chamber of Commerce, fearing severe antitrust and prolabor decisions, lent weight to the anti-court hysteria. Segregationists, business interests, and anti-Communists fell in behind a bill introduced by Virginia Congressman Howard W. Smith, the powerful chairman of the House Rules Committee. The bill proposed that no act of Congress be construed as preempting a field of legislation unless the act contained a provision to that effect. Had that been the federal law at the time the *Nelson* case was argued, the court could not have struck down the state statute.

Only a series of adroit parliamentary moves by the House leadership kept Smith's bill from coming to the floor for a vote, which would have been a victory for the anti-court movement regardless of the outcome.

The public furor diminished over the summer of 1956 with both the court and Congress in recess. Warren and Nina spent much of that summer traveling in Denmark and Switzerland with Santa Barbara newspaper publisher Thomas Storke and his wife, Marion. The Warrens broke off the vacation at the request of Secretary of State John Foster Dulles to accept an unanticipated invitation from the government of India to visit that country.

Warren's trip to India turned into a personal and diplomatic triumph. He found himself celebrated from Bombay and Calcutta to New Delhi as the man who had lifted America's color barrier. At the University of Delhi ceremony in which Warren received an honorary LLD, the audience broke into cheers at the first mention of *Brown*.

The widespread publicity that American newspapers devoted to the Warrens' triumphal sojourn, coupled with the congressional recess, helped mute criticism of the court. Earl and Nina returned in quiet triumph to a humid, somnolent Washington after Labor Day 1956. First to greet them was the news that conservative justice Sherman Minton, suffering from chronic anemia, had retired under orders of his doctor. With Minton's absence, Warren was losing not merely a friend but also a dedicated Chicago White Sox fan with whom the chief loved talking baseball.

On the other hand, with President Eisenhower's nomination of William Brennan as a replacement, Warren was gaining a critical legal ally. Brennan would go on to shape many of the intellectual arguments that defined the Warren Court.

But the slackening of the criticism of the post-*Brown* court through-out the summer of 1956 was not to last. With McCarthy's HUAC hearings unfolding daily, the American Bar Association allied itself with the sena-tor and his henchmen. Throughout the McCarthy era and the following years of desegregation, the ABA rarely had a kind word to say about the court. On the contrary, it did much to discredit the brethren. For years, the ABA had espoused support for southern racists who accused the court of improperly assuming power through its handling of a wide range of civil rights cases, particularly the *Brown* decision, and of being soft on crime and Communism.

This had been one organization from which Warren felt the court had a right to expect an enlightened appraisal of its work and a public defense of it where such support could be justified. In fact, the opposite proved true. At the ABA's annual meeting in London in 1957, one of the committees filed a report titled "Communist Tactics, Strategy and Ob-jectives." A political bombshell, it dealt little with those matters, instead alleging that the US Supreme Court was aiding the Communist cause through fifteen recent court decisions. It listed the "pro-Red" cases, giving biased outlines of their facts and the court's holdings, before concluding that the Brethren had given "great joy and comfort to the Communists."[11] In conclusion, the ABA report suggested that Congress act to pass legis-lation to guard the nation against the effects of these ominous Supreme Court decisions: "If the courts lean too far backward in the maintenance of theoretical individual rights it may be that we have tied the hands of our country and have rendered it incapable of carrying out the first law of mankind—the right of self preservation."[12]

The report generated widespread publicity and became the poster child for the convention and the ABA. The London press especially had a field day as it badgered Warren throughout the remainder of his stay over-seas. Instead of responding, Warren chose to ignore the questions to avoid entering into a bitter controversy within the group of which he was invited to be the leader. He believed that he was on a goodwill mission to affirm the unity of the United States and England in preserving freedom under law. The Paris edition of the *New York Herald Tribune* saw things differently. It circulated throughout Europe coverage typical of that featured on page one on Friday, July 26, 1957, under the headline, "BAR ASSOCIATION TOLD HIGH COURT WEAKENS SECURITY AGAINST REDS," and subheads such as "NEW LAWS TO PROTECT U.S. ASKED" and "DELEGATES ACCEPT COMMITTEE VIEW." The opening paragraphs revealed the paper's editorial slant:

The policy-making body of the American Bar Association accepted without protest here today a report stating that recent Supreme Court decisions threaten the right of the United States to "protect itself against Communist subversion" and that "serious consideration" must be given to corrective legislation.

The House of Delegates, the association's assembly of 236 policy-making members, heard former United States Sen. Herbert R. O'Conor, Md., cite reasons why a six-point legislative program must be erected against the new "resilience" of American Communists. . . .

The six-point legislative program asked by Mr. O'Conor's special Bar Association Committee on Communist Activities generally would undo, if enacted, the legal effect of 15 Supreme Court decisions in the last 15 months.[13]

"After that," Warren wrote, "I was more or less a pariah and several snide articles concerning me appeared in the press." He elaborated in his *Memoirs*:

[These articles] were of no importance to anyone else, and are not worthy of repetition here, but were designed to show that I was not only discredited by the Bar of the United States but was myself annoyed by the customs of England. This last insinuation was positively untrue. I was cordially treated by the English people, from Her Majesty the Queen and Sir Winston Churchill to the rank and file of the British Bar.

Never before have I discussed any phase of this affair, although I have been asked many times to divulge the story. I tell it here because it is indicative of the disservice the American Bar Association did to the Supreme Court, and I have no hesitancy in saying now that it was done designedly to besmirch the Court and to gain publicity for an otherwise rather unproductive convention. I say this because the Association apparently was later ashamed of it, and did not include it as given in its permanent report of the proceedings of that year. Volume 82 of the Reports of American Bar Association, 1957, carries an account of the convention. On page 179, it offers only an insipid summary of the committee action under the heading "Communist Tactics, Strategy and Objectives," and concludes with this statement: "The full report of the Committee which was received and filed appears on Page 328." Turning to page 328, we find a truncated version of that report, leaving out the castigation of the Supreme Court and concealing the real import and purpose of it.

There was no reason at all why this committee report should have been left for London. It could have been disposed of in New York. There was no debate on it, no action taken except to file it, but the implication was left that the American Bar Association approved of it, as indicated by the subheading of the article above referred to in the *Herald Tribune*, "Delegates Accept Committee View." This view was permitted to stand, and no official of the Association said a word to dispel that impression. It was not until the last night of the convention, at the banquet in Guild Hall, when Sir Winston Churchill spoke in high terms of the Court, that anything was said to soften the blow.[14]

The committee report painted a glowing portrait of the Commission on Government Security, headed by Loyd Wright, a former president of the American Bar Association. Warren felt that it, too, was a scare tactic, insinuating that the Supreme Court was legally responsible for a resurgence of Communist activity in the United States and ending with a recommendation that all court personnel be screened as to their loyalty. That meant the FBI would have had to check and pass each member of the court before he or she could be employed there. According to Warren, "The only other ABA committee report of any notoriety was that of the Individual Rights Affected by National Security Committee (page 340, Annual Proceedings) recommending that the district courts be empowered to send people to jail summarily for contempt if they failed to answer the Un-American Activities Committee of the House of Representatives. It approved HR 259, which would have accomplished the purpose without the benefit of an indictment or jury trial."[15]

The action was also a rebuke to the court for having held in *Watkins v. United States* that, although the Congress has broad powers of investigation to assist in determining what legislation should be enacted, it has no power to expose people for the mere sake of exposure. That was a direct slap in the court's face from the very worst elements of McCarthyism.

The reports at the time were devastating, arousing fears within Americans of a rising Red Scare. The court was regularly flogged after that by numerous officials of the ABA as well as members of Congress, where Senator McCarthy himself said, "I will not say that Earl Warren is a Communist, but I will say he is the best friend the Communists have in America."[16]

Warren was subsequently forced to admit that, if any prominent member in the American Bar Association condemned such comments, he hadn't heard of it. "The mood of the moment, I am sure," he opined, "prompted many people to agree. Others, while thinking such anti-Court overreaction was rather bizarre, treated it only humorously. But can you imagine the uproar that would have followed if the same things had been said about the President, the Vice-President, the Speaker of the House or some prominent senator?"[17]

After the ABA convention in London concluded, Warren and Nina took a month to visit Ireland, Scotland, and England, returning in late Au-

gust on the SS *United States*. During their tour, they traveled alone, exposed
to relatively little viciousness and derision, for which they were grateful.
Their time alone allowed Warren the opportunity to reappraise his association with the American Bar Association and to consider what his future
relationship with the ABA would be.

By the time they arrived back in Washington, according to Warren,
"I had concluded that I could no longer be a member of an organization
of the legal profession which would ask me to lead fifteen thousand of its
members overseas on a goodwill mission and then deliberately . . . contrive
to discredit the Supreme Court which I headed."[18]

But that wasn't the most critical decision of the young chief's life.
Author Ed Cray described the news reports that greeted the Warrens upon
their return to the states:

> The angry crowds churned along Park Avenue, stalking prey in the
> sweltering heat. Before them stood a line of raw Arkansas Air National
> Guard troops, drawn up before the entrance of Little Rock's Central
> High School.
>
> Arkansas governor Orval E. Faubus had "prayerfully" mustered the
> guard on September 2, 1957, the night before the fall semester be-
> gan. The nervous troops were "to protect the lives and property of
> citizens"—by barring nine handpicked black students from enrolling at
> Central under a federal court order.[19]

The guard stood an uneasy sentinel for twenty-four hours while
groups of white protesters roved the streets in anticipation of the "Little
Rock Nine," as the black students had come to be called. But no students
showed up. Finally, on the evening of September 3, Federal District Court
Judge Ronald Norwood Davies reaffirmed the order that Central admit its
first black students, but Faubus refused to recall the troops.

The following morning, September 4, with up to a thousand protesters
swelling the streets near the school, a cadre of white and black church leaders escorted a group of eight black students to the line of troops. A guard
(the officer in charge) demanded that they move away. Moments later, a
ninth student, fifteen-year-old Elizabeth Eckford, showed up at the school
without an escort. The crowd began shouting racial slurs as she twice came
to a halt before a guardsman's bayonet. The students turned away.

Finally, on September 20, Judge Davies enjoined Faubus from interfering with the integration plan for the school district. Faubus was forced to
withdraw the guard, and the following Monday, September 23, eight of the
black students successfully entered the school. But as the morning passed,

classes became more raucous as the protests mounted in the streets, and the students were forced to withdraw once more. The action provoked a showdown between Faubus and President Dwight Eisenhower, who had been following the antics nearly from the beginning. The following day, Eisenhower ordered the twelve-hundred-man 327th Airborne Battle Group of the US Army's 101st Airborne Division from Fort Campbell, Kentucky, to escort the nine students into the school. By the same order, he federalized the entire ten-thousand-man Arkansas National Guard to remove them from the governor's control.

Meanwhile, at nearby Camp Robinson, a hastily organized Task Force 153rd Infantry drew guardsmen from units all over the state. Most of the Arkansas Guard was quickly demobilized, but the ad hoc TF153Inf assumed control at Thanksgiving when the 327th withdrew to patrol inside and outside the school for the remainder of the school year. As Melba Pattillo Beals, one of the nine students, wrote in her diary, "After three full days inside Central [High School], I know that integration is a much bigger word than I thought."[20]

The event, watched by the nation and the world, was the site of the first critical test for the implementation of the US Supreme Court's *Brown v. Board of Education* decision of 1954. The crisis was the first fundamental test of the national resolve to enforce black civil rights in the face of massive resistance during the years following *Brown*. As to whether Eisenhower's specific actions to implement integration violated the Posse Comitatus Act, the Supreme Court, in *Cooper v. Aaron* (1958), indirectly affirmed the legality of his conduct. It was never expressly reviewed.

While members of the court withheld comments during the playing out of the drama in Little Rock, President Eisenhower wasn't quite so guarded. According to Attorney General Brownell, Ike "abhorred the idea of using troops, but he never contemplated that a governor of a state would defy the law and his oath." He had authorized the army's 101st Airborne to Little Rock, he wrote in a note to himself, "not to enforce integration, but to prevent opposition by violence to orders of a court."[21]

Central remained integrated while a suit by the school board to delay further integration worked its way to the Supreme Court. With the immediacy of the crisis abated, the protesters lost interest, and the paratroops began gradually withdrawing. On October 23, 1957, the nine black students entered a stilled Central High School for the first time without the presence of armed guards.

But the fight, while diminished, wasn't over as far as Arkansas officials were concerned. Rather than continue integrating at a snail's pace, the Little

Rock School Board asked the federal district court for permission to delay further integration until tempers cooled and a more reasoned schedule could be worked out.

The board's strategy, as Little Rock school superintendent Virgil Blossom explained, was "to get as little integration over as long a period of time as is legally possible."[22]

Public resistance, stirred by the governor and the state legislature, made compliance with *Brown* impossible, attorneys for the board argued in federal court. They asked to halt the current integration at Central High School and to delay further desegregation for two years.

Sympathetic District Court Judge Harry Lemley on June 20, 1958, granted the delay, giving the board until the opening of school in September 1960 to implement its plan. The NAACP immediately appealed.

A three-judge panel of the circuit court of appeals on August 18, 1958, agreed with the arguments of the NAACP's chief counsel, Thurgood Marshall, and reversed Lemley's order. "The time has not yet come in these United States," the court held, "when an order of a federal court must be whittled away, watered down, or shamefully withdrawn in the face of violent and unlawful acts of individual citizens."[23]

With the opening of the fall semester one week away, the school board quickly appealed to the Supreme Court. Time was short, and the brethren were scattered, the chief justice in Los Angeles for the annual convention of the American Bar Association at the invitation of his friend, ABA president Charles Rhyne. Throughout a long, warm reception for the chief at the Biltmore Hotel, Warren continually ducked from the receiving line to take telephone calls from Solicitor General J. Lee Rankin and Associate Justice William Brennan back in Washington. They were arranging an extraordinary special session, only the third in the court's history, to decide whether to hear the Little Rock appeal before school began on Tuesday, September 2, 1958.

As the justices scrambled to hold court in Washington, the Arkansas legislature was rallying behind Faubus by passing a clutch of bills to shore up his position. One measure compelled the governor to close any school facing integration; another permitted the transfer of funds from integrated public schools to white-only private academies.

Technically, school board attorneys had brought their suit on behalf of William Cooper, president of the Little Rock School Board. The respondents were the black parents who had sued the board to force the school's reopening, led alphabetically by John Aaron. They would be represented by the NAACP's Thurgood Marshall.

In fact, the real parties in the Supreme Court of the United States on August 28, 1958, were the president of the United States and the governor of the state of Arkansas. *Cooper v. Aaron* had become a great test of the Constitution and indicative of the word *federalism* in twentieth-century America.

Despite the importance of the case, then newly arrived law clerk Mike Heyman recalled that "there was a sense of summer lethargy" in the Supreme Court building. That venerable institution admitted to no sense of either urgency or crisis.

Little Rock attorney Richard C. Butler was to represent the school board before the high court. His task was to challenge a bedrock constitutional principle that dated to 1803 and *Marbury v. Madison*. A man of serene dignity polished by years as an unchallenged civic leader, Butler personally blamed the confrontation not on the governor, but on "some bad law created by the judiciary."[24]

Butler found himself in difficulty from the very beginning as he argued for a temporary stay of the circuit court order until the case could be argued on its merits. "May it please the Court," he began with the traditional introduction, "The people of Little Rock—"

He got no further before the chief justice interrupted. "What people? Which people of Little Rock are you talking about?"

The implication that Butler spoke only for white Arkansas hung in the marble courtroom, unanswered and damning.

Butler recovered to remind the justices that the two *Brown* decisions had "recognized that time was required for certain cultural patterns to change. . . . 'Deliberate speed,' as used by this Court, is certainly not just a phrase coined on the spur of the moment or developed as a philosophy of opportunism. . . ."

When Butler urged that Judge Lemley's two-year stay be approved, Warren quietly asked if the school board had made plans to desegregate if the stay were not granted.

"No, sir; it has not decided," Butler responded, "because it is almost compelled to see what statutes are passed by the General Assembly now in session. . . ."

"Well, as to these specific children, have they been assigned to any school?"

"Yes, sir; they have now been assigned," Butler said. "To the all-Negro school, the new high school there, Horace Mann."

"Well, isn't that action toward segregating them again?"

"Oh, yes, sir. It is, it is, and that was done under the order of Judge Lemley's decision."

"Yes." Warren seemed to sigh. And if the Supreme Court affirmed the integration order, "then the School Board will proceed to segregate these pupils who are plaintiffs in this case?"

"Yes, sir," Butler conceded. Little Rock would defy the Supreme Court of the United States.

Throughout his life, Warren dimly recollected the boyhood memory of an angry Los Angeles mob that had hung an effigy from the schoolyard flagpole in the light of a great bonfire. "It gave me a horror of mob action which has remained with me to this day," he recalled seven decades later.

One more time, the mob had assembled in force.

"Mr. Butler," Warren said with some sympathy, "I think there's no member of this Court who fails to recognize the very great problem which your school board has. But, can we defer a program of this kind merely because there are those elements in the community that will commit violence to prevent it from going into effect?"

Butler sought to argue that Faubus's very act of defiance had so clouded the legal issue that the school board was correct to delay. "Mr. Chief Justice, you have been the Governor of a great state, and if you—"

"I never tried to resolve any legal problem of this kind as Governor of my state," Warren broke in. As governor, he had abided by the decisions of the courts, state and federal.

"We all realize that, sir. The point I am making is this: That if the Governor of any state says that a United States Supreme Court decision is not the law of the land, the people of that state, until it is really resolved, have a doubt in their mind and a right to have a doubt."

Warren's voice was laced with cold fury. "But I have never heard such an argument made in a court of justice before, and I have tried many a case over many a year. I never heard a lawyer say that a statement of a governor as to what was legal or illegal should control the action of any court."[25]

Butler withered in the face of the chief's stinging rebuke. There would be no stay of the integration order. While he would return on September 11 to argue the case on the merits, the school board had no hope of winning.

Immediately after the September 11 argument, the brethren met in conference. They were unanimous. They were unbending. Under the Constitution, there was a single rule of law, and governors no less than judges were bound to it.

"We knew the kind of opinion we wanted," William Brennan told legal historian James F. Simon. "I remember Justice Harlan saying that this was the biggest crisis in Court history, since we were told that governors and other courts were not bound by our decision."[26]

Warren concurred with him in his *Memoirs*, recounting one regret he'd had throughout his judicial career:

> There was but one event that greatly disturbed us during my tenure, and that was the . . . Little Rock case [*Cooper v. Aaron*] which gave Governor Faubus the national spotlight. We were all of one mind in that case, which has already been discussed, but Mr. Justice Frankfurter called our attention to the fact that there had been a number of changes in the membership of the Court since *Brown v. Board of Education*. He suggested that in order to show we were all in favor of that decision, we should also say so in the Little Rock case, not in a per curiam or in an opinion signed by only one Justice, but by an opinion signed by the entire Court. I do not recall this ever having been done before. However, in light of the intense controversy over the issue and the great notoriety given Governor Faubus' obstructive conduct in the case, we thought well of the suggestion, and it was done.

But it wasn't, not entirely. Frankfurter told the brethren that, in addition to signing the Brennan opinion, he wanted to write a personal concurrence. Warren recalled, "This caused quite a sensation on the Court, because it was our invariable practice not to announce the decision in any case until all of our views had been expressed."[27] Regardless, Frankfurter made a rush to grab control of the court by circulating his opinion before the court's announcement had been made, lending the appearance that the court's unanimous decision was anything but united. The brethren were so upset with this violation of SCOTUS protocol that, afterward, Warren acknowledged, "[S]ome of the Justices stated that they would never permit a Court opinion in the future to be made public until it was certain that the views of all were announced simultaneously."[28]

10

JFK AND THE COURT

On January 2, 1960, Senator John Fitzgerald Kennedy of Massachusetts announced his candidacy for the Democratic presidential nomination. Although a number of voters questioned his youth and inexperience, his charisma and eloquence helped put aside many of their doubts. His most significant obstacle to winning the nomination was Kennedy's Catholic religion. Many Americans held anti-Catholic attitudes at the time—even if they didn't admit to them—but Kennedy's vocal support of the separation of church and state helped to defuse any potential problems there.

On the flip side, Kennedy's religion helped him win a devoted following among many millions of Catholic voters. Although facing several potential challengers for the Democratic nomination, including Senate Majority Leader Lyndon B. Johnson, perennial presidential candidate Adlai Stevenson II, and onetime Minnesota senator and former vice president Hubert Humphrey, he worked tirelessly to help build support among Democratic voters and elites.

At the time, party officials controlled most of the delegates, but several states also held primaries, and Kennedy sought to win several of those to boost his chances of winning the nomination. In his first critical test, the senator won the Wisconsin primary, effectively ending Midwesterner Humphrey's hopes of walking away with the presidency. Nonetheless, Kennedy and Humphrey faced each other in a competitive West Virginia primary in which Kennedy had no Catholic bloc behind him, as he'd had in Wisconsin. Kennedy won the West Virginia primary, impressing many in the party, but at the start of the 1960 Democratic National Convention, it was unclear whether he could win the nomination.

When Kennedy entered the convention hall, he had the most delegates committed to him but not enough to win the nomination. Stevenson, the

1952 and 1956 presidential nominee, remained a perennial dark horse while Johnson—with his many years in the US Senate—hoped to win the nomination with the support from party leaders. Kennedy's candidacy also faced opposition from former president Harry S Truman, who was concerned about the junior senator's lack of experience. Kennedy knew that a second ballot could give the nomination to Johnson or someone else, so his well-organized campaign team worked diligently at wrapping up the nomination on the first vote. In the end, they won the support of just enough delegates to do just that.

Ignoring the advice of his brother and party heavyweights, Kennedy passed over labor leader Walter Reuther as his vice presidential nominee and chose Johnson as his running mate. He knew the powerful Texas senator could help swing the South—the region of the country where Kennedy was most vulnerable—to his corner. With his "good ol' boy" appeal and his down-home charisma, Johnson could call in decades of favors with the governors of the southern states to help deliver the popular vote for his running mate.

In accepting the Democratic presidential nomination, Kennedy gave his well-known "New Frontier" speech, saying, "For the problems are not all solved and the battles are not all won—and we stand today on the edge of a New Frontier. . . . But the New Frontier of which I speak is not a set of promises—it is a set of challenges. It sums up not what I intend to offer the American people, but what I intend to ask of them."[1]

At the beginning of that fall's general election campaign, Kennedy's opponent for president, Republican nominee and incumbent Vice President Richard Milhous Nixon, held a six-point lead in the polls. The major issues looming before the candidates included the economy, Kennedy's Catholicism, the Castro takeover of Cuba, and beating the Soviets in the race for space. Allaying fears concerning his Catholicism, Kennedy told the Greater Houston Ministerial Association on September 12, 1960: "I am not the Catholic candidate for president. I am the Democratic Party candidate for president who also happens to be a Catholic. I do not speak for my Church on public matters—and the Church does not speak for me."[2]

Kennedy questioned rhetorically whether one-quarter of Americans were relegated to second-class citizenship just because they were Catholic and once stated: "No one asked me my religion in the South Pacific,"[3] where he served as a naval commander.

Between September and October, Kennedy squared off against Nixon in a series of the first televised presidential debates in US history. During the programs, Nixon suffered from a crippling wound ("five o'clock shadow") that made him look sloppy. He also sweated "profusely," reacting to the hot lights on the set, making him look less than presidential. Kennedy, on the other hand, wore stage makeup and appeared relaxed, which helped the sprawling television audience view him as a clean-cut young man and an up-and-coming political winner. On average, radio listeners thought that Nixon had won the debates based upon the substance of his answers, but television viewers believed just the opposite based upon what they saw.

After that first debate, Kennedy's campaign gained momentum. He pulled slightly ahead of Nixon in the polls, and by the time two more debates had passed and as the election drew near, Kennedy had expanded somewhat upon his lead. On Election Day, the popular young candidate defeated Nixon in one of the closest presidential elections of the twentieth century. In the popular vote, Kennedy led Nixon by most accounts by a slim two-tenths of one percent (49.7 percent to 49.5 percent), while in the Electoral College, he won 303 votes to Nixon's 219, with 269 required to win. Fourteen electors from Mississippi and Alabama refused to support Kennedy because of his support for the civil rights movement, choosing to vote instead for write-in candidate Senator Harry F. Byrd of Virginia, as did an elector from Oklahoma.

So, at the age of forty-three, John Kennedy became the youngest person ever elected to the presidency (although Theodore Roosevelt was a year younger, at forty-two, when he assumed the office after William McKinley's assassination in 1901). He was sworn in as the thirty-fifth president by Chief Justice Earl Warren at noon on January 20, 1961. In his inaugural address, he spoke of the need for all Americans to be active citizens, espousing the famous words: "Ask not what your country can do for you; ask what you can do for your country." He invited the nations of the world to join together to fight what he called the "common enemies of man: tyranny, poverty, disease, and war itself."[4]

One year later, in 1962, Warren found himself crossing the seventy-year threshold, still in good health and high spirits. By then, his life as chief justice had settled into a familiar routine. During the eight months that the court was in session, each of the justices wrote some fourteen majority opinions. They were free to write as many concurring or dissenting opinions as they wanted, although Warren, out of a sense of cohesiveness and in deference to his workload, wrote fewer dissents than his brethren.

In addition to his work on the bench, the chief justice had two other time-consuming duties: He was responsible for the administration of the court and its two hundred employees, and, because protocol dictated, he was a frequent host to foreign dignitaries. (In one instance, informed by

Margaret McHugh that the Indian delegation had arrived, Warren looked up to ask innocently enough, "Californian?")[5]

As Warren's reputation grew, so, too, did the number of visitors who laid claim to his time. Only by relying upon the skilled administrative talents of McHugh was he able to keep all his appointments and workload flowing. "He felt that was part of his job, to show the human side of the federal government," said law clerk Gordon Gooch. "He was very good, even in talking to high school students. He did it all willingly. He didn't seem to resent it."[6]

He was especially pleased to welcome visitors from his home state and often spent hours talking about the programs he had put into place as governor. Years after he was sworn in as chief justice, he still enjoyed asking guests about the University of California or the state's penal system or the ongoing preservation of the stately redwood groves in Mendocino County, for which Warren had always held a special fondness.

Among his favorite visitors, according to Ed Cray in *Chief Justice*, were Pat and Marge Patterson; the daughter and granddaughters of *Sacramento Bee* editor Walter Jones; Pacific Gas and Electric public relations executive Robert Gros; and Warren's World War I army buddy Tatsu Ogawa. The chief gave all of them personalized tours of the court.

Other guests with whom he enjoyed sharing apartment 1-140 at the Sheraton Park included CBS television commentator Eric Sevareid, ABC news director William Lawrence, and ABC radio commentator Edward P. Morgan, all trusted figures with the American public. Warren knew he could let his hair down and be frank with them, and they would respect his candor. Conversely, he relied upon their insights to share the latest gossip circulating the beltway for which Washington was so well known.

Other guests Warren favored included trial lawyer Edward Bennett Williams, who often spun yarns about clients as diverse as organized crime figure Frank Costello, Teamsters president Jimmy Hoffa, and Senator Joseph McCarthy. Williams, as notorious as the clients he chose to represent, held the chief justice spellbound.

Warren also enjoyed meeting with out-of-town journalists such as Irving Dilliard, editorial writer for the *St. Louis Post-Dispatch*, and editors Ralph McGill of the *Atlanta Constitution* and Harry Ashmore of the *Arkansas Gazette*, both of whom had put their papers at considerable risk by backing *Brown* during its most tumultuous days.

The Warrens' social circle expanded significantly when their oldest daughter, Virginia, married John Charles Daly, former ABC vice president for news, on December 22, 1960. The erudite host of the signature television game show *What's My Line?* was a staunch conservative. Throughout the passing years, both Warren and Daly enjoyed sparring over various court decisions, a tradition that Warren extended as well to his law clerks at their Saturday lunches at the court. Texan Gordon Gooch recalled,

> When we got into political disagreements—because I am more politically conservative than he was—he encouraged you. He enjoyed the debate.
>
> In those days they had the 'Impeach Earl Warren' billboards around. So when we would get in an argument and there would be an impasse, I would say, "Sir, you know, if you would just fire me, I could go back to Texas and run for governor unopposed on both tickets."[7]

That, Gooch recalled, always made the chief laugh.

The Warrens' circle of intimate friends grew steadily. With a courtesy call by newly elected Congressman James Corman, who had voted for Culbert Olson back in 1942, a lifelong friendship was formed. Whenever the Warrens were free, the Cormans hosted them at informal dinner parties in their Alexandria, Virginia, home.

"He was always so gracious," Corman said years later, "and it was such a thrill, particularly for young people, for anybody, to get to spend an evening with him."[8]

Walter Jones's occasional visits to Washington, according to Cray, invariably offered an excuse for a small group of California legislators from both parties to gather with Warren in a private setting and swap stories over a glass or two of Scotch—"always Cutty Sark, and always from a bottle stashed safely away" from prying eyes, according to Jimmy Lee Warren. While Nina didn't drink or approve of alcoholic beverages of any kind, "she never begrudged Papa Warren his favorite potable, usually no more than a finger or two served neat in a glass. He didn't imbibe regularly, and he rarely had more than one."[9]

At one typical Warren soiree, California Superior Court judge Harry Pregerson told the chief he was grappling with the idea of accepting a federal court appointment. While he'd had years of experience in state courts, he was concerned that he'd had very little in the federal system.

"Well, Harry, don't worry about it," Warren said in a marked overstatement. "I hadn't that much experience either when I went on the Supreme Court."[10]

As time passed, Warren found his Capitol Hill friendships shifting from Republican to Democrat, even though the chief's philosophical bent had remained basically unchanged. Representative Augustus Hawkins, a Republican, recalled that "Republicans soured on him. We wanted to give Warren a banquet in his honor and couldn't get the Republicans to agree."[11]

The reason for Warren's shifting preference was obvious. Back home in California, Republicans had grown less progressive and more conservative, which made them openly hostile toward the Warren philosophy. Nationally, the GOP was even less enamored with the Warren Court. Coincidentally, Democrat Pat Brown's policies as governor were more an extension of Warren's than of the liberal branch of his own party. "I instinctively followed Warren's political philosophy as governor," Brown acknowledged. "I tried to pattern my administration after his."[12]

From the beginning of Brown's first term in 1959, Warren had quietly advised the new governor to be "more forthcoming and candid than I sort of anticipated the chief justice would be," said Brown's chief of staff Fred Dutton. "I always thought they stopped short of overt politics. At the same time, Warren was being very fatherly, and frank, and helpful to Pat."[13]

When scuttlebutt began circulating that politico Richard Nixon, who had lost his bid for the presidency to Kennedy in 1960, intended to run against Brown in 1962, Warren threw his Stetson into the ring. News photogs caught the two men together, beaming, friendly, enjoying one another's company. The message was unspoken but clear.

"It was a very conscious show," said Hale Champion, Brown's finance director and campaign adviser. Friendship may have played a part, but "these two guys were very wily politically, and the political implications of this could not have been unknown to either of them."[14]

Lest the message be lost on anyone, Earl Warren Jr. changed his party registration from Republican to Democrat. He switched, he announced with some publicity, "for one reason only—to do everything I could to insure [*sic*] California's future as my father visualized it. Richard Nixon does not have that vision."[15]

Brown would go on to beat Nixon by three hundred thousand votes of 5.8 million cast in the general election. It was a stinging defeat for the former vice president, who bitterly announced his retirement from politics the morning after the balloting. (The value of Warren's "endorsement" of Brown lay in the fact that Republican senator Thomas Kuchel swept every county in the state and won reelection by seven hundred thousand votes. Brown, with Warren's subtle endorsement, had managed a million-vote turnaround.)

Three days after the California election, reporters on Air Force One spied a chortling Earl Warren and Jack Kennedy relishing once more the news stories of Nixon's defeat. "It would have been hard to say, watching their faces, who had enjoyed the downfall more, the Chief Justice or the President of the United States," newswoman Mary McGrory commented.

"They had their heads together over the clipping and were laughing like schoolboys over the contents."[16]

Warren's pleasure in Nixon's defeat was twofold. He considered Nixon "a bad man," according to Merrell "Pop" Small. Even more importantly, the state he loved was preserved from "ignorant mismanagement."[17]

Twice a year, summer and winter, the Warrens flew back to California, where they visited the governor's former office in Sacramento to shake hands with former staff members. Afterward, Warren stopped by Bob Tinsley's stand on J Street for a shoe shine and some baseball talk. Christmastime was crowded with family, football, and a drive to Wallace Lynn's Colusa Ranch to go duck hunting.

The very air of the Golden State seemed to restore him. "This is home," he said upon each trip. California was an emotional lodestone forever pulling them back. Any recollection of the governor's mansion brought fond tears to Nina's eyes. For both the primary and general each election year, husband and wife dutifully wrote Alameda County clerk-recorder Jack G. Blue for absentee ballots.

California, too, was still home to four of the Warren children. James had left the advertising business and, with his wife, Margaret, and their three sons, moved to St. Helena at the northern end of the Napa Valley. He was settled and prospering as a real estate agent. So, too, was Honey Bear in Beverly Hills, the mother of three, married to her physician husband.

After a conversation with his father, Earl Jr. had decided to leave his job as a farm adviser to attend law school at Boalt. He, his wife, Patty, and their children were back in Sacramento, where Earl decided to open his practice.

Warren also prodded son Robert, an athletic coach in the California prison system, to seek broader horizons. Bobby also secured a real estate license before opening an office in Davis.

In California, too, were the chief justice's closest companions—Bart Cavanaugh, Wally Lynn, and, more recently, hotelman Ben Swig.

Swig had met Warren shortly after World War II when he accidentally stumbled into then-Governor Warren's Pullman compartment on a cross-country train. The two struck up a conversation and ended up talking about investment opportunities in California.

Persuaded by the governor, Swig left Boston for the Golden State. He eventually purchased the swank Fairmont Hotel atop San Francisco's Nob Hill and became a prominent contributor to the Democratic Party.

Swig and Warren grew closer. For two weeks each Christmas, the hotelman turned over to the Warrens a suite at the Fairmont, first on the fifth floor and later the lavish penthouse with its glorious views of the Golden

Gate, the bay, and the city far below. In the summer, they spent three weeks together on a 115-foot yacht that Swig rented to cruise the Mediterranean with his family.

The cruises were unique. On the first one, Swig and Warren were present for the dedication of a forest planted in Israel. On another voyage, Swig arranged for the party to be presented to Pope Paul VI, which sent Nina and Swig's two granddaughters scurrying around Rome in search of the proper dresses.

"Uncle Chiefy and Auntie Nina were just up for everything," said Swig's granddaughter, Caroline Zecca. "We'd go into ports and they would be off seeing whatever they could—they were not young then—and swimming in the Mediterranean with all the ship's hands standing around in case they had to dive in quickly" in the event of sharks.[18]

The Warrens were undemanding guests, unassuming and unpretentious. On one voyage where they were short of fresh water, Nina offered to do everyone's laundry since she was washing Earl's underwear and socks daily.

If his wife doted over him, Warren, in turn, treated Nina with an endearing respect. She was "the best thing that ever happened to me," he often said.[19] He invariably stood whenever she entered the room. He held doors open for her, and he seated her at the dinner table. Although they were not publicly demonstrative, Warren's love for his wife was unquestioned.

A *New York Times* "story of human priorities" during the October 1962 Cuban missile crisis revealed some measure of Warren's affection for his spouse. With the United States and the Soviet Union poised on the brink of nuclear war, government officials issued laminated passes to admit key government figures to an ultra-secret "alternative seat of government" dug deep into a mountain in Appalachia.

When the earnest young man brought the chief justice his pass to this cavernous nuclear bomb shelter, Warren said he didn't see a pass for Mrs. Warren.

There was no room for wives, the courier informed him.

Well, in that case, Warren replied, now you have room for another VIP. Smiling, he handed back his pass.[20]

If Nina made his life run smoothly, Warren accepted his obligation as her financial protector. At the chief justice's request, Swig recommended a series of real estate investments intended to supplement Nina's pension in the event of Warren's death. The Warrens weren't wealthy. After a lifetime of public service, the chief had amassed a fortune garnered from the proceeds of their home at 88 Vernon when they sold it plus accumulated interest on that money. The total amounted to barely $50,000, according to a letter he wrote to Swig in 1957.

His paucity of finances troubled him, daughter-in-law Margaret recalled. One Christmas, the man she called "Papa" came out to the kitchen nearly in tears.

"You know, Jim," he confessed, "I lie awake at nights just thinking all the time. I've had many offers where I could have been a millionaire, and as it turned out, I always felt that I was a public servant and this was my life. And now I have nothing to leave my family."[21]

It weighed on him heavily, particularly with the family growing. By 1962, the Warrens had no fewer than fourteen grandchildren, the oldest of them eighteen. To know something of these youngsters, Earl and Nina decided to bring one grandchild to Washington each summer for two or three weeks.

The first visitor, in 1960, was sixteen-year-old James Jr. With a guide to lead them, Warren and his oldest grandson toured the Gettysburg battlefield on July 4, a brash and sunny day. Standing at the battle line that marked the high tide of the Confederacy, looking down at the green fields below, Warren spoke in wonder: "Just think, Jimmy, you are standing at the point in the war, that turned the tide, that created the nation that is now the United States of America."

Grandfather and grandson also visited the Lincoln Memorial, where they hiked slowly up the steep stairs in the front of the building, the great seated figure of the sixteenth president looming as they neared the top. Warren solemnly told the youth that the memorial was a continual inspiration: "He said he would come down there from time to time, and look at it because he was moved by Lincoln. He had seen people walk into that memorial with the same reverence they had when walking into a cathedral. He said it always struck him that way."[22]

Just as importantly, every chance he got, Warren took his grandchildren to a Washington Senators ballgame. Once, they were invited to sit on the Kansas City Athletics' bench by manager Hank Bauer, and Warren accepted. "It was quite a thrill for me," Jeffrey Warren recalled.

As game time neared, the umpire waved toward the dugout; major-league rules specified that only those in uniform were allowed inside. The two Warrens meekly retreated to their box seats as Bauer mounted the dugout steps and called, "Good goin', ump! You just threw out the chief justice of the United States."[23]

Sporting events remained a release from the burdens of the court. Warren not only attended Senators baseball games whenever he could but also traveled to the Penn Relays. His law clerk, Murray Bring, introduced him to hockey.

Seven Sundays each fall, Warren was a guest of Ed Williams at Washington Redskins football games. There, they squeezed into Williams's presidential box along with John and Virginia Daly, Robert and Ethel Kennedy, *Washington Post* editor Ben Bradlee, columnist Art Buchwald, diplomat Averell Harriman, and Tom Clark, all there cheering on a team of questionable talent and mediocre record.

Even among such heralded company, the chief justice ranked among Washington's elite; yet he never confused the office with the man. Though a stadium functionary stood ready to whisk the chief justice of the United States through a VIP gate, Warren always refused, saying, "No, no, I'll wait my turn in line with everyone else."[24]

Except for a few mandatory perks, such as a chauffeur-driven limousine and appropriate housing, Warren refused to take advantage of the perquisites of office. "He knew how important he was when he was governor and chief justice," said family friend Robert Gros, "but he didn't go around playing the role."[25]

When the Smithsonian Institution commissioned celebrated modernist Gardner Cox to paint a portrait of its honorary chairman, Earl Warren sat for him one morning before heading off to court.

"It took forever," the chief justice told Frankfurter law clerk Roland Homet Jr. "At the end, I showed it to my wife, and she still didn't like it."[26]

Warren had likewise been nonplussed when he was contacted in 1958 about the publication in book form of a collection of his speeches. Despite his reservations about the project, he turned over a box of materials. He refused to select those speeches he thought best or even to write an introduction, believing the public had the right to make up their own minds. Later, when the book came out as *The Public Papers of Chief Justice Earl Warren*, he shook his head. In a letter to Bill Brennan, he expressed "wonderment as to why the book was published."[27]

Because the chief justice would not presume upon his office, Warren summarily put an end to a "hobby" law clerks Gordon Gooch and Henry Steinman took up as a joke. Once mistaken as Warren's bodyguards at a baseball game, Gooch and Steinman began playing the role: "He'd be walking down the street, talking to whomever he was walking with, and Steinman and I would drop back, and drop back [*sic*]. Then we'd move out on the flanks a little bit, and whenever someone would approach, we would put our hands in our pocket like we were putting it on the butt of a pistol. People would just clear the path."

The two clerks chuckled over their charade "something fierce" until one day when the chief was walking over to the Washington Hotel to get a haircut. Steinman and Gooch fell into step behind him just as a derelict lugging two suitcases approached. "He looked up and saw Steinman and me with our hands on our [imaginary] pistols . . . and the man dropped his suitcases, went over and put his hands up against the wall."

Warren took one look at the man hugging the wall and looked back at Steinman and Gooch, recognizing instantly what they'd been up to. "Cut that stuff out!" he ordered.

"And we couldn't be police officers anymore," Gooch lamented. "He said he's never had a bodyguard in his life, and he wasn't going to start now."[28]

Until summer 1962, the court had remained relatively conservative. But in August, the replacement of Felix Frankfurter with Arthur Goldberg swung the court decidedly liberal. While Frankfurter had often proved a thorn in the side of the chief justice, he at least remained throughout his tenure decidedly conservative. He was a bulwark against the winds of change, and no one else could fill his role.

Indeed, with the appointment of Goldberg to the court, no one else did. A devoted judicial activist, Goldberg was at the opposite end of the spectrum from Frankfurter. Within weeks of his arrival, he began making his vote felt in several cases being reargued from the previous year's term.

His first contribution involved an appeal to ban the enforcement of a Virginia statute that declared illegal any organization retaining a lawyer in a cause in which it had no financial interest. During the previous term, Warren had argued in conference that the state law was intended to mute the implementation of *Brown v. Board of Education*. In fact, he said, the law would put the NAACP out of business in Virginia.

Despite his arguments, the brethren had voted in conference 5–4 to uphold the statute. But before Frankfurter's majority opinion could be issued, Justice Charles Whittaker resigned, and Frankfurter himself was felled by a stroke. With the vote now 4–3 to strike down the legislation, the court set the case for reargument.

So, in fall 1962, with Byron White and Arthur Goldberg occupying the seats once held by Justices Whittaker and Frankfurter, Goldberg voted to reverse the initial decision, going even further than Bill Brennan had in his opinion for the majority to uphold. White concurred in part and dissented in part. Clark, Harlan, and Stewart dissented, and the Virginia statute was struck down.

In another case, Goldberg proved to be the critical fifth vote challenging the Florida legislature's investigation into the Miami chapter of the

NAACP for Communist influence. Branch president Reverend Theodore S. Gibson refused to provide the committee with a membership list and financial records. He was found to be in contempt and sentenced to six months in jail and a $1,200 fine.

Argued first in 1961, this case might also have been decided by a 5–4 vote to uphold the contempt conviction. Once again, Warren, Black, Douglas, and Brennan were in the minority. But the illnesses of Frankfurter and Whittaker forced reargument of the case. Goldberg voted with the chief justice to reverse the results of the initial vote.

A third time Goldberg provided the deciding vote, and with it changed the outcome in a search-and-seizure case from San Francisco. Deadlocked at 4–4 with the hospitalized Whittaker not participating, the brethren put the case over for reargument in April 1962. White and Goldberg ended up splitting the vote, White voting with what had been the Frankfurter wing and Goldberg providing the activist members of the court a majority in favor of reversal.

Seven more times in that 1962 term, the junior justice joined Warren, Black, Douglas, and Brennan to form majorities in civil rights or civil liberties cases. With Goldberg's arrival, Earl Warren finally had his dream court.

The makeup of the brethren was, of course, a reflection of the philosophy of its chief. No case better demonstrated the court's new sensitivity to simple matters of justice than did the in forma pauperis petition of Clarence Earl Gideon, penciled in neat block letters on the lined paper provided by Florida's Raiford State Prison.

Gideon, an occasional drifter and convicted felon, had been found guilty of breaking and entering a Panama City poolroom on August 4, 1961, with the intent to commit a misdemeanor. He had broken into a cigarette machine for the change, but then he grabbed a bottle of wine and a six-pack of beer on the way out.

Denied a court-appointed attorney by the judge, Gideon's felony trial was short; its outcome, predictable. He was sentenced to the maximum sentence of five years in Raiford. The Florida Supreme Court summarily rejected his appeal.

"The question is very simple," Clarence Gideon argued in his handwritten petition to the US Supreme Court. "I requested the court to appoint me attorney and the court refused." Florida did not provide counsel for indigents except in capital cases.

Logged in by the court clerk's office, Gideon's five-page petition made its way to the in forma pauperis pile in the chief justice's chambers. When it eventually rose to the top of the stack, law clerk Henry Steinman picked it up.

The Sixth Amendment to the Constitution assured a right to counsel in criminal cases only in federal courts. Twenty years earlier, in *Betts v. Brady*, the Supreme Court had ruled that the Due Process Clause of the Four-teenth Amendment did not require that criminal defendants be represented by counsel in state courts. An attorney was required only if the absence of counsel constituted "a denial of fundamental fairness." The court in *Betts* had refused to set "hard and fast rules" stipulating in which cases the states had to provide counsel. Instead, in subsequent decisions, the court said the defendant had to be the victim of "special circumstances"[29]—his own illiteracy, youth, or mental illness, for instance, or the misconduct of the prosecutor or judge at the trial.

As he read Clarence Gideon's letter, Steinman became excited: "It was obvious to me. The guy had been denied counsel. In almost every case the Court had up to that time, the Court sent it back down because they [the justices] found there was some special circumstance—he had grown up poor, he was mentally unbalanced. They found something they could rely on without saying there was an absolute right to counsel."[30]

This one was "clean," Steinman realized, and might present an inter-esting challenge to the court. The clerk typed up a terse in forma pauperis memo to the justices: "Right to counsel case. There appear to be no ex-tenuating circumstances."

To the chief justice, he noted on the bottom of the page his recom-mendation to grant certiorari. "This may be it!" he concluded.[31]

When Clarence Gideon's petition came up in conference on June 1, 1962, eight justices voted to take up the case. Only Tom Clark voted to deny.

Three weeks later, Gideon requested counsel be appointed to argue his case in the high court, and Warren proposed Washington-based attorney Abe Fortas to do so pro bono. Such appointments in the Supreme Court are considered a great honor by attorneys. At the same time, the cases can be costly, not only in the unbilled hours devoted to them but also in the out-of-pocket investigative, printing, and travel costs associated with them. Pro bono may have been a great honor, but it was an expensive one!

Fortas was the perfect candidate for the job. He was one of the most influential attorneys in Washington, a veteran New Dealer with rock solid connections to the Democratic Party. More importantly, he was a seasoned courtroom advocate. Author Ed Cray related:

By the time the redoubtable Fortas argued the case on January 15, 1963, *Betts* hung by the thinnest of threads. The legal profession had long held it in faint regard, the law journals in even lower repute. The attorneys general of twenty-three states had prepared a friend-of-the-court brief asking that *Betts* be abandoned.

Thirteen states still had no legal requirement that counsel be provided in all felonies; in eight of these, however, the indigent found attorneys through informal systems. Only five states did not provide counsel for the poor except in capital cases: Alabama, Florida, Mississippi, North Carolina, and South Carolina. (Gideon, unfortunately, was not tried in one of Florida's three largest counties. These three did have countywide public defenders.)

In practical effect, the case would have comparatively small impact. Symbolically, it towered above the balance of the cases decided in the October, 1962, term.

Fortas's legal argument, the best Bill Douglas claimed to have heard in his thirty-six years on the bench, was more than enough. The Brethren voted unanimously to reverse *Betts*.

The question to be answered was whether the Fourteenth Amendment embodied a right to counsel in state trials. As Steinman later pointed out, "There is nowhere in the Constitution where it says you are entitled to legal counsel" in a state case.

"But if that is what you believe, you go to the Due Process or Equal Protection Clauses and find it."[32]

Warren saw an opportunity to produce a unanimous court decision, so he led the conference discussion following oral arguments with an ingenious suggestion. He knew that, if the court got bogged down on extraneous questions concerning state requirements to provide counsel in misdemeanor trials or for appeals, Clark, Harlan, Stewart, or White would likely dissent. So the chief proposed they leave those decisions to another day.

The Brethren agreed with his terms but rejected his additional suggestion that the decision should be made retroactive. After all, as they pointed out, the Florida deputy attorney general stated that nearly two-thirds of all inmates in state prisons were convicted without representation by lawyers at their trials.

In a gesture to placate Black, who had dissented twenty years earlier in *Betts*, Warren assigned *Gideon* to the senior justice. While there would be three concurring opinions, with Douglas embracing the incorporation of the entire Bill of Rights rather than the piecemeal approach they were taking into their ruling, the concurrences meant that once again the Warren Court was unanimous in the outcome of a significant case.

Clarence Gideon's long and unlikely road to the Supreme Court of the United States was a piece of storybook Americana: Even the lowliest drifter and convicted criminal could appeal to the highest court of the land to challenge shortcomings with the legal system—and win.

No tale affirmed the cause of American democracy any better. No story broadcast around the world so clearly proclaimed that it wasn't always only the rich who received justice in American courts.

The ruling in *Gideon* came down on March 18, 1963. It was the last in a series of decisions that critics of the decision dubbed the "Black Monday for states' rights."[33]

That day, the court also ruled in a case challenging Georgia's unpopular "unit system" in determining Democratic primary elections. The system assured that rural voters not only controlled the state legislature but also determined party nominees for governor. Such a winner-take-all system meant that as few as 11 percent of those voting statewide could elect the Democratic gubernatorial nominee given certain conditions. The apportionment system was so unfairly weighted that fewer than seven thousand residents of the state's three smallest counties had as much voting clout in primary elections as the more than half million residents of the city of Atlanta combined!

Disgruntled Atlantans had challenged the primary system in the courts before, only to suffer defeat. But this fifth assault on the system found its way all the way to the Supreme Court on an appeal by the state after a three-member federal panel struck down the malapportionment as unconstitutional.

Warren again set the direction of the court's discussion in conference. The Georgia unit system was defective, he reasoned, because it disproportionately favored some voters over others. So, too, were similar primaries in other states. The justices agreed 8–1, with John Harlan the lone dissenter. Warren assigned the decision to Douglas to write.

Two weeks later, Douglas had drafted his opinion. He wrote that "once a geographical unit for which a representative is to be chosen is designated, all who participate in the election are to have an equal vote. . . . The conception of political equality from the Declaration of Independence, to Lincoln's Gettysburg Address, to the Fifteenth, Seventeenth and Nineteenth Amendments can mean only one thing—one person, one vote."[34]

Warren immediately signed on, stating succinctly: "I agree. EW, 2/5/63." He asked for no changes as Douglas went through six revisions, making edits in each to accommodate the other justices' feelings on the matter.

Chief Justice Warren, when he was in the majority, made the assignment. When the drafts circulated, he wasted little time in signing on, requesting few, if any, changes. It was a philosophy that stemmed back to his earliest training in government: If it ain't broke, don't fix it. He left to others to work out the specific details and minutiae. His job, as he saw it, was to lead his brethren in conference, find common ground, and point a majority of justices to it. His focus was on the process and the result based upon the underpinnings of the legal principles to which he ascribed.

In private, Warren acknowledged that an occasional decision of the court might be "a little rough, or go too far. We know that, and we know future generations will tame it down."[35] But the Warren Court didn't often wait for those future generations, choosing instead to refine its own work. The clamor had hardly died down on *Engel v. Vitale* when the high court took up two more school prayer cases.

The first came in the form of an appeal to the Maryland state Supreme Court, which had upheld a Baltimore school order requiring that each day begin with the recitation of the Lord's Prayer and the reading of a selected Bible passage. In the second, a federal appellate panel had struck down a state law requiring that the school day begin with a reading of biblical verses.

The court could have disposed of both matters quietly. A short per curiam decision citing the previous year's school prayer decision would have resolved the Maryland matter, while a rejection of the appeal of the losing school board in the Pennsylvania case could have put that issue to bed. But the brethren did neither, choosing instead to grant certiorari. The misunderstood school prayer opinion had not been well received a year earlier, causing more confusion than it had resolved. Now the court was presented the perfect opportunity to revisit its ruling and answer the questions in the minds of the public in doing so.

Once again, Earl Warren's political sense played a role in shaping the opinion. The writing assignment would typically have gone to Hugo Black, who had written the first school prayer ruling. Instead, the chief assigned the majority opinion to Tom Clark, whom critics of the court considered a conservative, one of their own.

Bill Brennan, most likely with Warren's consent, informed the brethren he would write a concurrence in the Pennsylvania case. He would concentrate on the historical aspects of the court's church-state decisions over the years as a reminder that the Warren Court was not out of step with its precursors. Brennan, the sole Catholic on the court, asked that no one else join him. He was, in effect, appealing as a communicant to the hierarchy of the Catholic Church in America and to influential laymen for their support, which appeared to be dwindling.

Arthur Goldberg, with John Harlan joining, and William Douglas agreed to write additional concurring opinions. Only Potter Stewart dissented.

So, on the final day of the term, June 17, 1963, Tom Clark began reading the 8–1 majority opinion, affirming the previous year's *Engel v. Vitale* ruling. His holding extended even to the prohibition from the more nonsectarian King James prayer that the school district of Long Island had used to begin its day.

School District of Abington Township v. Schempp was a reaffirmation that the Warren Court would embrace "no breach of the wall between Church and State," as Ed Cray phrased it.[36] Public funds could not be used to support even mildly or voluntary religious activities.

With the court's latest ruling, the protests subsided. News stories and press commentators made a point of noting that Clark, a Methodist by upbringing; Brennan, a Catholic; and Goldberg, a Jew, had affirmed the decision in separate opinions. Forewarned by the outcry triggered by *Engel* the year before, the clergy was better prepared to back the court's finding when the second prayer decision came down.

That correction of the court's earlier finding had been simple. More difficult was the court's revisiting a group of cases arising out of sit-in demonstrations throughout the states of the old Confederacy. The sit-ins presented "a legal Gordian Knot because competing interests were at stake," as court historian Bernard Schwartz put it.[37]

The question came down to whether the state could prosecute private citizens for trespassing in the course of civil rights demonstrations staged by black activists. Or, put somewhat differently: could the state enforce a merchant's preference not to have blacks on his property?

The sit-ins had begun on February 1, 1960, when four freshmen at North Carolina Agricultural and Technical College sat down at the white-only lunch counter of the F. W. Woolworth store in Greensboro, North Carolina.

"They sell us merchandise from other counters," one of the four explained to a local reporter. "If they sell us other merchandise, we say they should serve us at the lunch counter."[38]

After having been denied lunch service, the students returned in ever-larger numbers the next week. They came in and took their seats at the counter in an orderly fashion until, one by one, no empty seats remained, thus ending lunch counter sales for the day. The age of the political sit-in had begun.

As sit-in movements spread across the South, the demands of the protesters exploded. By the beginning of the 1962 term, the brethren had agreed to hear six different sit-in cases involving scores of demonstrators.

The lead case was *Peterson v. Greenville*, in which ten black youths were appealing their arrest for unlawful trespass in Greenville, South Carolina. They, too, had violated the white-only practice at the lunch counter of the local S. H. Kress five-and-dime store. Their convictions for violating a city ordinance prohibiting the races from eating together were upheld in the state supreme court.

Warren opened the November 9, 1962, conference on the cases with the cautious suggestion that the court avoid the fundamental constitutional question of property rights versus civil rights. Instead, he proposed they reverse the convictions due to unlawful state action. In three of the cases, the cities had ordinances requiring separate seating of the races in restaurants.

The fourth, involving the Reverend F. L. Shuttlesworth, had two clergymen convicted of inciting a violation of a similar ordinance in Birmingham, Alabama. The fifth case was from New Orleans, which had no such local law but instead involved a mayor and a police chief pledging that sit-ins would not be allowed in their jurisdictions.

Finally, the sixth case involved a security guard deputized by a suburban Maryland county sheriff. The guard had arrested two black youths for entering a white-only amusement park and boarding a carousel.

Warren's suggestion as to how the court should proceed slowly took root as one justice after another joined ranks. According to notes Warren made at the conference, Hugo Black "believes a store owner as [does] a home owner has a right to say who can come in his premises, and how long they can stay. If he has that right he cannot be helpless to call the police."[39]

So if an individual wanted to discriminate, it was legal; if a state did the same thing, it was illegal. If that were the case, the court could reverse.

Bill Douglas emphatically disagreed with any defense of property rights. To accept Black's position, he felt, meant "we will have a new Plessy v. Ferguson." Rather, Douglas proposed the court plunge into uncharted waters. He wanted not only to reverse but also to "make the store owner a public utility"[40] by overturning the 1883 court decision holding that the Fourteenth Amendment did not apply to public accommodations. Failing that, he said, he would concur with the chief.

Clark, Harlan, Stewart, and Goldberg fell in with Black's position. Brennan suggested they rely on the fact that local ordinances were coercive; they did not give private property owners the right to integrate their lunch counters if they chose. Byron White seconded Brennan's position.

Warren was aware that the court was undermining not only decades of legal principle but also a century of southern social custom. Envisioning the social repercussions to the court's rulings, he decided to assign the sit-in cases to himself. Over the next seven months, he sought "as nearly a unanimous conclusion as possible," striving, as Stewart and Goldberg pointed out in a final two-hour conference on May 16, for "the great benefit that flowed from the unanimous decisions in the first school cases."[41]

To reach that goal, Warren accepted in his personally drafted opinions a series of editorial changes from Brennan, White, Goldberg, and Harlan. At the last moment, Clark nearly bolted, only to be brought back in line by Warren and Brennan.[42] In the end, only John Harlan dissented. While concurring in the result, he disagreed with the reasoning.

Warren delivered the basically written, easily understood majority opinion on May 21, 1963. His conclusion in disposing of cases from Greenville, South Carolina; Birmingham, Alabama; and Durham, North Carolina, was unequivocal: "When a state agency passes a law compelling persons to discriminate against other persons because of race, and the State's criminal processes are employed in a way that enforces the discrimination mandated by that law, such a palpable violation of the Fourteenth Amendment cannot be saved by attempting to separate the mental urges of the discriminators."[43]

In the fourth case—from New Orleans—neither city nor state had passed any law barring the races from eating together. Nevertheless, the mayor and the police chief had pledged they would not permit integration of lunch counters. Warren's opinion shredded their indefensible conduct, reversing the convictions of one white and three black college students for breach of the peace at a McCrory five-and-ten.

The outspoken mayor and police chief were adamantly opposed to desegregation; in effect, their orders were law, Warren wrote. Consequently, the city was to be treated as if it had adopted an ordinance prohibiting the races from eating together and could be enjoined from carrying out that ordinance.

Finally, the Warren Court wiped clean the convictions of Reverends Fred L. Shuttlesworth and Charles Billups for inciting two young men to commit criminal trespass at a Birmingham lunch counter. Although Birmingham had a segregation ordinance, the court that day ruled it unconstitutional. The convictions of the two youths for trespass under that ordinance were reversed. Since the two had therefore not committed a crime, Warren reasoned, the two clergymen could not be convicted of inducing them to break the law.

With that decision, the brethren were able to sidestep a land mine for another year before answering the real question: Could a private property owner call upon the political powers of the state to enforce his racial intolerance? And could a public merchant invoke nonracial trespass or "disturbing the peace" laws to advance his policy of discrimination? Because the Maryland amusement park case rested squarely on the answer to those questions, Warren agreed with Clark to put the matter over for reargument in the following term, allowing the justices more time for consideration.

And with that, Earl Warren put to rest his tenth term as chief justice of the United States Supreme Court. The press, in evaluating the success and failures of that term's court, fell along political lines.

The conservative *U.S. News & World Report* noted with barely throttled alarm that "the trend of the Warren Court in using its judicial authority to promote change in more and more fields shows no sign of abating." The magazine quoted California Democratic congressman Charles H. Wilson complaining that "[o]ur entire way of life in this country is being revised and remolded by the nine Justices of the Supreme Court."[44]

The *Milwaukee Journal*, championing Wisconsin's never-waning progressive vigor, applauded Warren editorially: "Court historians are already according him future rank as 'one of the great Chief Justices.'" With his vote and leadership, the editorial continued, the Supreme Court "has more profoundly influenced and shaped the course of individual human affairs than in any equal period of time before."[45]

One thing was certain. The court's decisions over the decade-long span had changed the nation while miring itself in controversy. A Gallup poll that year reported 10 percent of the public rated the court as doing an excellent job, 33 percent a good job, and 26 percent a fair job. Fifteen percent told interviewers they believed the court was doing a poor job.

In September 1963, shortly before the opening of the new term, the chief justice broke his ten-year moratorium on the court's activities with a general response to its critics. Speaking at the annual convention of the California Bar Association, Warren acknowledged that the court's docket had shifted from a quarter century before, when barely 1 percent of the court's opinions dealt with civil rights or civil liberties, to the present, when nearly half did.

But those who complained that the court was evolving too quickly and moving too aggressively, he continued, overlooked the fact that the court only reviewed cases decided by lower courts: "But really, where the supreme court of a state is vigilant in its protection of constitutional rights, as is the Supreme Court of California, few differences arise between it and the Supreme Court of the United States."[46]

He could have made that point more emphatically, although it might not have been judicious for him to point out that, if the legislative branch, consisting of Congress and the state legislatures, had done its statutory duty, the court or courts wouldn't have to be perpetually occupied with "making law" rather than interpreting it.

He did admit that those who had long been deprived of equality "are now testing all our institutions to make sure that they, too, will be the beneficiaries" of them.[47]

A week after Warren's speech, the *Washington Post*, owned in part by the Warrens' summertime traveling companion Agnes Meyer, rallied to the court's defense. According to the paper, four towering cases—*Brown, Baker, Mapp v. Ohio*, and *Engel*—highlighted the Warren decade, cases that had reached the court "tragically late" and so "ran counter to settled convictions and rooted practices among many Americans."

Under the studied guidance of Earl Warren, the Supreme Court had met its obligations and served the nation well, the editorial continued: "It was a piece of great good fortune that the chief justiceship was held during this trying period by a man of exceptional poise and strength and understanding. . . . He can be sure that in the perspective of history, he will have the deep gratitude of his countrymen."[48]

For Earl Warren, that gratitude was payment enough for a remarkably resilient performance on the bench. But for his countrymen, one question remained: In the end, would that gratitude be enough?

11

TRAGEDY IN DALLAS

Margaret Bryan heard it from a coworker in the Supreme Court cafeteria, shook her head, and walked away. The source had a reputation as "a terrible kidder," she recalled later. "I thought it was in bad taste."[1]

But when she realized the story was true, she raced up the stairs leading to the chief justice's offices and told Margaret McHugh the news. After several moments of silence, McHugh typed a brief note to the chief: "The President was shot while riding in a motorcade in Dallas. It is not known how badly he is injured."[2]

Alvin Wright, the robe room attendant who stood watch outside the massive oak doors of the conference room, knocked softly. Junior Justice Arthur Goldberg answered, and Wright handed him the note. Goldberg passed it on to Warren, who read it, turned suddenly ashen, and—tears staining his eyes—adjourned the conference. The justices shuffled off to their chambers, and several law clerks filed into Bill Brennan's office with its large-screen television set. They stared at the screen, watching, waiting. "It was a bizarre, and ultimately sad scene," Warren law clerk Frank Beytagh recalled. "There were people there who knew Jack Kennedy quite well, like Byron White and Arthur Goldberg."[3]

Warren retreated to his chamber to listen alone to the radio bulletins. Texas governor John Connally had been gravely wounded in the incident. Both he and the president were at Parkland Hospital, Dallas's premier emergency facility. A half hour later came the news: The president had died in the emergency room shortly after 1:00 p.m.

Stunned and tottering on the edge of denial, the chief opened the door from his office. With tear-stained eyes, he addressed the small staff assembled in the reception area. It all seemed so surreal. The entire court had seen JFK in the White House only thirty-six hours earlier, when he had held a reception for the brethren. The members and their wives had been invited to join the president and Mrs. Kennedy for refreshments in their private living quarters on the second floor while other guests mingled below.

Warren recalled Kennedy telling them he was scheduled to leave for Dallas the following morning, at which someone admonished him to be careful "down there with those wild Texans." Now, just that suddenly, that energetic young man was gone, his beacon of promise snuffed out by an assassin's bullet.

"The days and nights following were more like a nightmare than anything I had ever lived through," the chief justice wrote in reflection. Warren had viewed Jack Kennedy as more than the president. "It was like losing one of my own sons," he recalled later. "You know, he was just a little older than my oldest boy."[4]

A cloud hung over Earl Warren that afternoon, according to McHugh. "He was very, very upset."[5] The speedy apprehension of a suspect by Dallas police offered little consolation. The deed had been done. The unthinkable had happened. There was no turning back the hands of time.

One after another, people in the capital began filtering out of their offices, some to connect with friends to commiserate at a local bar, others to drive slowly, somberly home to seek the comfort of loved ones. Warren's chauffeur, in suburban Maryland with Nina, called to report that he was stuck in traffic.

Warren asked Beytagh if he would stay late that Friday. The court received word that Vice President Lyndon Johnson, while in Texas, had taken the oath as the thirty-sixth president of the United States, and that he and Mrs. Johnson were returning to Washington on the presidential plane with Mrs. Kennedy and the body of the late president. The plane arrived at Andrews Air Force Base around six o'clock. The public was not to be admitted to the base, but the justices were among those who were asked to be present. The chief asked Beytagh to drive him.

When the president's plane landed, Jacqueline Kennedy met Warren. She was still shrouded in her pink suit stained with her husband's blood. Tears slipped once more down the chief's face. The previous Wednesday night, the first lady had been his dinner partner, and he had exchanged pleasantries with her, so alive in a glittering formal hostess gown. Fewer than forty-eight hours later, he stood with a dozen others, watching as her husband's casket was lowered from the plane and loaded into a hearse.

The next few hours were a blur of shock and confusion. Warren recalled:

> The only thing that broke the gruesome television reports during the day was a visit Nina and I made, by invitation, to the White House Saturday morning with the other Justices and their wives to view the casket in the East Room. I then returned to the Court, and spent most of the day waiting for some information about what was to happen in the next few days. The entire governmental plant was closed. It was as though the world had stopped moving.
>
> About nine o'clock Saturday evening I was startled from my numbness by a call from the White House.[6]

It was Jacqueline Kennedy, asking if Warren would give a short talk in the rotunda of the Capitol the following day as her husband lay in state. He recalled being nearly speechless at hearing her voice. Naturally, he agreed. It turned out to be one of the most challenging things he'd ever done.

> After our brief conversation, I undertook to compose something, but it was simply impossible for me to put thoughts on paper. Accordingly, I went to bed around midnight, postponing until morning the writing of the statement I must have for the ceremony at one o'clock the next afternoon.
>
> It was again difficult to write in the morning, but there could be no further delay. I was still struggling with the words at 11:20 a.m. when my daughter Dorothy came running into my study and said, "Daddy, they just killed Oswald." A little annoyed, I said, "Oh, Dorothy, don't pay any attention to all those wild rumors or they will drive you to distraction." She replied, "But, Daddy, I saw them do it." I rushed into her room in time to see a replay of Jack Ruby shooting President Kennedy's assassin, Lee Harvey Oswald, on her television set.[7]

The news set Warren back even further, but he somehow managed to return to his desk and the task at hand, and when he'd finished writing, he enlisted the services of Nina to type up his words for him. Afterward, they hurried from midtown to the Capitol. Despite heavy traffic, they arrived on time for the simple but highly emotional ceremony. The three speakers included John W. McCormack, speaker of the House of Representatives; Senator Mike Mansfield, majority leader of the Senate; and Warren. The talks were all short.

Warren delivered his eulogy standing in front of the coffin that rested on the Lincoln catafalque in the Capitol rotunda. With each word, he could feel the emptiness struggling to engulf him, empathizing with the pain of the nation—not to mention the rest of the world—still rocked by the news. The president of the United States was gone. John Fitzgerald Kennedy, "a great and good President," was dead, snatched "from our midst by the bullet of an assassin." He wrote:

> What moved some misguided wretch to do this horrible deed may never be known to us, but we do know that such acts are commonly stimulated by forces of hatred and malevolence, such as today are eating their way into the bloodstream of American life.
>   What a price we pay for this fanaticism!

Without explicitly saying so, Warren appeared to be blaming the radical right and Texas's ultraconservative oil millionaires. He had known their allies in California, the William Kecks and the Tom Werdels and dozens more like them, all bitter men who preached a form of politics based on fear and hatred.

Warren could only close his eulogy to a fallen leader with a plea to

> abjure the hatred that consumes people, the false accusations that divide us, and the bitterness that begets violence.
>   Is it too much to hope that the martyrdom of our beloved President might even soften the hearts of those who would themselves recoil from assassination, but who do not shrink from spreading the venom which kindles thoughts of it in others?[8]

The accusation implied in the eulogy was a measure of his frustration and the haste with which he finally scribbled out his words. While many others predictably leaped to similar conclusions in those first days after the assassination, it was perhaps most surprising of all to find Warren pointing the finger of guilt.

Years later, after his father had passed from this life, son Earl Jr. said that, throughout those days, Warren alternated between sadness and fury: "He told me, at the height of his anger, 'I don't know who or what caused this or did the deed, but I sure know where the blame is.'"[9]

The day after the brutal slaying, a heavy-hearted Earl Warren walked behind the caisson that carried the body of the slain president first to the funeral service and then to the burial at Arlington National Cemetery. He returned to the court on Tuesday a different man, Margaret McHugh remembered: "He just wasn't like himself."[10]

On a dreary, rainy Friday, November 29, after the justices' weekly conference, Warren took a telephone call from Solicitor General Archibald

Cox and Acting Attorney General Nicholas Katzenbach. Warren recalled in his *Memoirs*:

> The public was becoming restive because the alleged assassin was dead, and the killing of him had been witnessed by more than a hundred million people over television. Things were moving to a crescendo when on Friday, November 29, there was a request to my office for a conference as soon as possible with the Deputy Attorney General, Nicholas Katzenbach, and Solicitor General Archibald Cox. I agreed to see them immediately, and they arrived . . . very shortly thereafter.[11]

Behind closed doors, the two explained that President Lyndon Johnson had sent them. "They told me that because of the rumors and worldwide excitement about the assassination, the President wanted to appoint a commission to investigate and report on the entire matter. The President wanted me to serve as chairman of the commission."[12]

In the conversation, Warren couldn't recall whether Cox or Katzenbach indicated that the Kennedy family had approved his nomination.

The newly sworn-in president had been contemplating such a commission since the previous Sunday. In the proceeding days, the US Information Agency had assembled a wide range of overseas reports expressing doubt regarding Oswald's guilt and hinting at a larger conspiracy. At the same time, the Communist press was "making a determined effort to attribute the assassination of President Kennedy to a rightist conspiracy, and the killing of Lee Oswald by Jack Ruby has given them new ammunition." Domestically, Johnson confronted a differing interpretation, an aide explained. It was "far more incredible for the American people to believe that one nut killed the president of the United States than if this was some plot masterminded in the Kremlin."[13]

By Friday morning, Johnson had reached a decision. He dispatched Cox and Katzenbach, both men close to the Kennedys and known to the chief justice. They were instructed not to take no for an answer. But their fortitude couldn't match that of the chief, who explained that the brethren had often discussed extrajudicial activities in the past, condemning them as being either politically motivated or perilously close.

As an example, in December 1941, Associate Justice Owen Roberts had agreed to investigate the Pearl Harbor attack, but his report to President Roosevelt led only to further investigations. Afterward, the justice admitted that his service had been a mistake.

Following World War II, Robert Jackson had accepted the assignment as a prosecutor at the Nuremberg war crimes trial. That, too, had ended in a whirlwind of public controversy about a justice's involvement in extrajudicial activity and stinging condemnation from the brethren.

In earlier discussions of a proposed constitutional amendment on presidential disability, Warren had publicly stated what he privately believed: The chief justice should not be one of the investigators to determine whether a sitting president was incapacitated and unable to fulfill his duties.

Following Warren's explanation to Katzenbach and Cox, the chief recalled, "I thought that settled it."[14]

When the two returned to Washington and informed Johnson of Warren's response, the president shook his head. Ninety minutes later, the president himself was on the telephone. He asked the chief justice to come to the White House.

The two men met privately in the Oval Office at 4:30 that afternoon for twenty minutes. The president personally asked Warren to serve as chairman. Johnson explained, "I told him that I had to have someone of his stature to head this commission."[15]

Sensing Warren's determination, the president went on to say that the problem was far more significant than anyone imagined. The FBI had obtained evidence of a Cuban who claimed to have offered Oswald $6,500 on behalf of Cuban premier Fidel Castro to kill JFK.

As Warren recounted the conversation, "The President told me that he felt that the assassination was such a torrid event that it could lead us into war, and that if it did it would be with another world power." As many as sixty million people would die in a nuclear war. "We don't know what this thing will bring forth."

Warren remained unconvinced. The brethren agreed that taking presidential assignments blurred the lines between the executive and the judicial branch. Besides, the justices had more than enough work to do without taking on extracurricular assignments.

But Johnson, who had served for years as US Senate strong man, was not to be denied. Cunning and manipulative, he resorted to the guilt-inducing tactic he called "jawboning," turning on Warren all the persuasive powers and authority of his office: "You're a man who occupies one of the most important positions in this country and this country has been good to you. And it's recognized you, and I know it hasn't made any mistake. I know that the merit that the country feels you have is justified."

Once launched, Johnson's ship soared: "I remember somewhere seeing a picture of you in an Army uniform when this country was under—involved in war, where you went out and offered your life to save your country. And now your services are more necessary at this moment than they were then to save this country."

Johnson's jawboning was an irresistible force. He had lined up the six other members of the committee, he said: senators Richard Russell and John Sherman Cooper; congressmen Hale Boggs and Gerald Ford; banker and frequent presidential counselor John McCloy; and former Central Intelligence Agency director Allen Dulles. All had agreed to serve on condition that Warren chair the commission, the president lied.

"And I'm not going to take no for an answer. And you're not going to tell me that if the president of the United States says to you that you must do this for your country so that we can resolve once and for all without any peradventure of a doubt what happened here, that you're going to say no, are you?"[16]

Under the pummeling, Warren gave way. As the president continued, embellishing freely as he went, tears welled up in Warren's eyes.

"Well, Mr. President, if, in your opinion, it is that bad, surely my personal views don't, shouldn't count. If you wish me to do it, I will do it."[17]

As a disconsolate chief justice returned to the Supreme Court that evening, law clerk Frank Beytagh recalled, "It took a lot to shake him, but he was pretty shaken that evening."

As Beytagh recalled the chief's explanation, he confessed, "I just don't want to do this thing."

Johnson's flattery had not seduced Warren. "I was told I am the only person who could do this, and I've lived long enough to know that's probably not true."

Instead, the chief's own sense of patriotic responsibility had led him to a change of heart. "I don't think it's the right thing to do, but I don't feel I had the right to tell the President, 'No.'"[18]

The president, in turn, had given his own concessions: Warren would remain on the Supreme Court and handle both court and commission duties simultaneously, and he would receive full cooperation from other government agencies along with whatever funding he needed to produce his report.

Johnson wanted a quick investigation by the commission, one based on the FBI report that Director J. Edgar Hoover had promised to deliver to the White House no later than the first of the week. Not only were there international implications to consider, but also rumors needed to be squelched—rumors that the new president had been involved in the assassination in some way.

That overriding concern helped to shape the commission. Five of its members were registered Republicans and only two were Democrats. That,

Johnson rationalized, would quell any rumors of political influence in the compiling of the report.

Johnson had chosen each of the commissioners for a specific reason— sometimes more than one—as he explained in a series of telephone calls he made on November 29 while lining up the panel.

Warren as chief justice lent the prestige of his office to the commission. Even Georgia senator Richard Russell, who disliked Warren, acknowledged, "I don't have much confidence in him though I realize he's a much greater man in the United States than almost anyone."

Russell had stubbornly refused to serve with Warren. "I just don't like that man," he insisted. (Warren was aware of Russell's harsh feelings, and attributed them to the court's racial decisions, he told a commission staff member.)

The Democratic senator—once Lyndon Johnson's mentor in the Senate—wavered when the president appealed to his patriotism. "You can serve with anybody for the good of America," Johnson insisted. "Now, by God, I want a man on that Commission and I've got one."[19] Russell reluctantly accepted.

John Sherman Cooper, the liberal Republican who had defended Warren and the court from William Jenner's attacks in 1957, was quick to sign on. Once ambassador to India, Cooper was sensitive to foreign policy implications, an important consideration when ambassadors at 125 overseas stations were anxious to know if a new president meant a new foreign policy.

Johnson selected two members from the House of Representatives, Hale Boggs and Gerald Ford. Boggs was the first in Congress to propose an investigation; Johnson felt it made sense to include him on the commission. Ford, eyeing leadership of the GOP in the lower house, was on good terms with J. Edgar Hoover and could help keep the FBI's shoulder to the wheel while protecting the bureau's reputation.

The two "civilians" Johnson named had been recommended by Kennedy's brother—Allen Dulles and John McCloy. Dulles had served as director of the Central Intelligence Agency for eight years under Eisenhower, thus assuring CIA cooperation. John McCloy had been the US military governor and high commissioner for Germany from 1949 until 1952 and had previously served as president of the World Bank (1947–1949) and as assistant secretary of war (1941–1945).

Johnson, still apprehensive about a potential plot to overthrow the government, ordered the Secret Service to extend its protection to numerous government officials, including the chief justice. Amused at such a fuss, Nina and Earl discounted it all as unnecessary, pointing out the armed agents with walkie-talkies as they tromped the Sheraton Park grounds at night. Somewhere between annoyed and amused by the security force, the chief and his clerks took to ducking into restaurants and abruptly leaving by the back door to throw off the agents.

As Warren prepared to step into his new position, he realized the sense of urgency that the president felt regarding the commission. LBJ made the appointments by Executive Order No. 11130 that very evening, November 29. According to Warren, "the press release announcing it was heard over the radio by Mrs. McHugh shortly after she arrived home from the office. Nina heard it before I arrived home for dinner."[20] It read:

> Office of the White House Press Secretary
> THE WHITE HOUSE
>
> The President today announced that he is appointing a Special Commission to study and report upon all facts and circumstances relating to the assassination of the late President, John F. Kennedy, and the subsequent violent death of the man charged with the assassination.
>
> The President stated that the Majority and Minority Leadership of the Senate and the House of Representatives have been consulted with respect to the proposed Special Commission.
>
> [The names of members of the Special Commission followed.] The President stated that the Special Commission is to be instructed to evaluate all available information concerning the subject of the inquiry. The Federal Bureau of Investigation, pursuant to an earlier directive of the President, is making complete investigation of the facts. An inquiry is also scheduled by a Texas Court of Inquiry convened by the Attorney General of Texas under Texas law.
>
> The Special Commission will have before it all evidence uncovered by the Federal Bureau of Investigation and all information available to any agency of the Federal Government. The Attorney General of Texas has also offered his cooperation. All Federal agencies and offices are being directed to furnish services and cooperation to the Special Commission. The Commission will also be empowered to conduct any further investigation that it deems desirable. The President is instructing the Special Commission to satisfy itself that the truth is known as far as it can be discovered, and to report its findings and conclusions to him, to the American people, and to the world.[21]

It was a critical move that the president made quickly in light of a Gallup poll at the time showing that more than half the American people believed that more than one person was involved in the assassination. The percentage overseas was most likely higher.

So the next task fell to Warren, who realized he had to build a reliable, hardworking staff. He chose as director Warren Olney, which wasn't surprising considering their history together in California but did create some blowback. As assistant attorney general in charge of the criminal division, Olney had butted heads several times with FBI director J. Edgar Hoover, whom he held in low esteem. On a more positive note, Olney was "the only guy who had balls enough to stand up to Hoover," as one FBI agent reportedly said.[22]

Olney had also helped push through Congress the Civil Rights Act of 1957, which angered some southern Democrats, including commission member Richard Russell.

In turn, Russell and Hoover, through Gerald Ford, lobbied against Olney's appointment, with Ford complaining that Warren was "attempting to establish a 'one-man commission' by appointing a chief counsel, Warren Olney, that [*sic*] was his own protégé."[23]

Slapped with infighting from the start, Warren asked for advice regarding a suitable replacement, and John McCloy said he had another man in mind.

Warren had known J. Lee Rankin as a former assistant attorney general in the Eisenhower administration. Later, he was solicitor general from 1956 to 1961. The chief particularly respected Rankin's principled stand against the cronyism and influence-peddling in the Dixon-Yates case.

Now practicing law in New York City, Rankin agreed to take on the critical role of the commission's general counsel. He proposed the organization of the investigative team, assigning a senior and junior counsel to each of five areas: gathering the basic facts of the assassination, identifying the assassin, researching Oswald's background, uncovering any potential conspiracies, and detailing the circumstances surrounding Oswald's death. (A sixth area addressing the necessity of providing the president with increased protection would be added later.) Relying on the FBI investigation, Rankin estimated they would wrap up their duties in three or four months.

So Rankin, after hearing recommendations from friends and associates, selected the staff. Of the eleven practicing attorneys he chose, only two actually knew the chief justice: Joseph Ball, senior counsel charged with determining the identity of the assassin; and Samuel Stern, the former law clerk who volunteered his services shortly after the commission was named. Stern was given responsibility for the subject of presidential protection.

A prominent trial lawyer in California, Joe Ball had known Warren as governor for a short period, mostly through their membership in the American College of Trial Lawyers. Their relationship expanded during

Warren's first years on the court. Ball's outspoken defense of "liberal" Warren Court decisions led to social meetings when the chief justice visited California. In 1960, the chief asked Ball to serve on a committee revising the federal rules of criminal procedure. Whenever Ball came to Washington, the two got together for a Washington Senators' baseball game. Warren even recommended that Ball handle the divorce of his daughter Dorothy.

For the ten months of the commission's life, Ball played a prominent role on the staff. "He was my father's right arm on that commission," Earl Jr. said. "Nothing would have come of that commission without Joe Ball."[24]

Ball's responsibilities broadened when the senior counsel charged with investigating the basic facts of the assassination began attending meetings only sporadically. Ball and his junior counsel, David Belin, joined forces with Arlen Specter to pick up the slack.

Warren as chairman of the commission met with the assembled staff for the first time early in January. His charge to them was straightforward: "Truth is our only goal."[25]

Because they would be handling classified documents, each of the men appointed had to receive security clearance by the FBI. A bureau report that one of Rankin's assistants, Norman Redlich, had once signed an ad opposing the House Un-American Activities Committee prompted Ford to demand that Redlich be fired. Warren dismissed the accusations as "nonsense," Ball said. "What do you think those files show on me?" Warren cracked.[26]

Ford, though, wasn't amused and persisted in his demand. Warren finally countered with, "Then we will have a public trial and give Redlich the same opportunity as anyone else to be heard in his own defense."[27] Ford's motion to hold a hearing died for lack of a second.

The commission waived the necessary clearances for Redlich and Ball, who had similarly opposed the committee, Ball said later, although the FBI apparently had no record of his stand.

So, beginning in January and ending in October 1964, Warren arrived each day at the commission's second-floor offices in the new Veterans of Foreign Wars building, kitty-corner from the Supreme Court, promptly at 8:00 a.m. He left shortly before 10:00 a.m. to attend the opening of the court to hear that day's arguments. He returned around 3:00 p.m. to work once more on the assassination investigation.

At the commission offices, the chief justice spent much of the time closeted with Rankin or Ball. Together they reviewed the staff work, Warren approving their accomplishments and occasionally suggesting follow-up investigations.

The chief devoted himself to the commission. Despite his responsibilities on the court and downplaying a bronchial infection through the winter that Sam Stern described as "a major strain on his health," Warren missed only one commission hearing plus part of a second.

The days were not easy on Warren, as Stern recalled: "The assassination was a terrible loss to him personally. He was terribly solicitous to Mrs. Kennedy and the family. It was a constant emotional drain on him."[28]

Initially, the commission had intended to rely on the FBI's report for the bulk of its investigation. The agency had assembled a narrative of the assassination reconstructed from hundreds of interviews. But Warren found the report to be a summary "in more or less skeleton form" of the evidence against Oswald.[29]

At Warren's urging, the commission adopted a resolution on December 16 asking all government agencies to produce the raw material on which the summary report was based. Concerned with what the commission might find—the FBI had its own secrets to protect, after all—agency director J. Edgar Hoover scrambled for a way out. He failed to find it.

Within the first week, staff counsel had turned up several problems with the supporting field investigations, justifying Hoover's worst fears.

The first was a missing page from Oswald's notebook. "We checked back and, sure enough, it was ripped out by FBI Special Agent James Hosty because it had Hosty's name and phone number [on it]," commission counsel W. David Slawson stated. "Hosty was afraid of his future career in the FBI if it came out that he had such close contact with Oswald and he [Hosty] had not warned the FBI that Oswald was such a dangerous person."[30]

The more than 25,000 pages of FBI reports proved frustrating to the commission staff in other instances, too. Frequently, questions that should have been asked were not, "because the agents didn't have any flexibility," Slawson assumed.[31] David Belin, working with Joe Ball on the identity of the assassin, found "a lot of inaccuracies, a lot of inconsistencies" in the twenty-three hundred FBI documents examined.

By the end of January, Ball said, he and Belin had concluded that the "FBI reports were insufficient to our minds. They were contradictory, and things that should have been explained in them weren't."

Faced with that, Ball recommended first to Warren and then to the commission that they investigate again the identity of the assassin. "All we got back was, 'Go ahead.'"[32]

Ball, Belin, and Specter set out to perform their own investigation of the case against Oswald, relying upon the FBI reports only marginally.

Once he realized his bureau's report was coming under fire from the commission, Hoover slipped into a state of sullen noncooperation. He refused to permit informal access to FBI agents and laboratory technicians. If staff members wanted to speak with them, Hoover insisted, the commission had to call them to appear. The commission called them to appear.

Far more critical, Hoover had withheld from the commission an internal FBI document of December 10, 1963, summarizing the censure of seventeen agents on the heels of the assassination. The seventeen men—field agents and supervisors in Dallas, New York, New Orleans, and Washington, DC—had failed to put Oswald on a security watch list. Thus, the Secret Service was not informed of Oswald's presence in Dallas on the day of the Kennedy motorcade.

Other members of the commission staff had uncovered problems as well. The Central Intelligence Agency was tight-lipped, failing to reveal that it had launched repeated efforts to assassinate Fidel Castro. As long as the commission did not ask—and the CIA's involvement in such intrigues was not yet public knowledge—CIA representatives did not tell.

The commission itself was embarrassed by a series of leaks. The Dallas Police Department was a sieve; ranking officers often talked off the record with pet local reporters. At least one member sold a portion of Oswald's "diary" for publication.

Not even Hoover was above such shenanigans. He slipped copies of the FBI's initial narrative report to friendly journalists before hinting that Warren was responsible for the leak. Finally, in late spring, *Life* magazine published an illustrated "inside account" of the assassination by Congressman Ford. The unauthorized story—for which Ford reputedly received $1 million—"was a real breach of confidentiality clearly done for personal profit and political motive," one staff member rightly concluded.[33]

Despite the distractions, Warren pressed on. But for whatever reason, attendance by commission members was spotty. Warren, as presiding officer, and McCloy were there for nearly every session. Dulles came almost as often, although, at age seventy, he grumbled that he had only two good hours a day. Senator Cooper and Congressmen Boggs and Ford were constantly leaving hearings to answer quorum calls on the Hill. Russell failed to attend but sent a stand-in at Warren's suggestion.

From early in the investigation, the chief decided "a surface case was established" against Oswald. The former marine worked at the book depository. He had disappeared after the shooting, the only depository employee to do so. An Italian rifle and spent cartridges were found on the sixth floor where Oswald worked.

These circumstances, followed by his quick exit from the building—getting on one bus and transferring to another, and then hailing a cab—were more than suspicious behavior. After "killing [Dallas policeman J. D.] Tippit, and running into a theater where he tried to shoot the policemen who came to get him, these made a case."[34]

Within days, law enforcement officers linked the Mannlicher-Carcano rifle to a mail-order house and then to Oswald through handwriting analysis. FBI ballistics tests linked the gun and spent cartridges to the bullet and lead fragments found in the president's body and on the stretcher of Governor Connally. With that, former prosecutor Earl Warren had his case.

"The facts of the assassination itself are simple, so simple that many people believe it must be more complicated and conspiratorial to be true," Warren later wrote in his *Memoirs*.

Warren personally had no doubts. "If I were still a district attorney and the Oswald case came into my jurisdiction, given the same amount of evidence I could have gotten a conviction in two days and never heard about the case again."[35]

Knowing how the majority of Americans were convinced of a conspiracy to assassinate the president, though, Warren remained grounded in reality. "One person [plus] the truth is a majority," he kept reminding his staff.[36]

Warren never doubted that Lee Harvey Oswald, the disenfranchised outsider, was the lone assassin. While others argued that a second rifleman was posted in Dealey Plaza, the chief justice said firmly, "No one could have fired from the knoll or the overpass without having been seen."[37]

He put no faith "in a conspiracy of any kind," Warren told the commission's historian. "The only thing that gave me any pause about a conspiracy theory was that Oswald had been a defector to Russia at one time."[38]

Still, a conspiracy was possible, he conceded. But Warren the former prosecutor relied on hard evidence, not supposition, in building a case.

"I don't doubt there were hundreds of people in the South who talked about killing President Kennedy," he told newspaper columnist Drew Pearson in the summer of 1967. "But the question is—were they in on the assassination in Dallas? We know what Oswald did, and I am quite satisfied that there is no evidence that anyone else did."[39]

But could a foreign power have put Oswald up to it? Warren didn't summarily dismiss the possibility. "I am quite prepared to believe that Castro wanted to kill Kennedy, and may have sent some teams here to do it. But there is no evidence that he did," Warren admitted.[40]

For the next ten months, Warren took a direct hand in the inquiry out of exasperation with the pace of the investigation, according to Earl Jr. A self-imposed deadline of July 1 was fast approaching; only Ball, Belin, and Specter had their draft reports completed.

So as not to miss a single session of the court in the packed closing days of the term, Warren compressed what Rankin estimated would be a week's worth of work in Dallas into a single day.

In the serene stillness of Sunday morning, June 7, 1964, Warren walked Dealey Plaza, talked to police officers and witnesses who had been in the Texas School Book Depository building, and retraced Oswald's footsteps from his boardinghouse to his sixth-floor "crow's nest." From there, Warren peered down through the trees to Elm Street below, just as Oswald would have done. He squinted through the four-power telescope on the same 6.5-mm Mannlicher-Carcano rifle Oswald had used. Meanwhile, staff lawyer Arlen Specter detailed his theory of the shooting.

As Specter reconstructed the event, Oswald's first shot struck the president in the back of the neck. It hit no bone but sliced through the trachea and exited the front, nicking the tie he was wearing.

Barely slowed, the bullet struck Governor Connally, who had been sitting on a jump seat in front of Kennedy. The shell entered to the left of his right armpit, sliced through a rib, and spiraled out, leaving a four-inch gash in Connally's chest below the right nipple. From there it passed through his wrist and came to rest in his left thigh.

Although such a proposition was scorned as far-fetched by critics once the report went public, the "single bullet" theory was supported by exhaustive laboratory tests.

Then came a second shot that proved fatal, striking the president in the back of the skull, spraying a mist of blood, bone fragments, and brain tissue over the limousine's interior.

A third shot missed the automobile entirely, struck a curb, and sent a chip of concrete flying off to nick a bystander's cheek. From first shot to last, slightly fewer than eight seconds had passed.

Although the commission was unable to determine conclusively which of the three shots had missed its mark, it made no difference. Warren personally believed in the sequence he detailed, although Connally maintained he heard the first shot, turned, and was wounded by the second, making the third shot the fatal one. However, in a statement released in Austin, Texas, on November 23, 1966, Connally stressed that, regardless of the sequence, he agreed wholeheartedly with the Warren Commission's findings that Oswald had acted alone.

When Specter had finished recounting the event, Warren turned from the window of the building. The distance from the rifle's muzzle to the president's limousine was approximately 175 to 270 feet. Divided by four (the magnification power of the telescopic gunsight), the range was effectively less than 70 feet—a simple shot for a practiced Marine Corps marksman, as even occasional sportsman/hunter Warren realized.

That completed, Warren, Ford, Rankin, and Specter arranged for an interview with Jack Ruby, convicted of Oswald's murder, in the basement of the Dallas city jail. Ruby had agreed to talk to Warren on the condition that he be given a lie-detector test. The exam, he felt, would prove he was not involved in a conspiracy. Even though Warren had little faith in the reliability of the polygraph machine, which he termed "Big Brother Paraphernalia," he reluctantly agreed.

The jailhouse meeting with Ruby was ethereal at best. Ruby at one point demanded that someone Jewish be in the room with him. According to Earl Jr., his father "felt that he and Ruby got along well together, that Ruby talked to him honestly as best he could under his mental condition. But he felt that Ruby's mental condition was very fragile."

Warren came away convinced that Ruby had not known Oswald before shooting him, that Ruby had acted alone, and that his decision to kill Oswald was made on the spur of the moment.

"But the fellow was clearly delusional when I talked to him," the chief justice commented. "He took me aside and he said, 'Hear those voices? Hear those voices?' He thought they were Jewish children and Jewish women who were being put to death in the building there."[41]

That afternoon, the men from the commission retraced Oswald's attempted escape route from the book depository to the Texas Theater on West Jefferson Boulevard, where he was cornered and apprehended. By nightfall, the four men were on their way home, Warren still reading witnesses' depositions.

In Washington, Warren took the initiative in questioning both widows, Jacqueline Kennedy and Marina Oswald. The chief justice and Rankin took Mrs. Kennedy's statement privately on Thursday, June 4, at her Georgetown home. Seeking to protect her from any renewed horror, Warren convinced his fellow commissioners to accept her statement without further questioning.

When "little Mrs. Kennedy" later asked Warren for the president's bloody clothing, he declined. He suspected she wanted to destroy it, and "we couldn't be in the position of oppressing or destroying any evidence."[42]

Members of the staff were unhappy that Mrs. Kennedy did not testify before the entire commission. Many were even more unhappy when the chief justice acceded to Attorney General Robert Kennedy's wishes to keep secret the X-rays and photographs of the autopsy conducted at Bethesda Naval Hospital. David Belin contemplated resigning in protest. If Officer Tippet's widow could not withhold evidence from the commission, why could the Kennedy family?

Warren explained that he feared souvenir hunters would turn the assassination into a ghoulish yard sale. Scavengers had offered $10,000 for the Mannlicher-Carcano and had asked to buy Oswald's clothes and the pistol with which he killed Tippit. Others had inquired about the president's bloody shirt.

The chief justice alone reviewed the autopsy photographs taken at Bethesda, color enlargements "so horrible that I could not sleep well for nights."[43] He did not want these exhibited in some touring sideshow devoted to the assassination.

He took responsibility for the decision—affirmed by the commission—not to make any of the items part of the public record. Instead, the commission relied on the testimony and sketches of the pathologists who performed the autopsy. "The public was given the best evidence available—the personal testimony of the doctors who performed the autopsy," Warren insisted.

The fifty-two autopsy photographs, fourteen X-rays, and the president's bloodstained clothes were turned over to the Department of Justice for permanent archiving; they would not be shown to anyone without the consent of the Kennedy family. "I am certain it was the proper thing to do," Warren wrote in his *Memoirs*.[44] That would be his final word.

Marina Oswald also received special consideration from the chief. The staff attorneys who had investigated Oswald's life and his disillusioned visit to the Soviet Union wanted to interview her more closely about several inconsistencies in her statements to the FBI. Warren assigned that task to Rankin, who lacked the detailed knowledge the others had. "So Marina Oswald was not questioned as thoroughly as she should have been," David Belin insisted. "In part, this was because Earl Warren was a compassionate person and I believe somewhat naive when it came to Marina Oswald."[45]

Marina, a newly widowed spitfire with two young children, impressed Warren. He told Drew Pearson off the record that he was convinced she was telling the truth.

The evening after she testified before the commission, Warren met briefly with reporters. In response to a question, he explained that all of the evidence gathered would be turned over to the National Archives. And then he made one of his rare verbal slips. Some of the evidence, he said, "might not be published in your lifetime."

Reporters' ears pricked and they jumped to the bait. Warren, regretting his words immediately, sought to explain: "I am not referring to anything especially, but there may be some things that would involve security. These would be preserved but not made public."[46]

He was referring to classified files from the FBI, the CIA, and the Department of State, but the seemingly bold confession cast doubts upon the commission's months of hard work. "I have never cussed myself so much for saying anything as I did that evening," Warren confessed to Drew Pearson. "I couldn't correct it. A denial never catches up."[47]

The commissioners and the staff understood the possibility that Oswald might be the point man in an international conspiracy. On June 24, CIA director Richard Helms informed Warren that the agency had custody of a defector who claimed to have knowledge of Oswald's activities in Russia. Former KGB lieutenant colonel Yuri Nosenko insisted that Oswald had acted without Soviet knowledge or participation.

Nosenko, Helms continued, was not a reliable source. To base any part of the commission's report on him was to risk the credibility of the entire document. Warren accepted Helms's explanation, and the commission agreed. Rankin made the final decision not to interrogate Nosenko on the grounds that the commission staff lacked someone with the expertise to do what a cadre of CIA interrogators could not.

Ironically, a foreign government conspiring to kill a national leader was not at all far-fetched. The CIA had hatched just such a plan, targeting Cuba's Fidel Castro under the encouragement of Attorney General Robert Kennedy. One of the schemes employed involved the enlistment of organized crime figures to assassinate the premier.

While the CIA volunteered nothing of this, Warren surreptitiously got wind of the plot. Near the end of the investigation, he wrote a letter to Robert F. Kennedy asking if he had "any additional information relating to the assassination" of the president. The carefully drafted letter asked specifically about information bearing on a conspiracy, foreign or domestic.

Kennedy returned an equally carefully drafted reply: All information in possession of the Department of Justice had already been turned over to the commission. His response was careful to exclude any reference to participation by the CIA and FBI.

As the investigation dragged on, the commission's self-imposed deadlines came and went. In the last two weeks of August and into September, twenty men sat down to finish the report. They included two incoming law clerks and two of Warren's clerks from the 1963 term who stayed on for a week to help check footnotes. Rankin and two assistants edited the incoming drafts.

After nine months of work, Warren, "relentless as a taskmaster,"[48] was worn down, putting in fifteen- and sixteen-hour days. "It was taking ten pints of blood a day from him," Earl Jr. said. "It was tearing him up; he was so emotionally involved."[49]

With the end of their monumental task approaching, Warren was suddenly dealt a new blow: Gerald Ford and Richard Russell refused to approve the document.

Warren invoked his diplomatic skills. "It would have been disastrous if we hadn't been unanimous," he explained.[50]

"Ford wanted to go off on a tangent following a communist plot," Warren revealed to Drew Pearson.[51] Castro was behind the assassination, the congressman insisted. Ford also objected to the report's sharp rebuke of the FBI for failing to report Oswald's presence in Dallas to the Secret Service. Although Warren had tempered that language, enough blame remained in the report to leave Hoover "furious about it."[52]

At Warren's request, Hale Boggs negotiated with Richard Russell, whose personal animosity toward the chief justice prevented him from reaching a compromise. Like Ford, Russell bolted at the draft's conclusion that Oswald had acted alone. The Georgian threatened to write a minority report because, as he saw it, there were "far too many unresolved questions for him to accept that as an incontrovertible fact."[53]

For the sake of unanimity, Warren personally drafted alternative language leaving an opening for the possibility of an as-yet-undiscovered conspiracy: "The Commission has found no evidence that either Lee Harvey Oswald or Jack Ruby was part of any conspiracy, domestic or foreign, to assassinate President Kennedy."[54]

With these changes to accommodate Russell and Ford, the commission's report was unanimous. "It was remarkable that the Commissioners all agreed to anything," Warren marveled later, perhaps with some pride. "Politically we had as many opposites as the number of people would permit."[55] In essence, the commission reached three conclusions: First, Lee Harvey Oswald was a lone assassin who had fired three shots from the sixth floor of the Texas School Book Depository building in Dallas, Texas, killing the president of the United States and wounding the governor of Texas. Second, the commission found no evidence of a conspiracy to assassinate President Kennedy. Third, the commission found no evidence that Oswald had assistance in planning or carrying out the assassination.

Beyond those basic conclusions, the commission dealt a mildly worded rebuke to both the FBI and the Secret Service, who had failed to develop adequate criteria to identify persons who might pose a threat to the president. Though the FBI had "considerable information" about Oswald, the agency "took an unduly restrictive view of its role in preventive intelligence work prior to the assassination."[56]

The commission's conclusion, spearhead by the chief justice, was based upon more evidence than even the other members of the commission realized. Members of the Warren family claim that the chief justice had developed covert sources of information that included a tightly knit cadre of FBI agents who were concerned about the quality of the investigation and who wanted the truth to come out. Others of Warren's "super sleuths" included Edward Bennett Williams, an attorney who had represented Mafia figures in the past and allegedly maintained an open line of communication; and Warren Olney, who had accumulated extensive law enforcement contacts from his days as a deputy attorney general and shared them with the chief.

"As far as Warren was concerned," said grandson Jeffrey Warren, the family's acknowledged expert on the commission, "the FBI was Inspector Clouseau,"[57] a reference to a bumbling detective in the Peter Sellers film series *The Pink Panther*.

So, after ten grueling months of investigative work, the commission delivered to President Lyndon Johnson its 888-page report on September 24, 1964, barely ten days before the beginning of the Supreme Court's October term. The immediate press reaction to the report was favorable, based in large part on the unquestioned reputations of the commissioners themselves, as well as on the obvious thoroughness of their investigation.

The report spanned twenty-six supplemental volumes and included the commission's publication of the testimony, depositions, and statements of the 552 witnesses it had reviewed. These were supplemented with numerous photographs, sketches, maps, and illustrations.

The seventeen appendixes to the report went so far as to include an analysis of Oswald's budget for the eighteen months before the assassination. Another appendix took thirty pages to deal with rumors ranging from the source of the shots to the claim that the army burial party had practiced for the Kennedy funeral a week before the assassination occurred.

Regardless, according to biographer Ed Cray, writing in *Chief Justice*:

> The report was a best-seller. The Government Printing Office sold more than 140,000 copies of the one-volume report, and 1,500 copies of

the supporting twenty-six volumes. Together, sales produced a profit of $191,400. A mass-market paperback edition sold hundreds of thousands of additional copies.

Warren, said a former law clerk who discussed with the chief justice the commission's work, believed "they had done as good a job as they could have under the circumstances." Still, "he was frustrated by the pressure to wrap it up as fast as he could."[58]

In a private conversation a year later, Warren conceded that the report "was probably done too quickly," but he affirmed his belief in the evidence pointing to Oswald's guilt. "There was great pressure on us to show, first, that President Johnson was not involved, and, second, that the Russians were not involved. These aspects were posed to us as the most important issues. And I do think our report conclusively proved these points."[59]

It was a tired man who delivered the commission report to the White House and Lyndon Baines Johnson. In the final weeks of its existence, the commission had met daily for hours on end, reviewing successive drafts, with Warren overseeing each session.

"One can't say too much about the Chief's sacrifice," commission assistant counsel Howard P. Willens said. "The work was a drain on his physical well-being."[60]

Warren's youngest son, Robert, reached a harsher conclusion: "That commission did more to age him than anything I've ever seen."[61]

A man of indomitable spirit and endless energy, Warren himself was forced to acknowledge the strain. "This has been a tough thing, living with this thing for ten months—along with my other work. Certainly I'm glad it is over."[62]

But if Warren thought the commission was behind him, he was mistaken. The critics were only beginning to circle the wagons. The conspiracy advocates couldn't wait to strike: Oswald had worked on behalf of the Soviets or at least the Cubans or, less likely but nowhere out of the realm of possibility, the powerful anti-Kennedy Texas oil cartel. No whisper, no rumor, no coincidence was too outlandish to be woven into ever more elaborate scenarios.

Rampant speculation along with procedural errors by the commission—taking Mrs. Kennedy's testimony in private, for example—played into the conspiracy theorists' hands.

When Joe Ball called Warren from California to ask what the chief suggested he do in light of the growing skepticism, Warren advised, "Nothing. We'll let history answer."[63]

His position was simple: The report was going to stand or fall on what they'd written because they'd done an accurate job.

When David Belin asked the chief's advice about replying to critics, Warren again advised against it. Warren reaffirmed that view until his death. "I don't think there is much left to be desired from the report," he told an interviewer. "We reported every bit of evidence we took in the case. . . . We got everything we wanted. We achieved as much proof as could be achieved."[64]

Warren's philosophy paid off. The conspiracy theorists were finally sidetracked—at least until 1966, when two books by prominent New York publishing houses came out. Critical of the commission's findings, Edward J. Epstein's moderate-in-tone *Inquest* was based in part on sketchy interviews with five commissioners and twelve staff members. Written originally as a master's thesis at Cornell University, it faulted the commission's work on several levels.

Epstein claimed the commission was inherently a political agency, faced with the problem of trying to have an unbiased investigation sans political interference. What he termed a "part-time staff and commissioners" who were removed from the day-to-day work frustrated the investigation. Finally, he found fault with the evidence itself, particularly an FBI observer's account of the autopsy he believed negated the official report by doctors.

The second book, by former New York state assemblyman Mark Lane, was a disastrous attempt by the author to litigate the act after the fact. Acting as Lee Harvey Oswald's defense attorney and political apologist, Lane proved himself competent as neither. A commission gadfly and journalistic scavenger, he nonetheless promoted his *Rush to Judgment* indefatigably.

Eventually, Lane's critics found that he had distorted evidence, used material out of context, and charged without facts a high-level government conspiracy to frame his "client" for the assassination.

Despite their obvious shortcomings, the two books disturbed Warren, according to law clerk Kenneth Ziffren, less for their contents than for what the chief justice considered the "underhandedness" of the critics themselves.[65]

Wesley Liebeler, the junior counsel assigned to investigate Lee Harvey Oswald's background, had provided Epstein with copies of the commission's working papers and a chronological file. "These were of particular importance in understanding the mechanics of the Commission," Epstein acknowledged in his book.[66]

For the chief, this was "the ultimate act of disloyalty," said Ziffren.[67] At their last meeting, Warren had specifically reminded staff counsel that their relationship to the commission was similar to that of attorney and client.

He blamed Liebeler for Epstein's *Inquest* and excoriated Epstein for exaggerating both his access and his sources. (In his book, for instance, Epstein inflated brief conversations with staff members such as Joe Ball into full-blown "interviews.")

Regarding Mark Lane and his *Rush to Judgment*, Warren had nothing but contempt. He saw Lane as nothing more than a publicity hound playing fast and loose with the facts.

Under these and other withering attacks, the commission report, with no one to speak in its favor, fell under increased attack.

As presidential press secretary George Reedy noted, Lyndon Johnson hoped to use the report "to do something impossible. The public can't believe a lone assassin with a mail-order rifle was capable of killing the president of the United States, no matter how easy it is, in fact, to do and how easy was the shot for Oswald. . . . The sheer banality of it makes for disbelief."[68]

By 1967, according to a Gallup poll, six out of every ten Americans doubted Oswald was the lone gunman at Dealey Plaza on that fateful day. Seven of ten concluded that there were still critical unanswered questions about the assassination, according to a Harris poll.

Charges of a cover-up plagued Warren, who lashed out. "What possible set of circumstances could get Jerry Ford and me to conspire on anything?" he asked in exasperation.[69]

That the chief justice would be party to a cover-up amused and, in some cases, angered the men who had served on the commission staff. Counsel David Belin, who would eventually become the most vigorous defender of the commission's work and its findings, recalled Warren's charge to them: Truth was to be their only goal.

"I took him at his word," Belin said. "I think the other people who were the lawyers on the staff also took him at his word. And I don't know of any single lawyer on the staff who at any time tried to bend the truth for any preconceived notion."[70]

In the end, the rampant speculation of intrigues surrounding the assassination reached all the way to the White House, frustrating Warren: "I have read everything that has come to my notice in the press and I read some of the documents that have criticized the Commission very severely, but I have never found that they have discovered any evidence of any kind that we didn't discover and use in determining the case as we did."[71]

Until three months before his death, Warren insisted the commission had left nothing uncovered and no witness uncalled. "There were no loose ends."[72]

But neither was there a resolution.

As the aftermath of the postcommission reaction dragged on, Warren felt the personal physical and psychological strain. According to son Earl Jr.:

Well I think I'd have to say more the effect I observed rather than directly what he said, and it was pretty obvious it was a highly traumatic experience for him. I don't think in all the years that I've known my father I've ever seen him go through a period that I felt was draining on him as this. Of course at the time he was carrying basically three loads. He was ax carrying a tremendously heavy workload with the Court itself. On the decision end of it. They had many crucial decisions at that time.

Secondly, he had tremendous administrative chores with the court. He's always been a strong man in the administration of the court and I think will go down in history as being as great [an] achiever in that arena as he will with his decisions. And at the same time he was spending every conceivable moment outside working on this . . . on this investigation and the report, and he's the type of man who doesn't have to sleep eight hours at a time, and I'm sure he's never done so, and probably at least the last fifty years. He can sleep for a few moments and then wake up and work at a hundred percent efficiency and then perhaps an hour or two later doze off again for a few moments and then resume his work and this he did constantly, too much so I think, and the full story of what went on in the . . . course has never come out, and I suspect that it was not an easy chore from the standpoint of the personalities involved. I imagine it was exceptionally difficult even to get the parties to agree on what form the investigation would take, and it was very noticeable to see that this was taxing him extremely heavily and I know that he personally had to relive constantly that assassination, and with his tremendous regard for the dead President, I just think that in itself was more than a man should be asked to do.[73]

12

FACING DOWN *MIRANDA*

By the mid–1960s, the Supreme Court's failure to address the "confession" rights in the case of *Escobedo v. Illinois* opened a floodgate of new appeals by incarcerated prisoners. Most were based upon rights the court had previously touched upon but not fully defined: When should an arrestee be advised of his rights, and, if he didn't already have a lawyer, was the government responsible for providing one?

From 170 "confessions" cases, the court distilled twenty of the most representative. Of those, the brethren granted certiorari to four. The lead case was from Phoenix, Arizona: an appeal by twenty-three-year-old convicted felon Ernesto A. Miranda, who was serving two concurrent twenty-to-thirty-year prison terms.

Police had located a 1953 Packard parked in front of Miranda's home. The car had been stolen from a woman who had been kidnapped and raped eleven days earlier. Because Miranda fit the description offered by the victim, Officers Carroll Cooley and Wilfred Young arrested him.

From a police station lineup, the victim identified Miranda as her assailant. At his interrogation, Miranda protested his innocence. Two hours later, he confessed.

At no time was he advised of his right to remain silent or his right to an attorney. In Miranda's case, those proved to be critical points.

Miranda was an example of an all-too-common arrestee. His English was limited. He had attended school only as far as the eighth grade. He suffered his entire life from what a psychiatrist described as a sociopathic personality disorder as a result of violent sexual fantasies. His history included a prior arrest for rape, half a dozen arrests as a Peeping Tom, military courts-martial for peeping and for being absent without leave, a dishonorable discharge, and a bizarre marital relationship.

There had been no coercion in Interrogation Room Number 2 that day, his attorney conceded at the oral argument, but Miranda "was called upon to surrender a right that he didn't fully realize and appreciate that he had." In cases such as that, continued attorney John Flynn, the Constitution "certainly does protect the rich, the educated, and the strong—those rich enough to hire counsel, those who are educated enough to know what their rights are, and those who are strong enough to withstand police interrogation and assert those rights."[1]

By contrast, Ernesto Miranda was poor, uneducated, and unprotected at the time of his arrest. Also, according to Arizona Assistant Attorney General Gary Nelson, Miranda had only a limited mental capacity. If anyone needed his constitutional rights protected, it was Ernesto Miranda.

At the March 4, 1966, conference, the chief justice began the discussion of the confession cases by proposing a major reform in criminal procedure. From the very instant that police focused on a specific suspect, he said, law enforcement officials were obligated to issue a four-part warning: The suspect had a right to remain silent. Anything he said could be held against him. He had a right to an attorney. If he did not have an attorney, the court would appoint one.

Warren rejected arguments that such warnings would hamper police investigations. Most states already mandated that arrestees be brought "promptly" before a magistrate so that the suspects might be informed of their rights. Few states enforced those statutes, though.

Warren had sufficient experience in law enforcement to tell him there was ample evidence that warning suspects would neither free the guilty nor send crime rates soaring. He reminded the brethren that, as district attorney of Alameda County, he had ordered his deputies to warn suspects of their right against self-incrimination. Federal police, including those in the District of Columbia, had long been giving that warning. The FBI used it routinely. It was time that the states did likewise.

That assertion from a onetime law enforcement official, as one of the brethren confided to Warren Court historian Bernard Schwartz, was pivotal: "I believe that was a tremendously important factor, perhaps the critical factor in the Miranda vote."[2]

The brethren divided 5–4. Black, Douglas, Brennan, and newly seated Abe Fortas joined the chief justice. Harlan, Stewart, White, and Clark voted against. Aware of the incendiary nature of the confession cases, Warren took upon himself the obligation of writing the opinion for the majority, which he did over the next ten weeks. He drafted a six-page outline to guide his three clerks. Then he edited and reedited their drafts of various sections.

On May 9, Warren sent a copy to Brennan asking for his comments. Brennan replied two days later with a detailed memorandum. "I feel guilty about the extent of the suggestions," he wrote, "but this will be one of the most important opinions of our time and I know that you will want the fullest expression of my views."[3]

Brennan recommended several changes, including one that shifted the focus of the opinion from civil rights to civil liberties. Warren's draft had also referenced prior Supreme Court cases in which "Negro defendants were subjected to physical brutality—beatings, hanging, whipping—employed to extort confessions." Brennan countered with the question of whether it was appropriate "in this context to turn police brutality into a racial problem. If anything characterizes the group this opinion concerns, it is poverty more than race."[4]

In effect, Brennan argued, the well-to-do who had an attorney were protected by the court's previous finding in *Escobedo*. The poor, like Ernesto Miranda, were not.

Warren understood that two systems of justice were at work in the United States. Noting the shoplifting arrest of actress Hedy Lamarr earlier that year, columnist Drew Pearson had sympathized, "It's a disease with which some people are afflicted."

"When poor people are afflicted with the disease, they are jailed," Warren retorted. "Richer people are given a chance to return the property."[5]

Warren empathized with the words and adopted Brennan's suggestion that differential treatment was more a factor of social class than of race and dropped his passage from the draft, which illuminated the subject in a brighter light.

Brennan also recommended relaxing the stringent rules Warren had proposed, to allow the fifty state legislatures some room in which to fashion responses. But Warren, usually quick to adopt Brennan's suggestions, declined to soften that mandate. The explicit warnings, he believed, were an absolute minimum necessary to protect against self-incrimination. Without them, the states would likely be awash in a sea of self-determination: What's constitutional and what's not?

Working in Warren's behalf was the fact the no one else on the court had his experience as a prosecutor and a governor in dealing with police and legislatures. He knew that his words carried the most weight.

With that, as Abe Fortas said, *Miranda* "was entirely his."[6]

As a result, the final opinion turned into a sixty-one-page interrogation manual that began with the sort of plain-language statement that marked the chief's tenure on the court:

[T]he prosecution may not use statements, whether exculpatory or inculpatory, stemming from custodial interrogation of the defendant unless it demonstrates the use of procedural safeguards effective to secure the privilege against self-incrimination. . . . Prior to any questioning, the person must be warned that he has a right to remain silent, that any statement he does make may be used as evidence against him, and that he has a right to the presence of an attorney, either retained or appointed. The defendant [*sic*] may waive effectuation of these rights, provided the waiver is made voluntarily, knowingly, and intelligently.[7]

As the chief justice read the majority opinion from the bench on June 13, 1966, he emphasized additional points of clarification for the police and the public:

One. We do not outlaw confessions, but permit their use when they are in fact voluntary.

Two. We do not outlaw police interrogations. We do require proper warnings and full opportunity for assistance of counsel if it is desired.

Three. We do not restrict the activities of the police in making on-the-scene investigations of crime and in interrogating the witnesses in the vicinity.

After reviewing dozens of police interrogation manuals, Warren understood that deceit and psychological pressure in hostile, unfamiliar surroundings (police stations) were not the exception but the norm. Cops were sometimes overzealous in nailing the bad guys. That didn't sit well with him, no matter how well-meaning their intentions. He addressed that problem, too: "It is obvious that such an interrogation environment is created for no purpose other than to subjugate the individual to the will of his examiner. This atmosphere carries its own badge of intimidation. To be sure, this is not physical intimidation, but it is equally destructive of human dignity."[8]

Although the Warren Court's prior criminal law decisions had been bold, *Miranda* stood out for its thoroughness, according to lawyer and Supreme Court reporter Fred Graham. "*Gideon v. Wainwright* had created a constitutional right [of the accused] to counsel in felony cases at a time when all but five states already provided it; *Mapp v. Ohio* had extended the exclusionary rule to illegal searches after roughly one-half of the states had adopted the same rule; *Miranda* was to impose limits on police interrogation that no state had even approached prior to the *Escobedo* decision."[9]

The outcry from police administrations was swift and predictable. Speaking for departments throughout Texas, Henry C. Ashley, chief of the Garland, Texas, police department, carped, "We might as well close up shop."[10] William C. Ransdell, the public prosecutor in Raleigh, North Carolina, labeled the court as "so detached from reality that they cannot possibly make a decision in the matter."[11] The *California Highway Patrolman* magazine touted *Miranda* as one of "the judicial rules that [is] making the law a shield for the criminal."[12]

Even conservatives picked up the flag. Although LA mayor Sam Yorty's own police department was already advising arrestees of their Fifth Amendment rights, he raked *Miranda* over the coals as "another set of handcuffs on the police department."[13]

Working in conjunction with J. Edgar Hoover and the FBI, Senator Robert C. Byrd lashed out at the court's "decisions which hamper effective law enforcement, elevate individual rights out of perspective, and relegate the over-all rights of society to a secondary position."[14] Hoover did, though, take time to express his appreciation for Abe Fortas's having worked into the *Miranda* opinion a glowing reference to the FBI's professionalism in having its agents routinely advise arrestees of their rights.

In open rebellion against the court, some prosecutors began releasing prisoners arrested before the *Miranda* decision. Although few in number, these cases made for splashy headlines: "Bronx Man Who Admitted Rape Set Free Under Miranda Ruling; Confessed Slayer of Wife and 5 Children Freed; Two Who Confessed Go Free in Slaying."[15] While there was nothing to prevent prosecutors from reinvestigating and trying those cases, the public relations damage had been done.

"The publicity seemed to paint a picture of nine unworldly judges," wrote Ed Cray in *Chief Justice*, "flinging wide the jailhouse doors in a burst of softhearted compassion."[16]

Those who knew Earl Warren as a hard-as-nails prosecutor of the Old School expressed surprise at *Miranda*. Warren's compatriot Oscar Jahnsen, for years an investigator in both the district attorney's and attorney general's offices, lamented that the Supreme Court was suddenly making unreasonable demands on police.

Oddly enough, the confession District Attorney Warren had extracted that proved instrumental in the 1936 Shipboard Murder Case of chief engineer George Alberts would have been inadmissible under Chief Justice Warren's *Miranda* opinion. To get that confession, Jahnsen had locked Frank Conner in a room at the Hotel Whitecotton for a full week, interrogating him for up to six hours at a time and denying him access to his own attorney. At one point, his "captors" kept him awake for twenty-one straight hours before obtaining a confession and arraigning him.

But Chief Justice Warren was not the same person as District Attorney Warren. As head of the court, he had greater responsibilities in defining the law than he'd ever had in enforcing it. And he took pride in *Miranda*. He was so proud of it that he sent a copy to Arthur Goldberg at the United Nations for his reaction. Goldberg praised the ruling: "This opinion will go down in history books as another great contribution by you to liberty under law."[17]

Miranda capped a series of reforms in criminal procedure that the Warren Court had visited. First *Mallory v. United States* and then *Mapp v. Ohio* had launched what was an irreversible revolution in the law by putting teeth into existing statutes or constitutional mandates: Arrestees had rights.

Later rulings, including *Gideon* and *Escobedo*, reinforced an accused's right to an attorney as guaranteed by the Sixth Amendment. Meanwhile, the court systematically overturned confessions that it deemed had been extracted by physical or mental coercion, many involving southern courts and black defendants.

While aggrandizing the constitutional protections afforded all American citizens, the court's rulings ensured continuing protests in the press in favor of stricter laws against arrestees and not lighter ones, as they interpreted the court's opinions to be.

Warren, particularly sensitive to the criticism that the court was moving "too fast," said in response that the court didn't look about for "sore spots" in society and proceed to operate upon them. That is not how the court worked. Instead, it waited until issues came before it. "[T]he times we are living in determine the kind of cases we hear. We reflect the burning issues of our society; we do not manufacture them."[18]

To the press and others who claimed the Supreme Court was a catalyst for the rising crime rate, Warren replied, "Thinking persons and especially lawyers know that this is not the fact. They know that crime is inseparably connected with factors such as poverty, degradation, sordid social conditions, and weakening of home ties, low standards of law enforcement and the lack of education."[19]

The charge that the Warren Court was coddling criminals particularly angered the chief justice. Why would he stand for such an action? he asked friends rhetorically. His own father had been murdered, and the case had gone unsolved for more than three decades!

Warren argued, "[N]one of us want to injure law enforcement in any way, but I am sure that if the police will play the game according to the rules and in the spirit of our Bill of Rights, the public will have great respect for the law, enforcement will be better, and the dignity of the police themselves will be greatly enhanced."[20]

Responding to police and politicians who complained about *Miranda* and its predecessors making law enforcement tougher, Warren went back to his lifelong dictum: Follow the law. Expanding upon that after his retirement, he said, "It is always easier to obtain a conviction if you are permitted to use excesses that are prohibited by the Constitution, and thereby avoid the necessity of going out and convicting a man on independent evidence."[21]

Providing an arrestee with access to an attorney, he said in a second postretirement interview, "is just so much a question of common humanity that nobody should want to avoid it."[22]

But *Miranda* was not without consequences for the chief, who was forced to revisit his past for the third time in two years. He had avoided potential embarrassment the first two times by declining to take part in cases from California. The first was when, by a 6–2 vote, the Supreme Court on April 28, 1965, ruled that the remarks by a judge and prosecutor about a murder defendant's failure to testify infringed on the Fifth Amendment's Self-incrimination Clause.

The second, three weeks later, involved the thorny question of ownership of the oil-rich California tidelands, in which the brethren held that Santa Monica Bay was entirely within state waters.

Amid all the court's reforms, Warren remained adamant about one procedural point: The chief justice banned television coverage of criminal trials. Warren insisted that cameras had no place in the courtroom. Law clerk James Gaither reflected that "he spent hours and hours working that one," more than any other case argued during the 1964 term.[23]

The issue arose in the appeal of Texas-sized confidence man Billie Sol Estes, convicted in a courtroom that, as *Time* magazine put it, had been turned into a broadcast studio.

Generally, a case such as Estes's, which involved the alleged sale of nonexistent fertilizer tanks and spraying equipment, would have generated scant attention in the press. But Estes had tenuous ties to Bobby Baker, secretary to the Senate majority leader, and, through him, to Baker's former boss Lyndon Johnson.

The media, upon learning of Estes's ties to DC, erupted in a frenzy. Reporters grabbed three-quarters of the seats in the courtroom. Another couple dozen stood along the walls. Estes had objected to the circus, with its television cameras, studio lights, and sound booth in the back of the courtroom, along with the audio cables slithering snakelike out beneath the door. The trial judge rejected a motion by Estes's attorney to ban the broadcasters and news photographers after a two-day hearing that was itself, ironically enough, televised.

Three decades earlier, District Attorney Warren had himself taken advantage of every opportunity to appear before the press. He rejoiced in his share of celebrated cases from the death of Bessie Ferguson and a raft of statewide graft trials to the Shipboard Murder Case as he posed with more than a few comely witnesses during court recesses.

But Warren never succumbed to the excesses exhibited in the trial of Bruno Hauptmann, accused of the kidnap-murder of the infant son of Charles and Anne Lindbergh, in which seven hundred eager, cutthroat reporters descended upon the tiny hamlet of Flemington, New Jersey. The courtroom burst at the seams with "more correspondents, sob-sisters, sports-writers, psychiatrists, cameramen, etc., etc. . . . than represented American papers in France during the World War." They transformed the trial into a public spectacle while a feckless judge looked on.

As a member of the American Bar Association's Section on Criminal Law, District Attorney Warren had reviewed a report of a special committee that condemned the "commercialization of the administration of justice" in the Hauptmann case. To curb such circuses in the future, the special committee recommended, among other things, that no cameras or "photo-graphic appliances" and no "sound registering devices" be permitted in the courtroom while the trial was in progress.[24]

Three decades later, Chief Justice Warren clung to the same position. "I think this violates due process," he said when the brethren met on April 2, 1965, to take up Estes's appeal. "To stage a trial this way violates the decorum of the courtroom, and TV is not entitled to special treatment."[25]

The initial vote in conference was 5–4 to uphold Estes's conviction and retain the presence of cameras in the courtroom. Harlan, Goldberg, and Douglas joined Warren in the minority.

Disturbed by the outcome, the chief justice, according to clerk James Gaither, went to work. He reviewed tapes of the trial "over and over again, to see if the judge and jurors were primping for the cameras." He visited the brethren, seeking a fifth vote, and when he finally convinced Tom Clark to switch sides, he made sure the opinion was worded strongly enough.

"Not only was he involved emotionally in the decision," Gaither said, "he was involved emotionally in the opinion. . . . [*Estes*] represented how hard it was for him to get up before a jury, and his sense of how jurors de-cided cases. It was quite clearly a product of his earlier career."[26]

Warren wrote an impassioned dissent when it appeared he would be in the minority. With little more effort, he could have converted it into a majority opinion. Instead, he slyly suggested that Clark write the decision, ensuring that his fellow justice would hold firm in his conviction for reversal.

Clark's ruling, issued on June 1, 1965, was moderate in tone. The chief's concurrence, by contrast, was unusually fiery. Televised trials, he wrote, influenced the conduct of trial participants. They turned a judicial proceeding into an ongoing soap opera, complete with a revolving cast and evolving storyline. They became vehicles for entertainment and "the commercial objectives of the television industry."[27]

Were the Supreme Court to sanction television coverage, Warren added, "trials would be selected for television coverage for reasons having nothing to do with the purpose of trial. . . . [T]he most important factor would be the nature of the case. The alleged perpetrator of the sensational murder, the fallen idol, or some other person who, like petitioner, has attracted the public interest would find his trial turned into a vehicle for television."[28]

The constitutional right to a public trial, Warren continued, conferred no special privilege on the press or broadcasters. A trial was "public" if there were a reasonable number of seats for members of the press and public.

A year after *Estes*, the court returned to the issue of fair trial versus free press, this time to lay out definitive rules to sanitize criminal proceedings from infection by publicity.

It happened when Bay Village, Ohio, osteopath Sam Sheppard was convicted of the 1954 murder of his pregnant wife, Marilyn, at their home outside Cleveland. In statements to police, Sheppard claimed a "bushy-haired" intruder had murdered his wife before attacking him and fleeing the scene.

As police focused their investigation on Sheppard, newspapers speculated about the evidence, trumpeting reports of "Dr. Sam's" extramarital affairs and raging about the slow-creeping pathway to justice.

The growing fury of the press reached a climax on July 30, 1954, with an editorial on the front page of the *Cleveland Press* screamed: "Quit Stalling and Bring Him In!"[29] The following day, the police arrested Dr. Sam.

Sheppard went on trial amid a buzz of national publicity. Out-of-town reporters joined the locals to fill the courtroom and commandeer the courthouse. It was, *Time* magazine concluded, "the biggest murder story in the US press since the trial of Bruno Hauptmann in 1935."[30]

Members of the jury pool followed the case against Dr. Sam daily as it unfolded in the newspapers and on television and radio. The jurors did the same. A reporter got word that the jurors were about to visit the murder scene, so he hired a helicopter to hover overhead while he photographed the event. Police investigators commented openly about how sure they were of Sheppard's guilt and eventual conviction.

The doctor was sentenced and spent ten years in state prison before the Supreme Court took up his appeal in 1966. Citing "increasingly prevalent" instances of prejudicial news coverage, Tom Clark wrote the 8–1 opinion reversing Sheppard's conviction and remanding the case for a new trial. The opinion went on to lay the groundwork for trial court judges to insulate juries from excessive publicity.

"The carnival atmosphere," Clark argued, could have been avoided had the judge better regulated press behavior in the courtroom.[31] Additionally, Clark advised that judges could prohibit witnesses, police, and lawyers from discussing a case with reporters, a gag rule that predictably incensed the media.

If a judge was ineffectual at curtailing pretrial publicity, Clark suggested, that judge needed to transfer the trial to another county or even delay its start until the din in the press died down. Once the trial began, the judge could sequester the jury to keep prejudicial news accounts from tainting the proceedings and their judgments.

Because of careful wording, Clark's opinion didn't affect the media's newsgathering procedures: They were free to publish whatever they obtained. The court was only making the fourth estate's job more difficult by limiting what those connected to the case were free to share with them. As such, *Sheppard* became a landmark case in due process rather than in First Amendment rights.

Despite the court's decisions from *Mallory* to *Sheppard*, granting specific rights to the accused, the Warren Court showed empathy toward the needs of law enforcement where the safety of police on the streets was concerned. When the high court turned to respond to that very question in 1968, both Warren and his critics claimed *Terry v. Ohio* as a victory.

The issue before the court was clear: Did a police officer have a right to stop and frisk a suspect on the street *before* arresting him for carrying a concealed weapon?

The question came to light when, on October 31, 1963, Cleveland detective Martin McFadden watched two men stroll back and forth past Zucker's clothing store, eyeing the building. "They didn't look right to me," McFadden testified.[32] It appeared the two were casing the store before attempting a holdup. When McFadden asked their names, they mumbled their responses.

McFadden grabbed the nearest man, John Terry, spun him around, and patted him down. He discovered a gun in the pocket of Terry's topcoat. He searched the second suspect, Richard Chilton, and found a weapon in his pocket, too.

Terry and Chilton were arrested and convicted of carrying concealed weapons. They appealed, their attorney claiming that Officer McFadden hadn't met the legal burden of proving probable cause: No crime had been committed for which they could reasonably have been suspects.

Until he frisked the two men, McFadden had no evidence of a crime; finding the guns, police claimed, gave him evidence both of the commission of a crime and the suggestion of the arrestees' guilt.

All throughout the state courts hearings and all the way to the United States Supreme Court, Terry's attorneys argued that the police procedure commonly known as "stop and frisk" was an illegal search. Under *Mapp*, the guns could not be used as evidence, and without them, the police had no case.

During the December 12, 1967, oral argument, it became clear that the justices were as sympathetic toward defending counsel's argument as Warren was. But the chief justice wasn't ready to throw the cops under the bus yet, as he might easily have done. Instead, he used his lifelong intuition and inquisitive knack for reason to ferret out a better solution. Injecting his concern for the safety of law enforcement officers, he remonstrated, "Police officers are very often in a position where they might not be able to make an actual arrest, but they are in a position of danger."[33]

That tipped off his fellow brethren to Warren's position as the chief opened the *Terry* discussion at conference three days after oral arguments. The issue wasn't whether McFadden had probable cause to arrest, he suggested, but the lower threshold of probable cause to fear harm. If so, then McFadden had a right to protect himself with a pat-down search or a frisk for weapons. If the officer felt a hidden gun, he would then have sufficient evidence to conduct a more thorough search.

It was a brilliant piece of "if/then" reasoning by the chief justice. To a one, the brethren concurred. Viewing *Terry* as a significant case in which the court should speak as one, Warren assigned the opinion to himself.

The decision did not come easy. In fact, Warren took six months to fashion it. His brother justices were concerned that whatever they wrote would be construed by police as a hunting license, particularly in minority communities where hostile attitudes toward police were already the norm. Besides, any stop-and-frisk law ran contrary to the Fourth Amendment, which required police to have specific justification for any search.

With Brennan's considerable aid—Warren had selected him to write the opinion for the majority—the chief found the necessary justification not in the behavior of the suspect but in the realities of police procedures. His opinion noted that fifty-five law enforcement officers were killed by gunshots in 1966 alone. He wrote, "In view of these facts, we cannot blind ourselves to the need for law enforcement officers to protect themselves and other prospective victims of violence in situations where they may lack probable cause for an arrest."[34]

As he had done in *Miranda* two years earlier, Warren turned his decision into a practical police manual. He laid out specific conditions that had to be met before a patrolman was justified in patting down a suspect: The police officer was required to identify himself, and he could search only the outer clothing where a hidden weapon might be accessible to a suspect. With those conditions met, any weapon discovered could be introduced as evidence against the arrestee.

Warren's opinion, with a last-minute change of heart by Douglas, found a compromise between a constitutional mandate and the need for protection by law enforcement in a society with ever more guns.

The *Terry* ruling was a practical response to a very real and serious social issue. The only problem with it was that it came too late to silence the court's critics.

13

ALL THE KING'S HORSES

With the last of its main opinions rendered, the Warren Court spent the remaining years of the tumultuous sixties tightening and illuminating its precedent-setting decisions. Once the framework for the machinations of the court had been laid out, what remained of the past several years, as well as the majority of the work of subsequent courts, began to fall neatly into place. These remnants included cases involving refinements to the rights of police officers from self-incrimination (*Garrity v. New Jersey*, 1967), freedom of speech allowing draft-card burning (*United States v. O'Brien*, 1968), and the illegality of double jeopardy (*Benton v. Maryland*, 1969). With the import of the court's influence upon the nation loosening, the chief breathed a sigh of relief and, for the first time, gave serious thought to his retirement.

Earl Warren Jr., in responding to his father's announcement in 1969, expressed it best in an interview that same year:

> My father basically is retiring as he said for reasons of age. His health is wonderful, both physically and mentally, but he feels I think as a matter of principle that men should not stay in public positions too long, at least past a point when there might be some question as to whether or not they're operating at maximum efficiency, and even though he has many years left, I think he felt at the age of 78, he shouldn't remain on any longer. I am also quite sure that he feels that this is basically the end of an era; the major decisions for the court probably now have been before the court and have been made—things like reapportionment, desegregation, cases of that sort—and from now on I think it's going to fall upon the court to interpret within those decisions. In other words, the umbrellas have been set up, and there is going to have to be interpretation within the scope of those umbrellas, they're going to have to

decide how prescribed they will be or how broad they'll be, and I think
he feels very strongly that younger men ought to make those decisions.
The day-by-day, step-by-step decisions under the broad framework that
has been established.[1]

Adding to the chief's decision, undoubtedly, was growing displeasure
in Congress over the Warren Court, which Capitol Hill had long since
deemed too far left. Congressional attempts to overturn or soften the court's
rulings on one man, one vote; school prayer; and desegregation failed—so,
as one statement of its displeasure with the brethren, Congress voted to
increase the justices' annual salaries by $4,500, to $39,500, less than half the
increase they appropriated to lower-court judges.

Adding to the fuel already thrown on the fire of the Warren Commission's report and the court's progressive decisions, Warren became involved
in yet another controversy not of his making. In early 1969, *Life* magazine
published an article detailing an agreement between Justice Fortas and a
foundation created by financier Louis E. Wolfson.[2] In it, Fortas committed
to serve as a consultant to the foundation in return for a fee of $20,000
a year in perpetuity. When Wolfson came under scrutiny for fraud by the
Securities and Exchange Commission (SEC), indictments were returned
against the financier.

The *Life* article, though, didn't contain the entire agreement between
Fortas and the Wolfson Foundation. Author Bernard Schwartz elaborated:

> The Justice Department had secured information about the contract that
> made it far more damaging to the Justice. Attorney General Mitchell
> discussed the new material with the President on the morning of May 7.
> Later the same morning, the Attorney General's limousine drove around
> to the rear entrance of the Supreme Court and pulled into the basement
> garage. Mitchell was met by a marshal who escorted him to the Chief
> Justice's chambers. The Attorney General had made his unceremonious
> back entry to avoid being seen by the press.
>
> The Warren-Mitchell meeting lasted less than thirty minutes, and
> the Attorney General did most of the talking.[3] He said later that he
> showed the Chief Justice "certain documents." From what Warren told
> the Brethren, this was a copy of the contract between Fortas and the
> foundation and the correspondence relating to it. The contract provided
> for an annual fee of $20,000 to be paid to Fortas for the rest of his life.
> After his death, the foundation would pay $20,000 a year to his wife.[4]

If Warren was concerned, he failed to show it, telling the attorney general only that he'd take the matter under consideration and thanking him

for bringing it to his attention. Then the chief called a conference and, with all the justices assembled, including Fortas, he related the contents of the contract that Mitchell had shown him. Fortas defended himself by insisting that he had paid back every penny of the funds he had received. When one of the justices asked why Warren had called the conference, the chief said simply, "I thought that you should know all that I know about the matter." Schwartz elaborated:

> Warren brought no other pressure on Fortas, but only because he did not have to. Fortas relied on two principal advisers, William O. Douglas and Clark Clifford. Douglas had been lecturing in Brazil when the *Life* article had appeared. As soon as he returned, he sat up with Fortas for two nights discussing the situation. Douglas urged Fortas to fight it out and not to resign. But Clifford persuaded him to step down, and Fortas sent a letter of resignation to the president on May 13, effective the next day, as well as a letter of explanation to the chief justice.[5]
>
> Had Fortas tried to heed Douglas's advice, there was no doubt that Warren would have done what he could to induce Fortas to leave the court. The chief had strict standards of right and wrong and looked upon Fortas's conduct as a "blot" on the court. "He can't stay," Warren told his executive secretary, Margaret McHugh, at the time. As Richard Nixon later wrote, Warren felt that the contract with Wolfson's foundation "represented a serious threat to the reputation of the Court; he was convinced that Fortas had no choice but to step down."[6]

As if that weren't enough to add to Warren's headaches, other issues continued to plague the chief and his brethren. The late sixties were a hotbed of antiwar and civil rights protests and unrest. When Julian Bond, a young black leader who had brought the civil rights movement to the Deep South, won a seat in the Georgia House of Representatives in November 1964, seventy-five members of the House filed petitions refusing Bond's right to be seated. Bond had only recently endorsed a proclamation by the militant Student Nonviolent Coordinating Committee (SNCC) advocating "sympathy with, and support [of] the men in this country who are unwilling to respond to a military draft."[7] Upheld by a three-judge panel that agreed that the legislature could deny membership on whatever grounds it deemed appropriate, the case made its way to the Supreme Court, where once again the brethren narrowly decided against legislative dictate and in favor of the constitutional rights granted to US citizens.

As the protests in the streets spread across the nation, a rash of other cases flooded the docket. The court predictably found in favor of personal rights at the expense of governmental overreach. Warren, meanwhile, grew increasingly concerned that both the civil rights movement and the protests against the Vietnam War were mounting in strength, not diminishing, as many social-justice observers had predicted they would.

Then, in January 1968, the Tet Offensive produced a battlefield victory for the United States but a global propaganda coup for North Vietnam. The US public, despite glimpses of military glory, was growing increasingly disenfranchised with the war and its prosecution. Faced with a quagmire from which there appeared no escape, President Lyndon Johnson announced he would not seek a second term as president that November.

Four months later, on April 4, a bullet from an assassin's rifle brought to an end the life of Rev. Martin Luther King Jr., the most prominent black leader in America, and the nation's ghettos exploded. Over the coming weeks, rioters torched several dozen neighborhoods. White middle-class America, which had just begun to settle into the comfort of integration afforded by the court's momentous decision in *Brown*, began concurring with some politicians that a broader, more malevolent motivation lay below the social turmoil. The moral fabric of America was unraveling faster than anyone could piece it back together. Wracked by insurrection, the nation witnessed riots in black communities across the nation. Students, homosexuals, environmental activists, women, and antiwar protesters all turned out. The evening news—long before the advent of cable television—ran red with blood as Americans of every ilk and socioeconomic status watched their nation ripped apart by radicals and Communists. More people than not blamed at least a good portion of it on the Warren Court for the permissiveness it used in rendering its decisions—permissiveness that led directly to civil unrest.

As time wore on, Warren learned of another Fortas-like entanglement in which Douglas had received an annual fee of $12,000 from a foundation financed mostly by income from gambling. He knew the time to nip such activities in the bud had come. Under pressure from the chief, the Judicial Conference adopted strict rules of judicial conduct, including a code of ethics, full financial disclosure, and restraints on income from off-the-bench activities. The new regulations did not apply to the Supreme Court, which alone has the power to prescribe rules for its members, but rather to lower federal judges. Warren was sure, though, that the enactment of the strict standards would spur the Supreme Court to act in cleaning up its own house.

He was wrong. Numerous press accounts at the time claimed that many federal judges resented the rules that the chief had rammed down their throats. The brethren felt even more strongly. At their June 13, 1969, conference, Warren moved that the court formally adopt rules of conduct similar to those that had just been applied to the lower courts. The majority rejected the chief's proposal, and the conference resulted in deferring further consideration until the new 1969 term—*after* Warren's retirement. Under the newly seated chief justice, the brethren did nothing about the matter. Indeed, without Warren there, the Judicial Conference itself felt free, at the beginning of November, to suspend the new rules for lower court judges, as well, for being "too strict."[8]

Meanwhile, the retiring chief justice had few doubts about the effect Richard Nixon's presidency would have upon the court. Nixon had made the Warren Court an even bigger personal target in his 1968 presidential victory than had Republican law-and-order candidate Barry Goldwater in 1964. As one observer expressed it, Nixon had run against Warren and his court as much as he had run against Senator Hubert H. Humphrey and the Democratic Party.[9] Nixon accused the court of "seriously weakening the peace forces and strengthening the criminal forces in our society." He vowed in public that his court appointees would be different. He promised to nominate only "strict constructionists" to "interpret, not to make laws."[10]

Warren commented later, "During the entire campaign, the principal issue was 'law and order.' It merely was an exercise in the rhetoric, accusation and recrimination which just increased division" across the land.[11] Now the architect of the anti-court campaign was to choose the new chief justice along with a replacement for Fortas. Warren knew that Nixon would use the opportunity to try to remold the court in his own, rather than in Warren's, image.

Still, Warren had faith in the work he had done in impacting the court. He confided to a former clerk that he knew Nixon would appoint justices of different temperaments to his own but added that "the pendulum swings back and forth" and that, in due course, it would swing back the other way. Even with whatever Nixon appointments the court embraced, Warren was confident that the solid work he had done would last forever.

So, as Warren moved on toward his last months in office, both the chief justice and the president were careful to observe the outward amenities. Nixon formally requested that Warren administer the inaugural oath and also swear in the president's new cabinet and some eighty-one members of the White House staff. Then, on April 23, 1969, the president honored the retiring chief justice and the Warren family at an elaborate White House dinner. The guest list included the entire court, most of the new cabinet, and virtually everyone who was anyone in Washington.

With "decorous insincerity," as one writer phrased it, Nixon toasted the chief and thanked him for his years of distinguished public service, after which Warren reciprocated, confessing his appreciation of the president's warmth, adding, "I approach retirement with no malice in heart toward anyone."[12]

After that, speculation turned to whom the president would nominate to be the next chief justice. Warren had already told his staff he expected it to be Warren Burger, and, sure enough, on May 19, 1969, Nixon announced Burger as the new chief justice. Warren had not been consulted and was informed "as a courtesy" only a few hours before the announcement. Two and a half weeks after being nominated, Burger was overwhelmingly confirmed by the Senate.

June 23, 1969, was the final day of the Warren Court's term and the last day of an era. Before the court's day began at 10:00 a.m., the president's limousine arrived at the basement entrance. Following several Secret Service agents, Nixon emerged and was escorted to the courtroom, where he sat quietly for eighteen minutes while the Warren Court announced its final three decisions. The chief justice welcomed the president, who was wearing a cutaway coat over striped trousers that looked too baggy on him regardless of how much tailoring had gone into their construction. Nixon crossed over to the lawyer's lectern facing the long, austere, mahogany bench. It was only his third time before the court, the first two coming when he argued *Time, Inc. v. Hill.*

Nixon, reflecting back upon his earlier disastrous appearances before the court, addressed the chief: "I can say Mr. Chief Justice, that there is only one ordeal which is more challenging than a presidential press conference and that is to appear before the Supreme Court." The balance of Nixon's seven-minute talk was devoted to praising Warren's career, after which he concluded, "this Nation owes a debt of gratitude to the Chief Justice of the United States for his example."

The chief justice thanked Nixon for his "most generous" words, which "are greatly appreciated, I assure you." Then Warren went on to read Nixon a virtual lecture on the court and its place in the constitutional order of the republic, stressing the crucial element of continuity: "I might point out to you, because you might not have looked into the matter that it is a continuing body. . . . [T]he Court develops consistently the eternal principles of our Constitution." Most clearly, Warren was reminding the president and everyone else in the room that the Warren Court and the principles it had laid down during the chief's tenure would endure despite Nixon's presidency. "We serve only the public interest as we see it, guided only by the Constitution and our own consciences." So long as the court was "manned by men . . . like those who sit today," the chief said he had no fears. "So I leave in a happy vein, Mr. President, and I wish my successor all the happiness and success."[13]

Then everyone rose as the retiring chief justice administered the oath of office to his successor. Warren turned to the audience and said, "I present the new Chief Justice of the United States."[14]

After the ceremony, Warren and Burger went into the conference room, where the clerk had left the necessary papers recording the administration of the oath for their signatures. They were alone in the room, and Burger recalled that Warren had tears in his eyes as the chief commented that the president's remarks had been warm and appreciated.[15]

Following Warren's retirement, the controversy over him dimmed. Even his long-term critics held their fire in the outpouring of the public's acknowledgments. And then, on June 29, with a national tribute scheduled at the steps of the Lincoln Memorial, the main paean was delivered by former Justice Arthur J. Goldberg, who hailed Warren as a "great emancipator of the law" whose achievements would long outlive any temporary criticism.[16] President Nixon had turned down an invitation to participate in the tribute, which was not unusual for Warren's political opponents. The year before, California governor Ronald Reagan had declined to attend the dedication of the Earl Warren Legal Center at Berkeley.

Warren himself held a final news conference just after his successor was sworn in. In response to a reporter, the former chief justice said that he hoped the decisions of the Warren Court would endure, adding "but I would not predict." He hoped his court would be remembered as "the People's Court."

A reporter asked him to describe the major frustration of his court years. Warren paused for several moments before breaking into his trademark wide grin. He couldn't think of any, he said. "It has not been a frustrating experience."[17]

The years Warren spent as retired chief justice of the United States Supreme Court passed all too quickly. The California press reported that the Warrens were house hunting in the San Francisco area or Sacramento, but

Warren eventually decided to retain his Washington apartment and remain in the capital. The new chief justice had given him a suite of chambers facing the Capitol, for which Warren was grateful. He was also assigned a law clerk to help him with his work.

But the work following his retirement was pedantic compared to what he'd done his entire public life. Warren attended some ceremonies and conferences, gave a few speeches, and traveled, often on behalf of the World Peace through Law movement. For one who had been active in government and the court for his entire adult life, going through the motions of maintaining meaningful activity was scarcely an adequate substitute for the real thing. A former law clerk recalled when he walked into the retired chief's chambers and found him reading the *Congressional Record*. Warren laughed when he saw his visitor and said that he wasn't reading it all *that* carefully.

On another occasion, Warren was reminiscing with grandson Jimmy Lee, who was visiting Papa and Mama Warren in Washington for the summer. Jimmy Lee, who would go on to become a sitting judge in California, asked the elder Warren why such an important case as *Brown* had taken so long to make its way to the Supreme Court. The young man watched his grandfather's expression, later recalling,

> He literally bristled. "Wait," he said. "That particular case had been to the Supreme Court three or four times and was bounced back, always kicked back." I asked him why, and he said that the courts generally have a method for not deciding the merits of a case. And then he told me about the three shiboleths of the law. Now, I didn't even know what a shiboleth was, but he said the three of them are *rightness, standing*, and *justiciability*. Those are legal words that mean the court that has the case in front of it [can decline to] decide the merits because the case isn't right yet (nothing bad has happened), because the person doesn't have standing and is not a person who has been individually hurt, or it's not a justiciable controversy. . . . Papa Warren said that by relying on one, and sometimes more, of those three shiboleths, the court can send the case back down below and let somebody else deal with the messy details. And he said that's what happened with the segregation cases. Those cases were batted down over and over and over and over again. . . . And he was mad about this. A judge's job, he said, is to decide the issue. "That's your job. And you don't kick it away and it keeps bouncing back." He was very angry about that in the case of *Brown v. Board of Education*.
>
> With *Brown*, which was his first big case, he told me two things were imperative to him: one, it had to be a unanimous decision—it could not be a split decision—and it had to be written by the chief justice.

Tom Clark, Hugo Black, Harlan, these people were from the south, and for all kinds of different reasons, they didn't like this [case], and Papa Warren would spend hours with them. Some legal scholars say [the decision] probably would have happened anyway, but if you look at the footnotes in the case, they address individual issues, states' rights issues, that were particularly dear to the individual justices. By being able to put the footnotes into the case that addressed a political or judicial matter of freedom, particularly for southern justices, he was able to get 100 percent on board. If you take the footnotes out, I don't think it would have happened. But he told them, "I understand you have a big concern here, and let's address this concern right here on the bottom, page 72; we'll put in a little footnote where we'll talk about state's rights, and it's great, and once that's in there, you're on board with the decision." He couldn't have any recurrent opinions. Not like it is today [when] you get a majority opinion and six concurring opinions. No. He had to have just a single one. That was a big deal. It was a really *huge* deal. It had to be. [*Brown*] was so important, it *had* to be. [He realized that people] had to feel the entire weight of the Supreme Court was behind the decision, and the entire weight meant unanimous, and that meant the chief justice had to write it.[18]

Papa Warren's candor with his grandson that day was typical of how he related to everyone in his life—not only his own family and friends but also anyone who crossed his path. The greatest joy he seemed to take from retirement was talking to college kids and law students. He had no paucity of concern for America's youth. He was indeed a hero to a generation that had lost the capacity for having heroes. To the young, he represented a person who had worked positively within the system—succeeding despite it. In the process, he effected lasting, meaningful changes for the betterment of the republic.

Warren was proud of his reputation among students. Once, after delivering a talk in the basement lounge of Notre Dame Law School, he decided to take questions. A student in the back of the packed lounge began: "Some people have suggested that you'll go down in history with Marshall as one of the two greatest Chief Justices—" Warren smiled broadly and interrupted, "Could you say that again—a little louder please? I'm having a little trouble hearing."[19]

While living the sedentary life of a former chief justice, Warren took umbrage with one issue that turned out to be controversial beyond expectations. It concerned the recommendation for a new court of appeals whose role would be to screen the cases that the Supreme Court would consider.

From the time of his appointment, Chief Justice Burger expressed concern over the Supreme Court's growing caseload. In mid-1971, Burger appointed a seven-member blue-ribbon panel led by Professor Paul A. Freund to study the problem. On December 19, 1972, the Freund Committee recommended the creation of a new National Court of Appeals to "screen all petitions for review now filed in the Supreme Court."[20] The new court's job would be to exercise the Supreme Court's certiorari jurisdiction to decide which cases would be considered by the highest tribunal and which would not.

Warren read about the Freund Committee recommendation and was furious. He fired off a letter to Peter D. Ehrenhaft, a former Warren law clerk and member of the Freund panel. "To put it mildly," Warren wrote, "I was shocked to read in the Sunday Star that you and the committee of which you are a member are expected to advance a scuttling of the Supreme Court. I can think of few things which could throttle the Court to a greater extent in its avowed purpose of establishing 'Equal Justice Under Law.'"[21]

On the same day, Warren shot off a memorandum to his former law clerks, enclosing copies of both an article on the committee's plan he'd read in the *Washington Star* and his response to Ehrenhaft: "I consider this to be of tremendous importance—as a matter of fact, as important as the 50-member Court of the Union which was proposed as a Constitutional Amendment some years ago but aborted because of its absurdity. In my opinion, this is the same thing in a different disguise."

Warren's memo noted that, while "it is reported that one of the law clerks is involved in the recommendation, I want all of you to know that it was not through any collaboration with me or in any respect with my concurrence."[22]

Once the Freund Committee report was published, Ehrenhaft sent a memorandum to the Warren law clerks, saying, "I hope that after reading the Report you realize that our Group hoped only to aid the Court in discharging its historic role. No denigration of the institution was intended; no retreat from the principles of justice for all it so forcefully developed while we worked with the Chief was even considered."[23]

Nevertheless, Warren failed to see it that way, looking at the Freund report as a direct attack on the work of his court, the Warren Court. His memo to his law clerks had asserted, "The news article is sketchy, but to me gives evidence of the real purpose behind it."[24] To Warren, the proposal was but the latest version of the continuing efforts to curb the powers, if not the influence, of the Supreme Court.

Warren had also been offended by the secretive procedure adopted by the Freund panel. He felt affronted by the committee's failure to meet with him. The group personally spent a day with each of the sitting justices. But it decided that only individual members would meet with former justices. Ehrenhaft was assigned to talk to Warren, who afterward remained unmoved.

Warren condemned the Freund proposal in the bluntest public attacks delivered by him since his retirement. On May 1, 1973, he delivered a Law Day speech that called the Freund report "naive" and "dangerous," saying that a new "case-screening court" would cause irreparable harm to the prestige, power, and functioning of the Supreme Court.[25]

Warren continued his vocal opposition to the Freund proposal for the rest of his life. Brennan, who saw Warren on his deathbed, recalls, "I last saw him only two hours before his death. He wouldn't talk with me about his health. He wanted an update on the status of the proposal to create a National Court of Appeals. He strongly opposed the proposal. Its adoption, he was convinced, threatened to shut the door of the Supreme Court to the poor, the friendless, the little man."[26]

Despite the procedural hiccup following his retirement, the Burger Court continued to show Warren the respect they understood he deserved. Warren appreciated the chambers that Burger had assigned to him and frequently met with him to discuss issues involved in running the court, often over lunch in one or the other's chambers. Not long after, Warren found his energy level beginning to wane, a prospect he might never have previously stopped to consider. When one day Burger sent him a note asking why he never joined the brethren for lunch anymore, where his opinions would surely be valued, Warren replied that the justices might want to discuss pending cases, and his presence wouldn't be appropriate.

Toward the end of 1973, Warren came to see Burger and said he hadn't been able to arrange his annual medical examination at Walter Reed Army Hospital. He had been informed that such services were no longer available to "retired officers." Warren, recalled Burger, "was quite annoyed, to put it mildly." Another member of the Warren Court said that Warren indignantly told him at lunch, "What do you know, the bastards have kept me out of Walter Reed."[27]

Burger was equally annoyed and placed a call to the secretary of the army. Howard Callaway told the new chief that it was obviously a mistake, since he alone had the authority to define the people entitled to medical services. The secretary said that it no more affected Chief Justice Warren than it would have a four- or five-star general.

Callaway offered to call Warren and apologize, but Warren had recently learned that his physician at Walter Reed had retired, so the former chief arranged for a physical with Dr. Oscar Mann, a private physician affiliated with Georgetown University Hospital.

Meanwhile, the problems facing President Richard Nixon continued to dominate the news. Following the president's haughtiness over his 1972 electoral sweep, the chief's old antagonist found himself sinking to his Watergate grave. Warren saw the scandal enveloping the White House as a confirmation of all his doubts about his fellow Californian. When Nixon's so-called enemies list was made public, Warren joked that he had his own list—"a one-man enemy list."[28]

Warren followed the news about Watergate with morbid fascination. A former law clerk remembers going to a meeting with the retired chief one morning during the height of the presidential scandal. Warren failed to show. After more than an hour, the staff member began to worry. He was about to call the chief's apartment when Warren came in and invited his guest to back to his chambers. When asked in light of his late arrival if Warren was feeling well, he grinned and said, "Oh, no. That's not the problem. My problem is I get in late because I have to read everything about Watergate. I look at my watch and see it's already late. But I just can't pass any of this stuff up."[29]

As the developing scandal began to reach into the Oval Office, Warren found it increasingly difficult to keep his views on the matter to himself. In his public speeches, he condemned those in the administration who had so dishonored the legal profession. In an April 1974 address in New Orleans, he noted, "Altogether twenty-one people in and around the White House have been indicted, and sixteen of these were lawyers.... The inner sanctum of the White House has been tarnished, and the end of the debacle is not yet in sight."[30]

Yet, Warren saw Watergate more as a vindication than a condemnation of the American political system. He told college audiences that Watergate showed that "a humble night watchman" could start the disclosures that might ultimately unseat a president. "The great virtue of our government," he said at Morehouse College in Atlanta on May 21, 1974, "is that people can do something about it. . . . When they have made a mistake, they can rectify it."[31]

Warren had no doubt that the American people had made a mistake in electing Nixon to the highest office in the land. Some months before he died, he expressed his feelings on the president with unusual frankness in an interview he gave to Alden Whitman of the *New York Times*.[32] The interview was to be off the record during Warren's lifetime, which accounts for the chief's candor. Whitman spent an entire afternoon in the retired chief justice's chambers. Toward the end of the interview, Whitman asked the chief what he felt about Nixon. Warren shook his head and replied, "Tricky is perhaps the most despicable President this nation has ever had. He was a cheat, a liar, a crook" who had abused both the office and the people. Warren spoke about the terrible state the country was in because of Nixon. Whitman remarked, "You sound like a man who regrets having left."

Warren turned to his interviewer and said, "I know now. I felt the Presidency would elevate him and he would make the right choice. It didn't work out that way." Then, his face growing increasingly inflamed and his voice choking with emotion, he added, "If I had ever known what was going to happen to this country and this Court, I *never* would have resigned. They would have had to carry me out of here on a plank!"[33]

In January 1974, Warren suffered a heart attack. He recovered within a week. But on March 19, as he began his eighty-fifth year, his health was failing. At the end of May, he was again hospitalized. Then, on July 2, Warren was admitted to Georgetown University Hospital after a third heart attack that was to prove fatal. Warren's seventh-floor room looked down on the Watergate apartments. And it was the scandal that started there that concerned him to the end.

On Tuesday, July 9, Warren's physician examined his patient and reported his condition as "satisfactory." By 5:30 that afternoon, Brennan, his closest associate on the court, paid a call on his friend. The justice used to call Warren "Super Chief," a title that was adopted by those in the court who were growing increasingly nostalgic about the Warren years.

Brennan found Warren alert and in good spirits. He had no idea that this would be the last time he would see the retired chief alive. The next day, Brennan told the brethren of his visit and what they had talked about. When Warren saw Brennan, he was eager to talk and, above all, wanted to know what was happening in the *Nixon* case that by then had come before the court.[34] The conference on that case had been held earlier that day, and Brennan relayed that the justices had decided unanimously against the president's claim that he could refuse to turn over crucial tapes to the district court based upon executive privilege.

"Thank God! Thank God! Thank God!" Warren cried out loud. "If you don't do it this way, Bill, it's the end of the country as we have known it."[35]

Soon after Brennan left, Warren suffered a cardiac arrest. He died at 8:10 p.m., his wife and youngest daughter sobbing softly at his side.

NOTES

INTRODUCTION

1. *Wikipedia*, s.v. "Saul," last edited April 9, 2019, https://en.wikipedia.org/wiki/Saul.

2. Robert W. Kenny, interview by Amelia Fry, Earl Warren Oral History Project, October 16, 1979; February 24, 1975, in *Earl Warren: The Governor's Family: Oral History Transcript and Related Material, 1970–1980* (Berkeley, CA: Bancroft Library, Regional Oral History Office, University of California at Berkeley, 1976).

3. McIntyre Faries, "McIntyre Faries: Warren: California Republicans, 1934–1953," interview by Amelia Fry, Earl Warren Oral History Project, in *Earl Warren: The Governor's Family: Oral History Transcript and Related Material, 1970–1980* (Berkeley, CA: Bancroft Library, Regional Oral History Office, University of California at Berkeley, 1976), 93.

4. James Warren, interview by Miriam Feingold Stein, Earl Warren Oral History Project, October 27, 1977, in *Earl Warren: The Governor's Family: Oral History Transcript and Related Material, 1970–1980* (Berkeley, CA: Bancroft Library, Regional Oral History Office, University of California at Berkeley), tape 1, side 2.

5. John Gunther, *Inside U.S.A.* (New York: Harper & Brothers, 1947), 18–21.

6. John Gunther, *Guide to the John Gunther Papers, 1935–1967* (Chicago: University of Chicago Library, Special Collections Center, 2006).

7. Alden Whitman, "Earl Warren, 83, Who Led High Court in Time of Vast Social Change, Is Dead," *New York Times*, July 10, 1974, https://archive.nytimes.com/www.nytimes.com/learning/general/onthisday/bday/0319.html.

8. James Warren, interview by Stein.

9. Ibid.

10. Felix Frankfurter, letter to Master Oliver Gates, October 29, 1953, Felix Frankfurter Papers, Library of Congress.

11. Harry S Truman, *Earl Warren—A Tribute*, 58 Calif. L. Rev. 3 (1970), 3–4.

12. Ed Cray, *Chief Justice: A Biography of Earl Warren* (New York: Simon & Schuster, 1997), 515.

13. James Warren, interview by Stein.

14. Ibid.

15. "Warren, Earl," Our Campaigns, last modified January 27, 2018, https://www.ourcampaigns.com/CandidateDetail.html?CandidateID=4976.

16. Robert Coughlan, "California's Warren & Family," *Life*, April 24, 1944, 100–110.

17. Earl Warren, *The Memoirs of Earl Warren* (Garden City: Doubleday, 1977), 7.

18. Earl Warren Jr., in correspondence with author, June 1995.

CHAPTER 1: UPON THIS ROCK

1. Ed Cray, *Chief Justice: A Biography of Earl Warren* (New York: Simon & Schuster, 1997), 17.

2. Earl Warren, *The Memoirs of Earl Warren* (Garden City: Doubleday, 1977), 14.

3. Cray, *Chief Justice*, 17.

4. Ibid., 16.

5. "Eugene V. Debs," *Time*, November 1, 1926.

6. Warren, *Memoirs*, 12.

7. *Wikisource*, s.v. "Page: Mexico, California and Arizona–1900.Djvu/428," last edited August 15, 2018, https://en.wikisource.org/wiki/Page%3AMexico%2C_California_and_Arizona_-_1900.djvu/428.

8. Jim Newton, *Justice for All: Earl Warren and the Nation He Made* (New York: Penguin, 2007), 20.

9. Ibid.

10. Ibid.

11. *Bakersfield Daily Californian*, February 12, 1900, 1.

12. Newton, *Justice for All*, 20.

13. Ibid.

14. Ibid.

15. Warren, *Memoirs*, 21.

16. Cray, *Chief Justice*, 22.

17. Russell Herman Conwell, *Acres of Diamonds* (New York: Harper & Brothers, 1915); available online at Russell Conwell, "Acres of Diamonds," American Rhetoric, https://www.americanrhetoric.com/speeches/rconwellacresofdiamonds.htm.

18. Leo Katcher, *Earl Warren: A Political Biography* (New York: McGraw-Hill, 1967), 116.

19. Ibid.

20. Warren, *Memoirs*, 25.

21. Ibid., 26.

22. Ibid., 30.

23. Ibid., 31.

24. John D. (John Downing) Weaver, *Warren: The Man, The Court, The Era* (Boston: Little, Brown, 1967); available online at https://archive.org/details/warren mancourter00weav/page/34?q=earl+warren?q=earl+warren.

25. Ibid.

26. Warren, *Memoirs*, 34.

27. Cray, *Chief Justice*, 26.

28. Ibid.

29. Warren, *Memoirs*, 40.

30. Cray, *Chief Justice*, 27.

31. Ibid.

32. Norman Stockwell, "From the Archives: Freedom Itself Is Radical," *Progressive*, June 14, 2016, https://progressive.org/magazine/archives-freedom-radical/.

33. Cray, *Chief Justice*, 28.

34. Ibid., 29.

35. Irving Stone, *Earl Warren: A Great American Story* (New York: Prentice Hall, 1948), 20.

36. Ibid., 30.

37. Ibid.

CHAPTER 2: LONG AND WINDING ROAD

1. LeRoy Reuben Hafen, Carl Coke Rister, *Western America: The Exploration, Settlement, and Development of the Region beyond the Mississippi* (Upper Saddle River, NJ: Prentice Hall, 1941), 646.

2. Jim Newton, *Justice for All: Earl Warren and the Nation He Made* (New York: Penguin, 2007), 27.

3. "Could You Survive a Natural Disaster?" Oxplore, https://www.oxplore .org/question-detail/could-you-survive-a-natural-disaster#2307.

4. Earl Warren, *The Memoirs of Earl Warren* (Garden City, NY: Doubleday, 1977), 34.

5. "Abe Ruef: America's Most Erudite City Boss," Virtual Museum of the City of San Francisco, archived from the original on June 4, 2013, http://www .sfmuseum.net/hist1/ruef.html.

6. Ibid.

7. Ibid.

8. Warren, *Memoirs*, 46.

9. Ibid., 46–47.

10. "The War To End All Wars," BBC News, November 10, 1998, http:// news.bbc.co.uk/2/hi/special_report/1998/10/98/world_war_i/198172.stm.

11. Warren, *Memoirs*, 47.

12. Ibid., 48.

13. Irving Stone, *Earl Warren: A Great American Story* (New York: Prentice Hall, 1948), available online at https://archive.org/stream/earlwarrengreata00ston#page/28/mode/2up.

14. Warren, *Memoirs*, 49.

15. Stone, *Earl Warren*.

16. Warren, *Memoirs*, 51–52.

17. Ibid., 52.

18. Ibid.

19. Newton, *Justice for All*, 72–73.

20. Ibid., 73.

21. Warren, *Memoirs*, 56.

22. Ibid., 58.

23. Stone, *Earl Warren*.

24. Warren, *Memoirs*, 60.

25. Ed Cray, *Chief Justice: A Biography of Earl Warren* (New York: Simon & Schuster, 1997), 42.

26. Stone, *Earl Warren*.

27. Cray, *Chief Justice*, 42.

28. Ibid.

29. Ibid., 42–43.

30. Ibid., 62.

31. Ibid., 67.

32. Ibid., 68.

33. Ibid.

34. John D. (John Downing) Weaver, *Warren: The Man, The Court, The Era* (Boston: Little, Brown, 1967); available online at https://archive.org/details/warrenmancourter00weav/page/34?q=earl+warren?q=earl+warren.

35. Stone, *Earl Warren*.

36. Ibid.

37. Ibid.

38. Ibid.

39. Ibid.

40. Nina Palmquist Meyers, interview by Amelia R. Fry, Earl Warren Oral History Project, December 12, 1978, in *Earl Warren: The Governor's Family: Oral History Transcript and Related Material, 1970–1980* (Berkeley, CA: Bancroft Library, Regional Oral History Office, University of California at Berkeley, 1976).

41. Warren, *Memoirs*, 64-65.

42. Ibid., 65.

43. Stone, *Earl Warren*, 49.

44. *Oakland Tribune*, editorial, September 20, 1931.

45. *Oakland Tribune*, December 22, 1943.

46. *Oakland Tribune*, May 16, 1938, 10.

47. Cray, *Chief Justice*, 95.

48. Jack Pollack, *Earl Warren: The Judge Who Changed America* (Upper Saddle River, NJ: Prentice Hall, 1979), 62.

49. Weaver, *Warren*, 237.

CHAPTER 3: MR. ATTORNEY GENERAL

1. Irving Stone, *Earl Warren: A Great American Story* (New York: Prentice Hall, 1948), 82.

2. Ibid.

3. *Los Angeles Times*, July 21, 1938.

4. Helen R. MacGregor, interview by Amelia Fry, June Hogan, and Gabrielle Morris, Earl Warren Oral History Project, September 17, 1969; October 30, 1969; June 17, 1971; and May 18, 1972, in *Helen A. MacGregor: A Career in Public Service with Earl Warren* (Berkeley, CA: Bancroft Library, Regional Oral History Office, University of California at Berkeley, 1973).

5. Ibid., 128.

6. Ibid.

7. Ibid., 128–29.

8. Earl Warren, *The Memoirs of Earl Warren* (Garden City: Doubleday, 1977), 130.

9. MacGregor, interview by Fry, Hogan, and Morris.

10. Ed Cray, *Chief Justice: A Biography of Earl Warren* (New York: Simon & Schuster, 1997), 100.

11. *Los Angeles Times*, July 24, 1938.

12. Cray, *Chief Justice*, 101.

13. Ibid.

14. Warren, *Memoirs*, 133.

15. Ibid., 134.

16. John D. (John Downing) Weaver, *Warren: The Man, The Court, The Era* (Boston: Little, Brown, 1967); available online at https://archive.org/details/warren mancourter00weav/page/78?q=earl+warren?q=earl+warren.

17. *Los Angeles Times*, July 29, 1939.

18. Cray, *Chief Justice*, 102–3.

19. *Los Angeles Times*, July 29, 1939.

20. Ibid.

21. "Homespun Titan of the Law," *True* magazine, June 1961, 24.

22. Warren, *Memoirs*, 134–35.

23. "Homespun Titan of the Law."

24. Warren, *Memoirs*, 135.

25. *Los Angeles Times*, August 3, 1939.

26. Ibid.

27. Warren, *Memoirs*, 135–36.

28. *Los Angeles Times*, August 4, 1939.

29. Ibid., August 6, 1939.

30. "Homespun Titan of the Law," 26.

31. *Los Angeles Times*, August 11, 1939.

32. New Jersey v. City of New York, 283 U.S. 473 (1931).

33. Ibid., 476.

34. *Los Angeles Times*, November 30, 1939.

35. MacGregor, interview by Fry, Hogan, and Morris.

36. Ibid.

37. Ibid., 137.

38. Alan Balbonifor, "Tony Cornero," *Las Vegas Review-Journal*, February 7, 1999, https://www.reviewjournal.com/news/tony-cornero/.

39. Warren, *Memoirs*, 103.

40. MacGregor, interview by Fry, Hogan, and Morris.

41. Cray, *Chief Justice*, 104.

42. Ibid.

43. Ibid.

44. Ibid.

45. Cray, *Chief Justice*, 105.

46. Ibid., 106.

47. Ibid.

48. Ibid.

49. Warren, *Memoirs*, 113–15.

50. Ibid., 117.

51. Cray, *Chief Justice*, 108.

52. Ibid.

53. Ibid.

54. Ibid.

55. Irving Stone, *Earl Warren: A Great American Story* (New York: Prentice Hall, 1948), 88–89.

56. Ibid., 109.

57. Cray, *Chief Justice*, 109.

58. Stone, *Earl Warren*.

59. Ibid.

60. Ibid.

61. Ibid., 110.

62. Ibid.

63. Ibid.

64. Ibid., 110–11.

65. Ibid., 111.

66. G. Edward White, "The Unacknowledged Lesson: Earl Warren and the Japanese Relocation Controversy," *Virginia Quarterly Review* (Autumn 1979): 613–29.

67. Carey McWilliams, interview by Willa Baum, Amelia Fry, and Hannah Josephson, Earl Warren Oral History Project, November 12, 1969–May 17, 1973, in *Earl Warren: Views and Episodes* (Berkeley, CA: Bancroft Library, Regional Oral History Office, University of California at Berkeley, 1976).

68. Weaver, *Warren*, 107.

69. Ibid., 109.

70. Eugene V. Rostow, "Our Worst Wartime Mistake," *Harper's*, September 1945, 193.

71. McWilliams, interview by Baum, Fry, and Josephson.

72. Earl Warren, *Earl Warren Papers, 1924–53*, F3640, compiled by David L. Snyder (Sacramento, CA: California State Archives, 2000).

73. Leo Katcher, *A Political Biography* (New York: McGraw-Hill, 1967).

74. Tom C. Clark, interview by Miriam Feingold, Earl Warren Oral History Project, August 12, 1972, in *Japanese-American Relocation Reviewed*, vol. 1, *Decision and Exodus* (Berkeley, CA: Bancroft Library, Regional Oral History Office, University of California at Berkeley, 1976).

75. McWilliams, interview by Baum, Fry, and Josephson.

76. Weaver, *Warren*, 109.

77. Ibid.

78. Warren, *Memoirs*.

79. Ibid., 155.

CHAPTER 4: NEW LIFE

1. Earl Warren, *The Memoirs of Earl Warren* (Garden City, NY: Doubleday, 1977), 155–56.

2. Ed Cray, *Chief Justice: A Biography of Earl Warren* (New York: Simon & Schuster, 1997), 125.

3. Ibid.

4. Ibid.

5. Ibid.

6. Ibid.

7. Ibid., 126.

8. Ibid.

9. Ibid.

10. Warren, *Memoirs*, 156.

11. Cray, *Chief Justice*, 126.

12. *Los Angeles Times*, April 10, 1942.

13. *Oakland Tribune*, April 11, 1942.

14. Robert E. Burke, *Olson's New Deal for California* (Berkeley, CA: University of California Press, 1953), 216.

15. *Los Angeles Times*, April 10, 1942.

16. Warren, *Memoirs*, 157.

17. Ibid.

18. Ibid., 157–58.

19. Ibid., 127.

20. Cray, *Chief Justice*, 128.

21. Ibid.

22. Ibid., 128.

23. Ibid.

24. Ibid., 129.

25. Ibid., 130.

26. Ibid.

27. Ibid.

28. Ibid., 131.

29. Ibid.

30. Ibid.

31. Jack Pollack, *The Judge Who Changed America* (Upper Saddle River, NJ: Prentice Hall, 1979), 102.

32. Cray, *Chief Justice*.

33. Pollack, *The Judge*, 83.

34. Warren, *Memoirs*, 166.

35. Robert Coughlan, "California's Warren & Family," *Life*, April 24, 1944, 100–112.

36. James L. Warren, interview by the author, May 20, 2019.

37. Ibid.

38. Ibid.

39. Edmund G. Brown, interview by Amelia R. Fry, Earl Warren Oral History Project, October 17, 1969, March 20, 1975, April 7, 1975, in *Earl Warren: Fellow Constitutional Officers* (Berkeley, CA: Bancroft Library, Regional Oral History Office, University of California at Berkeley, 1979).

40. John D. (John Downing) Weaver, *Warren: The Man, The Court, The Era* (Boston: Little, Brown, 1967), 55; available online at https://archive.org/details/warrenmancourter00weav/page/78?q=earl+warren?q=earl+warren.

41. Coughlan, "California's Warren & Family."

42. Ibid.

43. Ibid.

44. Warren, *Memoirs*, 76.

45. "Muskie Congressional Record: Death of Former Chief Justice Earl Warren," Bates Archives and Special Collections Library, July 11, 1974, http://abacus.bates.edu/muskie-archives/ajcr/1974/Earl%20Warren%20Death.shtml.

46. Weaver, *Warren*, 147.

47. Pollack, *The Judge*, 105.

48. Robert W. Kenny, interview by Amelia R. Fry, Earl Warren Oral History Project, October 16, 1969; February 24, 1975, in *Earl Warren: Fellow Constitutional*

Officers (Berkeley, CA: Bancroft Library, Regional Oral History Office, University of California at Berkeley, 1979).

49. Charles H. Titus, "The Two Major Conventions in 1948," *Western Political Quarterly* 1, no. 3 (1948): 252–60.

50. Warren, *Memoirs*, 240.

51. Titus, "Two Major Conventions," 252–60.

52. Merrell Farnham Small, interview by Amelia R. Fry and Gabrielle S. Morris, Earl Warren Oral History Project, February 24, March 18, and April 8, 1970, and January 17, 1971, in *The Office of the Governor under Earl Warren* (Berkeley, CA: Bancroft Library, Regional Oral History Office, University of California at Berkeley, 1972).

53. Warren, *Memoirs*, 240–41.

54. Ibid.

55. Ibid., 241.

56. Ibid.

57. Earl Warren Jr., interview by Amelia R. Fry, Earl Warren Oral History Project, July 8–9, 1970, in *Earl Warren: The Governor's Family: Oral History Transcript and Related Material, 1970–1980* (Berkeley, CA: Bancroft Library, Regional Oral History Office, University of California at Berkeley, 1976).

58. Warren, *Memoirs*, 246.

CHAPTER 5: PRIME TIME

1. Bernard Schwartz, "Chief Justice Earl Warren: Super Chief in Action," *Tulsa Law Review* 33, no. 477 (2013).

2. Robert Coughlan, "California's Warren & Family," *Life*, April 24, 1944, 101.

3. Ibid.

4. Ibid.

5. Ibid., 102.

6. James L. Warren, interview by the author, May 20, 2019.

7. Ibid.

8. Coughlan, "California's Warren & Family," 105.

9. Warren, interview by the author, May 20, 2019.

10. Ibid.

11. Coughlan, "California's Warren & Family," 105.

12. Ibid., 112.

CHAPTER 6: ON THE ROAD

1. Earl Warren, *The Memoirs of Earl Warren* (Garden City, NY: Doubleday, 1977), 202.

2. Ibid., 182.

3. Edmund G. Brown, interview by Amelia R. Fry, Earl Warren Oral History Project, October 17, 1969, March 20, 1975, April 7, 1975, in *Earl Warren: Fellow Constitutional Officers* (Berkeley, CA: Bancroft Library, Regional Oral History Office, University of California at Berkeley, 1979).

4. Earl Warren Jr., in correspondence with author, June 1995.

5. Brown, interview by Amelia R. Fry.

6. Warren, *Memoirs*, 249.

7. Herbert Brownell, "Earl Warren's Appointment to the Supreme Court: A Retrospective Memorandum," interview by Amelia R. Fry, Earl Warren Oral History Project, October 29, 1974, in *Earl Warren: The Chief Justiceship* (Berkeley, CA: Bancroft Library, Regional Oral History Office, University of California at Berkeley, 1977).

8. Thomas J. Mellon, interview by Amelia R. Fry, Earl Warren Oral History Project, November 11, 1971, and November 16, 1973, in *Earl Warren's Campaigns*, vol. 2 (Berkeley, CA: Bancroft Library, Regional Oral History Office, University of California at Berkeley, 1977).

9. Ibid.

10. Dwight D. Eisenhower, *Mandate for Change 1953–1956: The White House Years* (Garden City: Doubleday, 1956), 228.

11. John D. (John Downing) Weaver, *Warren: The Man, The Court, The Era* (Boston: Little, Brown, 1967), 183; available online at https://archive.org/details/warrenmancourter00weav/page/78?q=earl+warren?q=earl+warren.

12. Richard M. Nixon, "Checkers" speech, delivered and broadcast live on television September 23, 1952, available online on American Rhetoric, https://www.americanrhetoric.com/speeches/richardnixoncheckers.html.

13. Warren, *Memoirs*, 246.

CHAPTER 7: SCOTUS MEETS *BROWN*

1. Earl Warren, *The Memoirs of Earl Warren* (Garden City, NY: Doubleday, 1977), 260.

2. Ibid.

3. Ibid., 261–62.

4. Ibid., 262.

5. Ibid., 264.

6. Ibid., 268.

7. Herbert Brownell, "Earl Warren's Appointment to the Supreme Court: A Retrospective Memorandum," interview by Amelia R. Fry, Earl Warren Oral History Project, October 29, 1974, in *Earl Warren: the Chief Justiceship* (Berkeley, CA: Bancroft Library, Regional Oral History Office, University of California at Berkeley, 1977).

8. Ed Cray, *Chief Justice: A Biography of Earl Warren* (New York: Simon & Schuster, 1997), 247.

9. Cray, *Chief Justice*, 250.

10. Ibid.

11. Ibid.

12. Bernard Schwartz, *Super Chief: Earl Warren and His Supreme Court: A Judicial Biography* (New York: New York University Press, 1983), 4.

13. Cray, *Chief Justice*, 249–50.

14. Ibid.

15. Warren, *Memoirs*, 270.

16. Timm Herdt, "Warren Milestone Eclipses Brown's Big Day," *San Francisco Examiner*, October 6, 2013, 14.

17. Jack Pollack, *Earl Warren: The Judge Who Changed America* (Upper Saddle River, NJ: Prentice Hall, 1979), 156.

18. Warren, *Memoirs*, 270–71.

19. *New York Times*, October 5, 1953, 1.

20. Earl Warren: The Governor's family: Oral History Transcript and Related Material, 1970–1980 by Bancroft Library. Regional Oral History Office; Earl Warren Oral History Project (Bancroft Library); Amelia Fry, Nina Palmquist Warren, James Warren, Earl Warren Jr., Nina Warren Brien, Robert Warren, Miriam Feingold Stein.

21. Gerald T. Dunne, *Hugo Black and the Judicial Revolution* (New York: Simon & Schuster, 1977), 297.

22. Kent A. Zimmerman, interview by Gabrielle Morris, Earl Warren Oral History Project, May 26 and October 9, 1970, in *Earl Warren and the State Department of Public Health* (Berkeley, CA: Bancroft Library, Regional Oral History Office, University of California at Berkeley, 1973).

23. *Wikipedia*, s.v. "Oyez," last edited November 25, 2018, https://en.wikipedia.org/wiki/Oyez.

24. Earl Warren and Michal R. Belknap, *The Supreme Court under Earl Warren, 1953–1969* (Columbia: University of South Carolina Press, 2005), 1.

25. Brown v. Board of Education of Topeka, Kansas, 347 U.S. 483 (1954). (Majority Opinion, Earl Warren, United States Supreme Court, May 17, 1954.)

26. "Brown v. Board of Education Issue: Racial Segregation in Public Schools," PBS, https://www.pbs.org/jefferson/enlight/brown.htm.

27. "(1953) Thurgood Marshall, 'Argument Before the U.S. Supreme Court in Brown v. Board of Education,'" Black Past, January 16, 2012, https://blackpast.org/1953-thurgood-marshall-argument-u-s-supreme-court-brown-v-board-education.

28. Stephen Higginson, "Thurgood Marshall: Cases in Controversy," *George Mason Law Review* 15, no. 3 (2008): 741–74, http://www.law.nyu.edu/sites/default/files/upload_documents/Higginson-Thurgood-Marshall-George-Mason-Law-Review.pdf.

29. Cray, *Chief Justice*, 286.

30. Lisa Aldred, *Thurgood Marshall* (New York: Chelsea House, 1990), 18.

31. Brown v. Board of Education of Topeka, Kansas, 347 U.S. 483 (1954). (Majority Opinion, Earl Warren, United States Supreme Court, May 17, 1954.)

32. Warren, *Memoirs*, 287.

33. Aldred, *Thurgood Marshall*, 81.

34. Ibid.

35. Warren, *Memoirs*, 291.

36. Ibid.

37. Robert A. Diamond, *The Supreme Court: Justice and the Law*, 2nd ed., *Congressional Quarterly* (Washington, DC: CQ Roll Call, 1960), 13.

38. Ibid.

39. Felix Frankfurter to C. C. Burlingham, January 15, 1954, in Felix Frankfurter, Frank W. Buxton, and William H. Moody, *Felix Frankfurter Papers* (Washington, DC: Library of Congress, 1846–1966).

40. *New York Times*, February 26, 1954, 18.

CHAPTER 8: ONE MAN, ONE VOTE

1. Samara Freemark and Joe Richman, "'Segregation Forever': A Fiery Pledge Forgiven, But Not Forgotten," NPR, January 10, 2013, https://www.npr .org/2013/01/14/169080969/segregation-forever-a-fiery-pledge-forgiven-but -not-forgotten.

2. Earl Warren, *The Memoirs of Earl Warren* (Garden City, NY: Doubleday, 1977), 290–91.

3. Ibid., 306.

4. Ibid., 306–7.

5. Ibid., 307.

6. Ibid., 308.

7. Ibid.

8. Baker v. Carr, 369 U.S. 186 (1962), 258.

9. Ibid., 251.

10. Ibid., 217.

11. Ibid., 237.

12. Ibid., 254.

13. Ibid., 267.

14. Warren, *Memoirs*, 310–11.

15. Ibid., 311.

16. Ibid., 312.

17. Edward G. White, *Earl Warren: A Public Life* (New York: Oxford University Press, 1987), 243.

18. Warren, *Memoirs*, 313.

19. Ibid., 315.

20. Ibid.

21. Ibid., 315–16.

22. Ibid., 316.

23. Ibid., 316–17.

24. Ibid., 317–18.

25. Ibid., 318.

26. Ibid., 318–19.

27. Ibid., 319.

28. Ibid., 319–20.

CHAPTER 9: UNDER EVERY BED

1. 102 Cong. Rec. 4459 (1956) (Southern Manifesto on Integration), available online at https://www.thirteen.org/wnet/supremecourt/rights/sources_docu ment2.html.

2. Ed Cray, *Chief Justice: A Biography of Earl Warren* (New York: Simon & Schuster, 1997), 320.

3. Ibid., 321.

4. Ibid.

5. Ibid.

6. Ibid.

7. Ibid., 321–22.

8. Ibid.

9. Earl Warren to L. Harold Anderson, May 28, 1956, in "Personal Correspondence—A," *Earl Warren Papers, 1864–1974* (Washington, DC: Library of Congress, 1974), Box 1.

10. Cray, *Chief Justice*, 322.

11. Earl Warren, *The Memoirs of Earl Warren* (Garden City, NY: Doubleday, 1977), 322.

12. Ibid., 322.

13. Ibid., 323.

14. Ibid., 323–24.

15. Ibid., 324.

16. Ibid., 325.

17. Ibid.

18. Ibid.

19. Cray, *Chief Justice*, 342.

20. Melba Patillo Beals, *Warriors Don't Cry* (New York: Simon & Schuster, 2007), 113.

21. Cray, *Chief Justice*, 344.

22. *Newsweek*, October 7, 1957.

23. Cray, *Chief Justice*, 345.

24. Richard C. Butler, "Reminiscences of Richard C. Butler," Oral History, interviewed by John Luter, August 17, 1971, as part of Eisenhower administration project and available at Eisenhower Presidential Library.

25. Cooper v. Aaron 358 U.S. 1 (1958), transcripts of hearing, August Special Term, *Earl Warren Papers* (Washington, DC: Library of Congress, 1974), Box 584, 49–50.

26. James F. Simon, *The Antagonists: Hugo Black, Felix Frankfurter and Civil Liberties in Modern America* (New York: Simon & Schuster, 1989), 230.

27. Warren, *Memoirs*, 298–99.

28. Ibid., 299.

CHAPTER 10: JFK AND THE COURT

1. John F. Kennedy, "New Frontier," speech, acceptance speech given at the Democratic National Convention in the Los Angeles Memorial Coliseum, 1960, available online at https://www.shapell.org/manuscript/jfk-1960-new-frontier -speech/.

2. John F. Kennedy, speech on his religion given to the Greater Houston Ministerial Association, September 12, 1960; transcript available online at https://www.npr.org/templates/story/story.php?storyId=16920600.

3. Ibid.

4. John F. Kennedy, "Inaugural Address of President John F. Kennedy," Washington, DC, January 20, 1961, record available online at the John F. Kennedy Presidential Library, https://www.jfklibrary.org/archives/other-resources/john-f-kennedy-speeches/inaugural-address-19610120.

5. Ed Cray, *Chief Justice: A Biography of Earl Warren* (New York: Simon & Schuster, 1997), 395.

6. Ibid., 395–96.

7. Ibid., 396–97.

8. Ibid., 397.

9. James L. Warren, interview by the author, May 20, 2019.

10. Ibid.

11. Ibid.

12. Ibid.

13. Ibid.

14. Ibid., 398.

15. Ibid.

16. Ibid.

17. Ibid.

18. Ibid., 399.

19. Earl Warren, *Memoirs*, iv.

20. Cray, *Chief Justice*, 299–300.

21. Margaret Warren, in interview with Ed Cray, in *Chief Justice*, 400.

22. James Warren, in interview with Ed Cray, in ibid.

23. Jeffrey Warren, in interview with Ed Cray, in ibid., 401.

24. Murray Bring, in interview with Ed Cray, in ibid.

25. Robert Gros, in interview with Ed Cray, in ibid.

26. Roland Homet Jr., in interview with Ed Cray, in ibid.

27. Earl Warren to Brennan, October 5, 1959, in "Brennan '56–'59" file, in *Earl Warren Papers* (Washington, DC: Library of Congress, 1974), Box 348.

28. Gordon Gooch, in interview with Ed Cray, *Chief Justice*, 401

29. Betts v. Brady, 316 U.S. 455 (1942).

30. Cray, *Chief Justice*, 403.

31. Ibid., 404.

32. Ibid., 404–5.

33. Ibid., 406.

34. Gray v. Sanders, 372 U.S. 368 (1963).

35. McIntyre Faries, in interview with Ed Cray, July 25, 1991.

36. Cray, *Chief Justice*, 408.

37. Bernard Schwartz, "Chief Justice Earl Warren: Super Chief in Action," *Tulsa Law Review* 33, no. 477 (2013): 479.

38. *Charlotte Observer*, February 3, 1960.

39. Earl Warren's undated notes in "Sit-In Cases" file, in *Earl Warren Papers* (Washington, DC: Library of Congress, 1974), Box 604.

40. Cray, *Chief Justice*, 409.

41. Earl Warren to Bill Douglas, May 18, 1963, in "Sit-In Cases" file, in *Earl Warren Papers* (Washington, DC: Library of Congress, 1974), Box 604.

42. Cray, *Chief Justice*, 409.

43. Ibid., 409–10.

44. *U.S. News & World Report*, July 1, 1963, 72.

45. *Milwaukee Journal*, September 29, 1963.

46. Quoted in *Congressional Record*, October 21, 1963, 19849.

47. Ibid., 19853.

48. *Washington Post*, October 5, 1963.

CHAPTER 11: TRAGEDY IN DALLAS

1. Margaret Bryan, in interview with Ed Cray, in *Chief Justice: A Biography of Earl Warren* (New York: Simon & Schuster, 1997), 412.

2. Earl Warren, *The Memoirs of Earl Warren* (Garden City, NY: Doubleday, 1977), 351.

3. Frank Beytagh, in interview with Ed Cray, *Chief Justice*, 412.

4. Earl Warren, in interview with John Weaver, January 1, 1966, in *John Downing Weaver Collection of Materials Concerning the Article "The Honorable Earl Warren" published in* Holiday *magazine in April, May and June of 1966* (Berkeley, CA: Law Library, University of California at Berkeley, 1966), File 60, Box 171.

5. Margaret McHugh, in interview with Ed Cray, *Chief Justice*, 413.

6. Warren, *Memoirs*, 352.

7. Ibid., 353.

8. Reprinted in *Congressional Record*, November 25, 1963, 22695.

9. Earl Warren Jr., in correspondence with author, June 1995.

10. McHugh, in interview with Ed Cray, *Chief Justice*, 413.

11. Warren, *Memoirs*, 355–56.

12. Earl Warren, in interview with Alfred Goldberg, Warren Commission historian, "Warren Commission General Correspondence File," in *Earl Warren Papers* (Washington, DC: Library of Congress, 1974), Box 758.

13. Richard H. Nelson, interview by Michael Gillette, LBJ Library Oral Histories, July 20, 1978, LBJ Presidential Library, 44.

14. Warren, interview with Goldberg.

15. Drew Pearson, "The Chief Justice," unpublished manuscript, in *Earl Warren Papers* (Washington, DC: Library of Congress, 1974), Box 6.

16. Warren, interview with Goldberg.

17. Earl Warren, in interview with Abraham Sacher, in *Earl Warren Papers* (Washington, DC: Library of Congress, 1972), Box 846, 18.

18. Frank Beytagh, in interview with Ed Cray, *Chief Justice*, 413.

19. Telephone conversation between President Lyndon B. Johnson and Senator Russell, November 29, 1963, 8:55 p.m., LBJ Presidential Library.

20. Warren, *Memoirs*, 358–59.

21. Ibid.

22. Warren Olney IV, in interview with Ed Cray, August 26, 1992.

23. Memorandum from Cartha DeLoach to "Mr. Mohr," December 12, 1963, FBI file number 62-109090-36.

24. Earl Warren Jr., in correspondence with author, June 1995.

25. David Belin speech, National Press Club, March 26, 1992.

26. Joseph Ball, in interview with Ed Cray, *Chief Justice*, 419.

27. Drew Pearson diary entry, October 26, 1966, in "Earl Warren No. 2" file, Drew Pearson Papers, LBJ Presidential Library.

28. Sam Stern, in interview with Ed Cray, *Chief Justice*, 420.

29. *New York Times*, December 17, 1963.

30. W. David Slawson, in interview with Ed Cray, *Chief Justice*, 420.

31. Ibid.

32. David Belin, in interview with Ed Cray, *Chief Justice*, 421.

33. Slawson, interview with Ed Cray, *Chief Justice*, 421.

34. Warren, interview with Goldberg.

35. *New York Times*, November 22, 1966.

36. David Belin, speech at the National Press Club, March 26, 1992.

37. Warren, interview with Goldberg, 5.

38. Ibid., 3.

39. Undated notes in file "Warren, C J, Earl #1," Drew Pearson Papers, LBJ Presidential Library.

40. Ibid.

41. Earl Warren, interview by Joe B. Frantz, LBJ Library Oral Histories, September 21, 1971, LBJ Presidential Library, 22.

42. Drew Pearson diary entry, Wednesday, October 26, 1966, in Drew Pearson Papers, LBJ Presidential Library.

43. Warren, *Memoirs*, 371.

44. Warren, interview with Goldberg, 4.

45. David W. Belin, *Final Disclosure* (New York: Scribner, 1988), 47.

46. Drew Pearson, "The Chief Justice," unpublished manuscript in *Earl Warren Papers, 1864–1974* (Washington, DC: Library of Congress, 1974), Box 6.

47. Ibid.

48. Howard P. Williams interview, April 9, 1965, in Folder 60, Box 171, John Weaver Papers, Department of Special Collections, University Research Library, UCLA.

49. Earl Warren Jr., in correspondence with author, June 1995.

50. Notes in "Proposed Book 'The Chief,'" August 21, 1967, file, in Drew Pearson Papers, LBJ Presidential Library.

51. Ibid.

52. Warren, interview with Goldberg, 7.

53. William H. Jordan Jr., interview 1 (I), December 5, 1974, by Michael L. Gillette, LBJ Library Oral Histories, LBJ Presidential Library, accessed April 25, 2019, https://www.discoverlbj.org/item/oh-jordanw-19741205-1-78-38.

54. *The Warren Commission Report (President's Commission on the Assassination of President Kennedy), New York Times* editorial, September 28, 1964, 41.

55. Warren, interview with Goldberg, 7.

56. *Warren Commission Report*, 44.

57. Jeff Warren, in interview with Ed Cray, March 3, 1994; Earl Warren Jr., in interview with Ed Cray, July 29, 1991.

58. Fred Warner Neal, in interview with Ed Cray, March 23, 1993.

59. Ibid.

60. Howard P. Willens interview, April 9, 1965, in Folder 60, Box 171, John Weaver Papers, Department of Special Collections, University Research Library, UCLA.

61. Robert Warren, interview by Amelia R. Fry and Mortimer D. Schwartz, Earl Warren Oral History Project, January 28, 1971, in *Earl Warren: The Governor's Family: Oral History Transcript and Related Material, 1970–1980* (Berkeley, CA: Bancroft Library, Regional Oral History Office, University of California at Berkeley, 1976), 38.

62. *Sacramento Bee*, ca. October 1, 1964, in John Weaver Papers, Department of Special Collections, University Research Library, UCLA.

63. Notes for Earl Warren biography in Earl Warren file, Drew Pearson Papers, LBJ Presidential Library.

64. Warren, interview with Goldberg, 10.

65. Kenneth Ziffren, in interview with Ed Cray, September 9, 1992.

66. Edward Jay Epstein, *Inquest: The Warren Commission and the Establishment of Truth* (New York: Viking, 1966), xviii.

67. Ziffren, in interview with Cray.

68. George Reedy, in interview with Ed Cray, April 15, 1994.

69. John Weaver Papers, File 37, Box 69, Department of Special Collections, University Research Library, UCLA.

70. Belin, interview with Ed Cray.

71. Warren, interview with Sacher, 19.

72. Warren, interview with Goldberg, 4.

73. Earl Warren Jr., interview by Amelia R. Fry, Earl Warren Oral History Project, July 8–9, 1970, in *Earl Warren: The Governor's Family: Oral History Transcript and Related Material, 1970–1980* (Berkeley, CA: Bancroft Library, Regional Oral History Office, University of California at Berkeley, 1976).

CHAPTER 12: FACING DOWN *MIRANDA*

1. Peter H. Irons and Stephanie Guitton, *May It Please the Court* (New York: The New Press, 1993), 217.

2. Bernard Schwartz, "Chief Justice Earl Warren: Super Chief in Action," *Tulsa Law Review* 33, no. 477 (2013): 589.

3. William J. Brennan to "Dear Chief," May 11, 1966, in Brennan Papers (Washington DC: Library of Congress, 1966), File 2 of 4, Box 45.

4. *Earl Warren Papers, 1864–1974* (Washington, DC: Library of Congress, 1974), Box 617.

5. Drew Pearson diary entry, February 4, 1966, in Drew Pearson Papers, LBJ Presidential Library.

6. Schwartz, "Chief Justice," 589.

7. Miranda v. Arizona, 384 U.S., 436 (1966) at 444.

8. Earl Warren's reading copy of the opinion, in *Earl Warren Papers, 1864–1974* (Washington, DC: Library of Congress, 1974), Folder No. 3, Box 617.

9. Fred P. Graham, *The Self-Inflicted Wound* (New York: MacMillan, 1970), 158.

10. Ed Cray, *Enemy in the Streets* (Garden City, NY: Doubleday, 1972), 152.

11. Ibid.

12. Quoted in *Congressional Record*, August 22, 1966, 20128.

13. *Los Angeles Times*, June 16, 1966.

14. Cray, *Enemy in the Streets*, 152.

15. Graham, *Self-Inflicted Wound*, 185.

16. Ed Cray, *Chief Justice: A Biography of Earl Warren* (New York: Simon & Schuster, 1997), 461.

17. Arthur Goldberg to Earl Warren, June 14, 1966, in "Goldberg, 1964–1969" file, in *Earl Warren Papers, 1864–1974* (Washington, DC: Library of Congress, 1974), Box 354.

18. Earl Warren, speech at Bohemian Grove, July 30, 1965, in *Earl Warren Papers, 1864–1974* (Washington, DC: Library of Congress, 1974), Box 818.

19. *New York Times*, September 12, 1965.

20. Earl Warren to Edward P. Morgan, June 25, 1966, in Miranda No. 4 file, in *Earl Warren Papers, 1864–1974* (Washington, DC: Library of Congress, 1974), Box 617.

21. Anthony Lewis, "A Talk with Warren on Crime, the Court, the Country," *New York Times Magazine*, October 19, 1969, 35.

22. "A Conversation with Chief Justice Earl Warren," interview by Morrie Landsberg, McClatchy Broadcasting, June 24, 1969, video, 58:00, https://cali sphere.org/item/2b3c2ac84efe7d958632f07ae6697127/.

23. James Gaither, in interview with Ed Cray, *Chief Justice*.

24. "Report of Special Committee on Publicity in Criminal Trials to the Section of Criminal Law of the American Bar Association," n.d., ca. 1935–36, 7, in F3640:17603, in *Earl Warren Papers, 1864–1974* (Washington, DC: Library of Congress, 1974).

25. Schwartz, "Chief Justice," 544.

26. Gaither, interview with Cray.

27. Estes v. Texas, 381 U.S., 532 at 571 (1965).

28. Ibid.

29. *Cleveland Press*, July 30, 1954.

30. *Time*, November 22, 1954.

31. Sheppard v. Maxwell, 384 U.S. 333 (1966).

32. Terry v. Ohio, 392 U.S. 1 (1968).

33. Irons and Guitton, *May It Please the Court*, 203.

34. Terry v. Ohio, at 24.

CHAPTER 13: ALL THE KING'S HORSES

1. Earl Warren Jr., in interview on his father's career, retirement, and family life, Sacramento, 1969. Interviewer unknown, possibly for NET program on Chief Justice Warren.

2. "Fortas of the Supreme Court: A Question of Ethics," *Life*, May 4, 1969.

3. Robert Shogan, *A Question of Judgment: The Fortas Case and the Struggle for the Supreme Court* (Indianapolis: Bobbs-Merrill, 1972), 248–49.

4. William O. Douglas, *The Court Years 1939–1975: The Autobiography of William O. Douglas* (New York: Random House, 1980), 259.

5. Ibid.

6. Shogan, *Question of Judgment*, 249.

7. Anthony Lewis, *Make No Law* (New York: Random House, 1991), 235.

8. *New York Times*, November 2, 1969.

9. Jack Harrison Pollack, *Earl Warren: The Judge Who Changed America* (Englewood, NJ: Prentice Hall, 1979), 283.

10. Ibid.

11. Ibid.

12. Ibid., 286.

13. I. 395 U.S. VII. Warren's sure-handed draft of the statement is in Warren Burger Correspondence File, *Earl Warren Papers, 1864–1974* (Washington, DC: Library of Congress, 1974), Box 347.

14. Bernard Schwartz, *Super Chief: Earl Warren and His Supreme Court—A Judicial Biography* (New York: New York University Press, 1983), 765.

15. Ibid.

16. *New York Times*, June 30, 1969, 44.

17. *New York Times*, June 23, 1969, 24.

18. James L. Warren, interview by the author, May 20, 2019.

19. Pollack, *Earl Warren*, 309.

20. Federal Judicial Center, *Report of the Study Group on the Caseload of the Supreme Court* (Washington, DC: Federal Judicial Center, 1972).

21. Earl Warren, in letter to Peter D. Ehrenhaft, November 8, 1972.

22. Earl Warren, "Memorandum to My Law Clerks," November 8, 1972.

23. Peter D. Ehrenhaft, Memorandum to the Law Clerks of Chief Justice Warren, December 21, 1972.

24. Schwartz, *Super Chief*, 768.

25. Earl Warren, 59 A.B.A.J. 724 (1973).

26. William Brennan, "Chief Justice Warren," *Harvard Law Review* 88, no. 1 (1974).

27. Bernard Schwartz, "Chief Justice Earl Warren: Super Chief in Action," *Tulsa Law Review* 33, no. 477 (2013): 769.

28. Pollack, *Earl Warren*, 288.

29. Schwartz, *Super Chief*, 770.

30. Pollack, *Earl Warren*, 319–20.

31. Ibid., 321.

32. *New York Times*, March 23, 1975, section IV, 6; Alden Whitman, "Alden Whitman's Golden Oldies," *Esquire*, April 1, 1975, 82.

33. Pollack, *Earl Warren*, 333.

34. United States v. Nixon, 418 U.S. 683 (1974).

35. Schwartz, *Super Chief*, 772.

INDEX

ABA. *See* American Bar Association

activism: Goldberg and judicial, 193–94; social, 30–31

AEC. *See* Atomic Energy Commission, US

AG. *See* Attorney General

Alabama: Black as from, 156, 248; bus-segregation by, 171; malapportionment of, 156; Parks in, 170; segregation laws of, 147; Shuttlesworth in, 200–201; Wallace as Governor and, 5, 154

Alameda County: Board of Supervisors legal adviser for, 46, 48–50, 54; crime in, 61–64, 80; DA for, 43, 45–46, 48–50, 55–58, 61–62, 80–81, 105, 115, 229; home as, 189; Young Lawyers' Club of, 38–39

Alberts, George, 80–81, 97, 232–33

American Bar Association (ABA): HUAC and, 174–76; reapportionment and, 161–62; Rhyne and president of, 179; southern politicians supported by, 174; Warren Court discredited by, 174–77; Warren Court not supported by, 161–62

American Legion, 42, 83, 96

American Railway Union (ARU), 10–12

anti-Asian sentiment, 86–88

anti-court hysteria: communism and, 176; constitutional amendments against SCOTUS and, 160–61; segregationists, anti-Communists, business in, 173

antitrust laws, 11, 164–65, 173

Arkansas: discriminatory laws of, 147; *Marbury v. Madison* and desegregation in, 180; school desegregation challenge by, 177–82

arrogant justice system, 166–68

ARU. *See* American Railway Union

Atomic Energy Commission (AEC), US, 163

Attorney General (AG), of California: cross-filing and bipartisan support for, 59–60; dog track cases as, 63–65; gambling ships shut down as, 65–74; issues dealt with, 75; on Japanese concentration camps, 86–88, 92, 97; law enforcement agency coordination as, 61; MacGregor working for, 60–61, 72–73, 75–76; National Association of Attorneys General and, 78–79; Native Americans case as, 77–78; nonpartisan politics during, 88–89; on Radin, 83–86; slot machine cases as, 63; staff and